2025年度版

福岡県・福岡市・北九州市の英語科

過去問

協同教育研究会 編

協同出版

本書には，福岡県・福岡市・北九州市の教員採用試験の過去問題を収録しています。各問題ごとに，以下のように5段階表記で，難易度，頻出度を示しています。

難　易　度

非常に難しい　☆☆☆☆☆
やや難しい　☆☆☆☆
普通の難易度　☆☆☆
やや易しい　☆☆
非常に易しい　☆

頻　出　度

◎　ほとんど出題されない
◎◎　あまり出題されない
◎◎◎　普通の頻出度
◎◎◎◎　よく出題される
◎◎◎◎◎　非常によく出題される

※本書の過去問題における資料，法令文等の取り扱いについて

本書の過去問題で使用されている資料や法令文の表記や基準は，出題された当時の内容に準拠しているため，解答・解説も当時のものを使用しています。ご了承ください。

はじめに～「過去問」シリーズ利用に際して～

教育を取り巻く環境は変化しつつあり，日本の公教育そのものも，教員免許更新制の廃止やGIGAスクール構想の実現などの改革が進められています。また，現行の学習指導要領では「主体的・対話的で深い学び」を実現するため，指導方法や指導体制の工夫改善により，「個に応じた指導」の充実を図るとともに，コンピュータや情報通信ネットワーク等の情報手段を活用するために必要な環境を整えることが示されています。

一方で，いじめや体罰，不登校，暴力行為など，教育現場の問題もあいかわらず取り沙汰されており，教員に求められるスキルは，今後さらに高いものになっていくことが予想されます。

本書の基本構成としては，出題傾向と対策，過去5年間の出題傾向分析表，過去問題，解答および解説を掲載しています。各自治体や教科によって掲載年数をはじめ，「チェックテスト」や「問題演習」を掲載するなど，内容が異なります。

また原則的には一般受験を対象としております。特別選考等については対応していない場合があります。なお，実際に配布された問題の順番や構成を，編集の都合上，変更している場合があります。あらかじめご了承ください。

最後に，この「過去問」シリーズは，「参考書」シリーズとの併用を前提に編集されております。参考書で要点整理を行い，過去問で実力試しを行う，セットでの活用をおすすめいたします。

みなさまが，この書籍を徹底的に活用し，教員採用試験の合格を勝ち取って，教壇に立っていただければ，それはわたくしたちにとって最上の喜びです。

協同教育研究会

C O N T E N T S

第1部 福岡県・福岡市・北九州市の英語科　出題傾向分析 …3

第2部 福岡県・福岡市・北九州市の教員採用試験実施問題 …9

▼2024年度教員採用試験実施問題 ……………………………10

▼2023年度教員採用試験実施問題 ……………………………43

▼2022年度教員採用試験実施問題 ……………………………82

▼2021年度教員採用試験実施問題 ……………………………117

▼2020年度教員採用試験実施問題 ……………………………150

▼2019年度教員採用試験実施問題 ……………………………184

▼2018年度教員採用試験実施問題 ……………………………215

▼2017年度教員採用試験実施問題 ……………………………289

第１部

福岡県・福岡市・北九州市の英語科出題傾向分析

福岡県・福岡市・北九州市の英語科 傾向と対策

福岡県の2024年度の筆記試験で出題されたのは，文法・語法問題が大問で1問，英作文問題，会話文問題が大問で1題，読解問題が3題である。中高別で，学習指導要領に関する問題がそれぞれ大問で3題ずつ出題されている。構成は，前半がOCR式の択一式問題，後半が記述式(一部択一式を含む)である。また，筆記試験(配点100点)とは別にリスニングテスト(配点50点)が実施されている。2023年度に比べると，わずかに読解問題の配点が減り，文法・語法問題，英作文問題そして会話文問題の配点が増えたが，問題数や配点等に大きな変更はない。全体的には，難解な問題がないので，時間配分などに気を配りながらミスをしないように取り組めばよい。

福岡市は，福岡県と共通問題であるが，前半の択一式問題のみ(文法・語法問題，英作文問題，会話文問題，読解問題のうち大問6まで)を解答するようになっている。

文法・語法問題は，空所補充の形式で出題されている。配点は計10点で，語彙力が問われている。選択肢の中には難易度が高い語彙も含まれているが，高頻度語も含まれているため，正答がすぐにわからない時は，不適切な選択肢を冷静に削除していくことも必要である。語彙を学習する際には単語レベルではなく，必ず自動詞か他動詞かわかるようにコロケーションで覚えることが重要である。

英作文問題は，整序英作文の形式での出題である。配点は計9点。日本語が与えられており，並べ替える部分もごく短いので，その部分に対応する日本語を見て英訳を考えつつ前後の語との繋がりを考えれば容易に解ける。苦手な人は，同レベルの問題集で数をこなしておくとよい。

会話文問題は，会話文を正しく並べかえるという整序形式である。配点は計6点。会話整序問題はまず第一文を決めることがポイントだが，基本的には，ItやThatなど代名詞や指示語が含まれている文，Yes，NoやThat's right，I agreeなどの，相手の質問や発言を受けた返答で始まる文を除いていけば比較的容易に決められる。その後は，文中の指示語に注意して読んでいくことで容易に会話が繋がる場合が多い。過去問題を解いて，そのあたりのコツをつかんでおくことが必要である。

読解問題は3題出題されており，配点はそれぞれ計12点，12点，16点である。一致文選択や内容に関する問いに選択肢で答える形式が多く出題されている。また，例年，パラグラフの空所を埋める問題が出題されているが，短文自体は難解な語彙もないため，英文の流れを追っていけば容易に解答できる。読解問題はいずれも400～500語程度の長さであり，内容は教育や心理学に関するものや，科学分野などの軽い読み物などである。特に難解なものはないが，各々，自身の英文を読むスピードを確認し，時間内に解答できるよう長文問題に慣れることとともに，新聞のコラムや雑誌などを多読して英文を読むことに慣れておくことが望ましい。

学習指導要領に関する問題は校種別で，内容に関する空所補充問題が択一式と記述式の両方で出題されている。ただし，2024年度は中学校は全てが記述式であった。配点は中学・高校それぞれ計35点で，配点が高い。学習指導要領に精通していれば対処できる問題が多いが，学習指導要領解説の細かいところも問われている。ただ，過去には，指導方法に関する自分の考えを日本語で書くというものや，国立教育政策研究所の指導資料等からの出題もある。また，文部科学省のリーフレットから英語で出題された年度もある。学習指導要領について理解を深めるためにも，教育に関する関係文書をひろく当たって情報を頭に入れておくと安心である。

リスニングテストは，大問数が4題で，解答はすべて択一式である。配点は2023年度と同様であり，順に，9点，21点，12点，8点。最初の2題は選択肢が印刷されているが，あとの2題は選択肢も読まれる形式である。ただし，第4問は内容一致文を選ぶ問題であるため，音声で設問を理解する必要はない。様々な形式のリスニング問題に慣れておくとよいだろう。第1問はダイアローグ，それ以外はモノローグである。250～350語程度の長さであり，解答にあたっては細部まで内容を把握する必要がある。選択肢の英文も比較的長いので，集中力を必要とする。音声付きの読解問題など，まとまりのある英文を聞いて内容を把握する学習を積むことを勧める。リスニング教材で学習する際は，必ず自分の実力で無理なく聞き取れるレベルのものから順次レベルを上げていき，確実に実力をつけていくこと，何度も繰り返し学習して慣れることなどが重要である。

過去5年間の出題傾向分析

福岡県中高・北九州市中学共通＝◎
福岡県・北九州市中学＝● 福岡県高校＝▲ 福岡市＝○

分類	設問形式	2020年度	2021年度	2022年度	2023年度	2024年度
リスニング	内容把握	◎	◎	◎	◎	◎
発音・アクセント	発音					
	アクセント					
	文強勢					
文法・語法	空所補充	◎	◎○	◎○	◎○	◎○
	正誤判断					
	一致語句					
	連立完成					
	その他					
会話文	短文会話	◎	◎○	◎○	◎○	◎○
	長文会話					
文章読解	空所補充	◎	◎○	◎○	◎○	◎○
	内容一致文	◎	◎○	◎○	◎○	◎○
	内容一致語句			◎	◎○	◎○
	内容記述					
	英文和訳					
	英問英答					
	その他	◎	◎○	◎○	◎○	◎○
英作文	整序	◎	◎○	◎○	◎○	◎○
	和文英訳					
	自由英作					
	その他					
学習指導要領		●▲	●▲	●▲	●▲○	●▲

第２部

福岡県・福岡市・
北九州市の
教員採用試験
実施問題

2024年度　実施問題

※福岡市を志望する場合は，【中高共通】の【5】～【10】を解答して下さい。

【中高共通】

【１】次に読まれる英文を聞き，1～3の設問に対する答えとして最も適切なものを，四つの選択肢の中から一つ選びなさい。

(英文及び設問は2回読まれる。)

Staff : Good morning. Are you checking in for a flight?

Cathy : Good morning, yes.

Staff : May I have your name?

Cathy : I'm Cathy Green, here is my booking on my phone. I think my flight will be leaving soon, and would like to board as quickly as possible.

Staff : OK, let me check. Flying to California, flight 328, economy… Sorry, we can't find your name. Perhaps, we are overbooked.

Cathy : What? I don't understand. I booked properly, so please prepare another seat.

Staff : Sorry, there aren't any available seats in economy, but I can book you on the next flight.

Cathy : Is there anything else you can do? My sister had a baby girl three years ago. I'm going to see her for the first time. Could you please try to get me a seat in business class?

Staff : Let me check. Wow, you're lucky! There's only one seat in business class and it was cancelled 5 minutes ago.

Cathy : Amazing! I'II pay the difference. How much is it?

Staff : You don't need to worry about that. In this case, we, the airlines, are responsible for reserving alternative seats for our passengers.

Cathy : Thank you for the upgrade.

Staff : My pleasure.

Cathy : I've never flown business class before, I'm very excited!

Staff : Oh, that's nice. You can watch a movie or enjoy a fine meal in your comfortable seat.

Cathy : The first thing I want to do in my comfortable seat is to have a good sleep.

Staff : Have a safe and pleasant flight. Here's your boarding pass.

(275 words)

Question 1: Who is Cathy going to see in the U.S for the first time?

① Her brother. ② Her nephew. ③ Her niece.

④ Her cousin.

Question 2: Why was Cathy unable to get an economy seat for her flight?

① Because she had not completed her flight reservations.

② Because she was mistaken and tried to get on the wrong flight.

③ Because she was too early to start check-in procedures.

④ Because the economy seats had already been taken.

Question 3: What is the first thing that Cathy is most likely to do on board?

① She'll order water. ② She'll get some rest.

③ She'll watch movies. ④ She'll enjoy a meal.

(☆☆☆◎◎◎◎)

【2】次に読まれる英文≪A≫及び英文≪B≫について，それぞれの1～3の設問に対する答えとして最も適切なものを，四つの選択肢の中から一つ選びなさい。

(英文及び設問は2回読まれる。)

≪A≫

In today's society, which is undergoing drastic changes due to IT innovations, it is necessary to have the ability to collect information and make various decisions based on that information. Therefore, the demand for ICT education is increasing worldwide. Some countries overseas have been focusing on ICT education from an early stage. What kind of ICT education is practiced overseas?

Finland is a small country with a population of about 5.5 million people, but it is attracting attention as the world's number one educational country. They respect children's autonomy and value how they learn, rather than how teachers teach. In Finland, the right to connect to the Internet is a citizen's right, and IT is indispensable in life. That's why programming education is required from the first year of compulsory education in order to acquire basic knowledge of IT.

In Denmark, in parallel with improving the ICT environment, efforts are being made to promote ICT education for teachers. In other words, there is a rich learning environment where instructors can improve their IT skills. A learning platform has also been introduced to allow teachers, children and parents to easily share learning progress.

The Ministry of Education, Culture, Sports, Science and Technology of Japan is also focusing on ICT education, such as distributing one tablet to each child. For children living in a digital society, a PC tablet is now a necessity along with pencils and notebooks. In addition, teaching methods have been changing significantly. Focusing on ICT education will undoubtedly lead to a major turning point in Japanese education and greatly expand the possibilities for students and teachers.

(268 words)

Question 1: According to the passage, why is programming education required from the first year of compulsory education in Finland?

① Because they want to keep Finland the number one educational country in the world.

② Because they want to foster ICT engineers who can compete with other countries.

③ Because there is a possibility of failing if they do not acquire basic IT knowledge.

④ Because it is a citizen's right to connect to the Internet, and it is indispensable to life.

Question 2: According to the passage, what is possible with a learning platform in Denmark?

① It is possible for each child to receive a tablet.

② It is possible for teachers to provide parents with information on their children's learning progress.

③ It is possible for parents to take classes along with their children.

④ It is possible for teachers to get higher ICT skills in classes.

Question 3: According to the passage, which statement is true?

① In Finland, they emphasize how to learn rather than how to teach.

② Denmark is attracting attention as the world's number one educational country.

③ A PC tablet is now more necessary than pencils and notebooks.

④ Even in ICT education, class contents should not be changed in the future.

≪B≫

Sightseeing tours in India often visit the Ganges River, which flows through the city of Varanasi, which is considered a sacred place. The Ganges River in this region flows as a wide river.

Bathing in the Ganges River is a lifelong dream for Hindus as the waters of the Ganges River are believed to wash away all sins. It is also believed that the waters of the Ganges River purify all things, so it is a wish of Hindus to burn the bodies to ashes and float them down the Ganges River. One of the attractions of the Ganges River is that you can learn about the Hindus' views on life and death.

Therefore, many people gather at the Ganges River in Varanasi, and from early morning until late at night, people pray and bathe in the river. There are various bathing styles, such as those who rinse their mouths and those who wash their bodies, and some children play in the water using floats.

Many tourists visit during the day, usually taking a boat to see the bathing scenery. Cars are not allowed in the intricate city of Varanasi, which is already quiet, but aboard a traditional wooden rowboat makes it even quieter. Only the squeak of the oars can be heard, and the landscape of the Ganges River has remained unchanged for hundreds of years.

Some people say that going to India will change their outlook on life, but it is certain that anyone who visits the Ganges River will be greatly surprised and impressed. Visit the Ganges River, experience a world of surprises, and feel the wonderful culture of India.

(273 words)

Question 1: According to the passage, why do Hindus want to bathe in the Ganges River?

① Because they believe that the Ganges River washes away all sins.
② Because they believe that the Ganges River leads to heaven.
③ Because they believe that the Ganges River makes them a saint.
④ Because they believe that the Ganges River brings good luck.

Question 2: According to the passage, what can you learn when you visit the Ganges River?

① How to make a traditional wooden rowboat in Varanasi.
② Many kinds of swimming styles popular all over India.
③ Hindus' perspective on life and death in their belief in the Ganges River.
④ A ritual of carrying ashes on the boat to the inner city of Varanasi.

Question 3: According to the passage, which statement is true?

① These days, the Ganges River is rarely visited by sightseeing tours.
② As the Ganges River is sacred, it is forbidden to play in the river.

③ The city of Varanasi can be explored by car.

④ The landscape of the Ganges River does not seem to have changed in hundreds of years.

(☆☆☆◎◎◎◎)

【3】次に読まれる英文を聞き，1～3の設問に対する答えとして最も適切なものを，その後に読まれる四つの選択肢の中から一つ選びなさい。
(英文，設問及び選択肢は2回読まれる。)

Keiko, a first-year high school student, has a goal of working at an international organization such as the United Nations and contributing to world peace in the future. It all started with a research activity on the theme of "international conflict" in her junior high school social studies class. Therefore, she wants to study abroad for a year while she is still in high school and acquire the language skills that she will need in the future.

One day, Keiko told her parents that she wants to study abroad to learn English, but they didn't agree mainly for two reasons. One was that studying abroad for a year would prevent her from studying for the entrance examination in Japan, which would give her a disadvantage. The other was that they felt uneasy about sending her abroad alone due to the unstable social situation in the world. Moreover, they said that she can take online classes and acquire language skills in Japan as well.

She could understand her parents' thoughts, but couldn't give up her dream of studying abroad, so she consulted with her homeroom teacher. The teacher advised her to research on studying abroad by herself and discuss it with her parents and convince them. Then, the teacher also told her that if her parents allowed her to study abroad, they would have a meeting all together at school.

After talking with the teacher, Keiko gathered information on the Internet. As a result, she realized that the university that Keiko hopes to enter uses a variety of selection methods for entrance examinations and studying abroad may not be a disadvantage. In addition, she is now sure that studying abroad will enable her to acquire not only language skills but also the ability to adapt to different cultures. This skill will be very important when working in an international society.

Now she is heading to school with her parents to meet with her homeroom teacher. She has some anxiety about making a different choice than the other students, and her heart is now full of hope.

(343 words)

Question 1: According to the passage, why did Keiko's parents object to her studying abroad?

① Because they couldn't afford to let her study abroad.

② Because they were worried about her grades in subjects other than English.

③ Because they want her to enter a university abroad.

④ Because they believed that studying abroad would be safer than taking online classes.

Question 2: According to the passage, what did she notice while researching about studying abroad?

① She noticed that she can enter university without taking the entrance examination after returning from studying abroad.

② She noticed that language skills are the most important when working in an international society.

③ She noticed that the ability to adapt to different cultures will be useful in the future.

④ She noticed that it is easier to work at the United Nations after graduating from a Japanese university.

Question 3: According to the passage, which statement is true?

① Her goal was inspired by an article on "international peace" she read in English class.

② She was completely angry when her parents objected to her studying abroad.

③ When she asked about studying abroad, her homeroom teacher collected materials for her.

④ In the end, her parents are likely to allow her to study abroad.

(☆☆☆☆◎◎◎◎)

【4】次に読まれる英文を聞き，英文の内容に合致するものを，その後に読まれる六つの選択肢の中から二つ選びなさい。

(英文及び選択肢は2回読まれる。)

Do you have animals at home? Dogs have long played the role of man's best friend and this is evident in the appearance of dogs in Japanese folktales like *The Peach Boy*. However, this is changing. According to the results of the 2022 National Dog and Cat Breeding Survey, the number of cats being kept as pets exceeds that of dogs. Cats are familiar animals, but they have some special abilities.

First, they know how to effectively drink water. A study by an American university revealed that cats use the balance of gravity and inertia to drink water. The researchers found that cats drink water by curling the tips of their tongues into a "J" shape, sticking it out into the water, and pulling it back into their mouths. More importantly, they only skim the surface of the water in doing so. When a cat drinks this way, a column of water rises between the tip of their tongue and the surface of the water due to the "delicate balance between gravity and inertia." Once the tip of the water column is in their mouth, they quickly close their mouth to drink. This method is said to allow them to drink water without wetting their chin.

Second, they have leg whiskers. Most of you are probably thinking, "what are leg whiskers?" We all know that cats have whiskers around their mouths, and it's arguably one of their most attractive features, but they actually also have whiskers on their legs. Like the whiskers around their mouths, the whiskers on their legs allow them to sense the flow of air and help them to maintain their sense of balance, A cat's eyesight is only one-tenth that of a human's on average, so their whiskers play an important role in their ability to move agilely. Once you have been enlightened to these abilities, perhaps you will be more interested in cats. Given how peculiar yet functional they are, it is no wonder that the ratio of dogs to cats being kept at home has reversed. Next time you come across a cat, why not look a little closer at their behavior? It's fascinating!

(360 words)

1　Thanks to the folk tale of *The Peach Boy*, dogs became man's best friend.

2　The survey in 2022 shows that there are more people who have dogs than cats.

3　The balance of inertia and gravity is used when cats drink water.

4　While cats are drinking water, they always wet their chins because of the column of water that they create.

5　Cats have whiskers both around their mouths and on their legs.

6　On average, a human's eyesight is ten times worse than that of a cat's.

(☆☆☆☆◎◎◎◎)

【５】英文の意味が通るように，(　　)内に入る最も適切なものを選びなさい。

問1　Before Marie and I launched an ICT business, we wrote a legally (　　) contract detailing our responsibilities.

①　inaccurate　②　desperate　③　opponent　④　shallow
⑤　binding

問2　Our company strives to respond (　　) to all inquiries by email or fax.

①　accidentally　②　promptly　③　reluctantly　④　cruelly
⑤　inappropriately

問3　In contrast to a strong (　　) in the second half of last year, the first half of this year turned out to be very poor.

①　performance　②　disturbance　③　interference
④　preservation　⑤　integration

問4 The residents of this area complained to the city that they were not given (　　) notice of the community center being closed.

① insecure　② offensive　③ intellectual　④ sufficient
⑤ honored

問5 Due to renovations, the use of the gym's restrooms will be (　　) for the next month.

① accomplished　② accelerated　③ refunded
④ restricted　⑤ spread

(☆☆☆◎◎◎◎◎)

【6】次の各問の日本文の意味を表す英文を作るために，(　　)内のA～Eの語句を正しく並べかえたとき，2番目と4番目にくる最も適切な組合せを選びなさい。ただし，組合せの左側を2番目，右側を4番目とする。

問1 乗客たちが飛行機に搭乗しようとしたまさにその直前，悪天候による運行中止がアナウンスされた。

Just (A to B about C passengers D before E were) board the plane, it was announced that it would be canceled due to bad weather.

① C－A　② C－B　③ E－D　④ E－A　⑤ D－E

問2 チームメンバーの懸命な努力がなければ，彼らはこのプロジェクトを完成させることはできなかっただろう。

They would not have been able (A the B without C complete D project E to) the hard work of their team members.

① A－C　② C－A　③ A－E　④ D－C　⑤ C－D

問3 近年，この町の多くの中小企業では，有能な労働者の不足が深刻な問題となっている。

In recent years, the (A has B of C labor D qualified E shortage) become a serious problem for many small businesses in this town.

① E－A　② E－D　③ C－D　④ B－C　⑤ B－D

(☆☆☆◎◎◎◎)

【7】次の各問のA～Fの英文を二人の会話として意味がつながるように並べかえたとき，2番目と4番目にくる最も適切な組合せを選びなさい。ただし，組合せの左側を2番目，右側を4番目とする。

問1　A : I'm really sorry, sir. Could you give me your name and registration number, please?

B : Yes, I had the kitchen plumbing repaired last Saturday. But it started leaking again this morning.

C : Thank you. But we are going out now. So I'd appreciate it if you could come and check it in the evening, maybe around six o'clock.

D : That's okay. I'll check your number and then I'll have a staff come up and take a look at it for you right now.

E : My name is Steven Brown. Oh, sorry I don't know the registration number...

F : Hello, This is the customers call center, Patrick Smith. Can I help you?

① B－C　② E－B　③ B－E　④ C－A　⑤ C－E

問2　A : Do you think you'd like to work there? Our Hanoi branch is looking for a new manager.

B : All right, think about it. Let me know if you'd like to apply.

C : Well, I don't know. It was fun for a trip, but I think living there is different. I don't think I could make it actually living there.

D : Hey, Sarah. I heard you visited Vietnam, right? How was your trip?

E : It was wonderful. The food, the architecture, the art, the religion, it was quite a different culture there. I had a great time in Vietnam.

F : OK. I'll be sure to do that.

① E－F　② E－C　③ C－E　④ B－E　⑤ A－C

(☆☆☆◎◎◎)

【8】次の英文を読んで，以下の問に答えなさい。

Given the option to say "No," it certainly is not easy to say "Yes." For example, when I have a job beyond my ability, will I immediately say "No," or will I say "I'll try anyway" ? This may be related to our way of growing up. Are you familiar with the proverb "Nothing ventured, nothing gained" ?

My father took me to a local baseball club when I was an elementary school fourth grader. (　A　) Until then, I had repeatedly been joining and quitting several sports clubs. (　B　)

The first reason why I quit sports clubs was simple. (　C　) It was because I was not too fond of the practice. One day my dad said to me, "Let's just try it for a month and see how it goes."

Two weeks later, the baseball coach told me, "Why don't you make your debut as an outfielder in a practice game in two months?" I thought to myself, "Can I already play in a game?"

I decided to practice hard to be a good player. The coach said to me as he was leaving, "Enjoy Practice! Have fun! Just do your best!" (　D　)

Two months later, at my debut game, I stood in the batter's box three times at-bat, but I did not hit the ball even once. Moreover, my last chance was a strikeout. Still, my team won the game 3-2, thanks to my teammates.

After the game, we all rejoiced and I said to my dad, "We won! But I want to contribute to the team next time." (　E　)

Now, as an adult, I face challenges at work. Sometimes I unintentionally gaze out the window and remember my childhood and think back to that day when I first started playing baseball. Thirty years have passed since then. From that experience, I'm willing to try anything at first. Now, I am coaching a baseball team in another community. I always tell the children as they first visit the team, "Come on, just try it. Now is the time to give it a try. Nothing ventured, nothing gained."

問1　Put the following sentence in the correct placement in the passsage from (　A　) to (　E　).

Through my experience, even if we don’t know the outcome, the important point is we should take action and always try our best.

① A　② B　③ C　④ D　⑤ E

問2 According to the passage, which of the following is true about the author’s father?

① The author’s father convinced him to take up baseball until he won a game.

② The author’s father saw him devote himself to training, saying that training was most important.

③ The author’s father encouraged him to play baseball for at least a month.

④ The author’s father told him to play on this team first, and when he could get many hits, he would join the regional selection team.

⑤ The author’s father told him to stop playing baseball and start playing several sports during his fourth grade year of elementary school.

問3 According to the passage, which of the following is true?

① Until the fourth grade of elementary school, the author liked practicing baseball but disliked playing in games.

② The author contributed to the score for his team.

③ In grade school, the author regretted not being involved in a strategic game like chess, not baseball.

④ Trying to play baseball taught the author the value of attempting anything, even though he may not know the outcome.

⑤ When the author became an adult, he realized that when faced with a challenge he should just give up.

(☆☆☆◎◎◎◎◎)

【9】次の英文を読んで，以下の問に答えなさい。

When you go shopping, how do you make purchases? The first thing to consider may be the price. If you do not plan how much money you will spend and continue to buy anything you want, your budgets will quickly become strained.

The second would be its quality. Sometimes quality has priority compared to the price. When purchasing something, we are likely to consider the balance between budget and quality. However, if you add one more perspective, what would it be?

It should be “sustainability”. Most of the food we eat is supplied by imports from abroad. These include coffee, tea, flour, and corn. Some of these products that are sustainable for farmers are priced slightly higher. The price is set at a certain level so that farmers can get paid fairly for their hard work. Such products are called “Fairtrade” and are marked for consumers to purchase.

In addition to well-known Fairtrade products such as coffee and cacao, various other materials are marked as Fairtrade. One example is bamboo. Many bamboo products, such as baskets and shelves, are made in Cambodia and Thailand, and exported to Japan. Many expenses are included in the price of the product. For example, part of the profits are used to train bamboo artisans in each country.

It is certain that these goods are not inexpensive and are somewhat overpriced. However, in the producing countries, even in cases of extreme depression, these Fairtrade products can boost their economy. As I mentioned at the beginning, when we buy a product, we consider the balance between affordability and quality. I suggest that people in modern society should also think consistently about the possible impact of their purchase.

It may not be easy to do all the time, but I believe that thinking about sustainability when shopping can positively contribute to society.

問1　According to the passage, how do Fairtrade bamboo products contribute to artisans?

① Bamboo is cut in Cambodia, and assembled into baskets and shelves in Japan.

② The cost required to produce bamboo products is not included in Fairtrade prices.

③ The production of bamboo products has led to supporting their jobs in Cambodia and Thailand.

④ Processing bamboo is too difficult and is no longer a Fairtrade product.

⑤ Fairtrade products made from bamboo are so inexpensive that they do not support artisans' livelihood.

問2 According to the passage, which of the following is true about purchasing behavior?

① A rumor is used to help people think about some budgetary issues.

② Quality is the only factor to keep in mind when purchasing goods.

③ One deciding factor in purchasing a product is if it's within a budget.

④ Only daily necessities have been targeted for price increases in recent years.

⑤ Fairtrade products are becoming cheaper and cheaper than other products these days.

問3 According to the passage, which of the following is true about Fairtrade?

① All products are required to be Fairtrade products in some countries.

② Fairtrade products are unnoticed by consumers even when they are on display.

③ Purchase of Fairtrade products is one effective way to improve sustainability of the people involved.

④ Fairtrade products are no longer discussed for their sustainability aspects.

⑤ Fairtrade products are only limited to food and do not include other crafts or productions.

(☆☆☆◎◎◎◎◎)

【10】次の英文を読んで，以下の問に答えなさい。

Making a choice to make better decisions is based on the accumulated experience of the past and the possibilities of the future. It is also the output of complex information processing. Outputs are, to a certain extent, a direct product of choice. It is about acquiring a wide range of information and perceptions of a situation, organizing them, and choosing specific actions.

It often occurs that some kinds of obstacles, such as uncertainty and tiredness, hinder the process of decision making. Then how about sleep shortage? We know it can affect us mentally or physically in our daily lives. For example, when we are sleep deprived, we have a reduced appetite. Moreover, our performance at work also deteriorates. In the morning, we manage to finish the tasks we are assigned, but in the afternoon hours, our work pace suddenly decreases. Our output quality likely goes down due to lack of sleep because our brains become incapable of using a proper decision making method. But is it always true?

Let's consider cooking and travel. Most people, while wandering around the supermarket, probably consider the balance between what is better and what is burdensome. Then they make the appropriate choice without too much effort by checking their memories and knowledge from the past. Sleep deprivation should have some impact. However, many people may decide what to have for dinner spontaneously rather than carefully considering what they had yesterday or the day before. They can make exciting new choices.

What about traveling? Let's consider a case of independent travel. We enjoy the excitement of being in a place completely different from our everyday lives, making unexpected choices, starting in new directions, and thinking about where to have lunch. We enjoy the excitement of making new choices, not based on past knowledge, but the anticipation of our future. At such times, even if one is sleep deprived, the anticipation and excitement of the journey can easily overcome that condition. The lack of sleep will have little effect on the choices and decisions that will be made.

Thus, when we make choices, whether for work, dinner, or travel, we make judgements by comparing them to past experiences or anticipating the future. Just as the amount of sleep, anticipation, and excitement also appears to influence our choices, the influence between judgment and sleep should be different for every individual. Recognizing the different factors that influence our decision making helps us considerably.

問1　According to the passage, which of the following is true about making choices?

① Making choices is only based on one's previous experiences.

② One can reflect on the accumulation of past experiences and choose what is now considered better.

③ When putting a choice into action, it is recommended that failure should always be considered.

④ Although it is essential to make choices that everyone finds acceptable, it is also sometimes appropriate to make choices based on one's preferences.

⑤ Making choices has no connection with an individual's past experiences of success or failure.

問2　According to the passage, which of the following is true about appetite?

① Appetite has no direct causal factor to sleep deprivation.

② Sleeping in concentrated periods does not necessarily lead to a regain of appetite.

③ Appetite is affected more by physical activity than sleep, so moderate exercise is required.

④ For the author, lack of sleep affects appetite and decision making.

⑤ Sleep shortage definitely has nothing to do with our choice about cooking.

問3　According to the passage, which of the following is true about traveling?

① Traveling is never affected by lack of sleep and tiredness.

② Too much sleep in the afternoon cannot be recommended because our output quality easily deteriorates.

③ The effect of sleeplessness far exceeds excitement and anticipation when we make choices while traveling.

④ Lack of sleep has a possible correlation with decision making process, but the degree depends on each person.

⑤ Traveling with others makes it easier where to eat lunch.

問4　Which is the main topic of this passage?

① Effects of appetite on the brain.

② Comfortable sleep while traveling.

③ Change in efficiency of work between morning and afternoon.

④ Difference between individual and group behavior.

⑤ Various factors that affect our choices.

(☆☆☆◎◎◎◎◎)

【中学校】

【1】次の文は，「中学校学習指導要領解説　外国語編」(平成29年文部科学省)「第2章　外国語科の目標及び内容」「第1節　外国語科の目標」の一部である。次の(　①　)～(　⑤　)に当てはまる語句を書きなさい。ただし，同じ番号には同じ語句が入る。

> 第1節　外国語科の目標
>
> 外国語科では，次のように目標を設定した。
>
> －　中　略　－
>
> 「外国語によるコミュニケーションにおける見方・考え方」とは，外国語によるコミュニケーションの中で，どのような(　①　)で物事を捉え，どのような考え方で(　②　)していくのかという，物事を捉える(　①　)や考え方であり，「外国語で表現し伝え合

うため，外国語やその背景にある(　③　)を，社会や世界，(　④　)との関わりに着目して捉え，コミュニケーションを行う目的や場面，状況等に応じて，情報を整理しながら考えなどを形成し，(　⑤　)すること」であると考えられる。

(☆☆☆☆◎◎◎)

【2】次の文は，「中学校学習指導要領」(平成29年3月告示)「第2章　各教科」「第9節　外国語」「第2　各言語の目標及び内容等」「英語」「1目標」の一部である。次の(　①　)～(　⑤　)に当てはまる語句を書きなさい。ただし，同じ番号には同じ語句が入る。

第2　各言語の目標及び内容等

英語

1　目標

英語学習の特質を踏まえ，以下に示す，聞くこと，読むこと，話すこと[(　①　)]，話すこと・[発表]，書くことの五つの領域別に設定する目標の実現を目指した指導を通して，第1の(1)及び(2)に示す資質・能力を一体的に育成するとともに，その過程を通して，第1の(3)に示す資質・能力を育成する。

－　中　略　－

(2)　読むこと

ア　日常的な話題について，簡単な語句や文で書かれたものから必要な情報を読み取ることができるようにする。

イ　日常的な話題について，簡単な語句や文で書かれた短い文章の(　②　)を捉えることができるようにする。

ウ　(　③　)な話題について，簡単な語句や文で書かれた短い文章の要点を捉えることができるようにする。

－　中　略　－

(4)　話すこと[発表]

ア　関心のある事柄について，簡単な語句や文を用いて(④)で話すことができるようにする。

イ　日常的な話題について，事実や自分の考え，気持ちなどを整理し，簡単な語句や文を用いて(⑤)のある内容を話すことができるようにする。

ウ　(③)な話題に関して聞いたり読んだりしたことについて，考えたことや感じたこと，その理由などを，簡単な語句や文を用いて話すことができるようにする。

(☆☆☆☆◎◎◎)

【3】次の文は，「中学校学習指導要領」(平成29年3月告示)「第2章　各教科」「第9節　外国語」「第2　各言語の目標及び内容等」「英語」「3　指導計画の作成と内容の取扱い」の一部である。次の(①)～(⑤)に当てはまる語句を書きなさい。

3　指導計画の作成と内容の取扱い

－ 中　略 －

(2)　2の内容に示す事項については，次の事項に配慮するものとする。

－ 中　略 －

エ　文法事項の指導に当たっては，次の事項に留意すること。

－ 中　略 －

(イ)　文法はコミュニケーションを支えるものであることを踏まえ，コミュニケーションの目的を達成する上での必要性や有用性を実感させた上でその(①)を活用させたり，繰り返し使用することで当該文法事項の規則性や(②)などについて気付きを促したりするなど，言語活動と効果的に(③)指導すること。

－　中　略　－

キ　生徒が身に付けるべき資質・能力や生徒の実態，教材の内容などに応じて，視聴覚教材やコンピュータ，情報通信ネットワーク，教育機器などを有効活用し，生徒の興味・関心をより高め，指導の(　④　)や言語活動の更なる充実を図るようにすること。

ク　各単元や各時間の指導に当たっては，コミュニケーションを行う目的，場面，状況などを明確に設定し，言語活動を通して育成すべき資質・能力を明確に示すことにより，生徒が学習の(　⑤　)を立てたり，振り返ったりすることができるようにすること。

(☆☆☆☆◎◎◎)

【高等学校】

【1】次の文は，「高等学校学習指導要領解説　外国語編　英語編」(平成30年文部科学省)「第1部　外国語編」「第2章　外国語科の各科目」「第2節　英語コミュニケーションⅠ」「2　内容」の一部である。文中の(　①　)～(　⑤　)に当てはまる語句を書きなさい。ただし，同じ番号には同じ語句が入る。

〔思考力，判断力，表現力等〕

(2)　情報を整理しながら考えなどを形成し，英語で表現したり，伝え合ったりすることに関する事項

具体的な課題等を設定し，コミュニケーションを行う目的や場面，状況などに応じて，情報を整理しながら考えなどを形成し，これらを(　①　)に適切な英語で表現することを通して，次の事項を身に付けることができるよう指導する。

ここでは，本科目において身に付けるべき資質・能力の柱の一つとして，「思考力，判断力，表現力等」の内容を示している。

小学校の外国語科では，音声で十分に慣れ親しんだ語彙や基本的な表現を用いて，自分の考えや気持ちなどを伝え合う基礎的な力を養うことが求められている。

中学校では，外国語で簡単な情報や考えなどを理解したり，これらを(②)して適切に表現したり伝え合ったりすることができる力を養うことが求められている。

高等学校では，外国語で，情報や考えなどの(③)や要点，詳細，話し手や書き手の意図などを(④)に理解したり，これらを(②)して適切に表現したり伝え合ったりすることができる力を養うことが求められている。そのために，「具体的な課題等」の(⑤)に向けた英語を用いた言語活動の中で，「(①)に適切な英語で表現すること」を通して，以下のアからウの3点を身に付けることができるよう整理した。

－ 省 略 －

(☆☆☆☆◎◎◎)

【2】次の文は，「高等学校学習指導要領」(平成30年3月告示)「第2章 各学科に共通する各教科」「第8節　外国語」「第3款　英語に関する各科目にわたる指導計画の作成と内容の取扱い」の一部である。文中の(①)～(⑤)に当てはまる語句を以下の語群から一つずつ選んで記号で答えなさい。

3　教材については，次の事項に留意するものとする。

(1)　教材は，五つの領域別の言語活動及び複数の領域を結び付けた(①)な言語活動を通してコミュニケーションを図る資質・能力を総合的に育成するため，各科目の五つの領域別の目標と2に示す内容との関係について，単元など内容や時間の(　②　)ごとに各教材の中で明確に示すとともに，実際の言語の使用場面や言語の働きに十分に配慮した題材を取り上げること。その際，各科目の内容の(1)に示す(　③　)事項などを中心とした構成とならないよう十分に留意し，コミュニケーションを行う目的や場面，状況などを設定した上で，言語活動を通して育成すべき資質・能力を明確に示すこと。

(2)　英語を使用している人々を中心とする世界の人々や日本人の日常生活，風俗習慣，物語，地理，歴史，伝統文化，自然科学などに関するものの中から，生徒の発達の段階や興味・関心に即して適切な題材を効果的に取り上げるものとし，次の観点に配慮すること。

(ア)　多様な考え方に対する理解を深めさせ，公正な(　④　)を養い豊かな心情を育てるのに役立つこと。

(イ)　我が国の文化や，英語の背景にある文化に対する関心を高め，理解を深めようとする態度を養うのに役立つこと。

(ウ)　社会がグローバル化する中で，広い視野から国際理解を深め，国際社会と向き合うことが求められている我が国の一員としての自覚を高めるとともに，(　⑤　)の精神を養うのに役立つこと。

(エ)　人間，社会，自然などについての考えを深めるのに役立つこと。

≪語群≫

A　区切り　　B　判断力　　C　文法　　D　国際平和
E　指導　　F　国際協調　　G　包括的　　H　まとまり
I　統合的　　J　行動力

(☆☆☆☆◎◎◎)

【3】次の文は,「高等学校学習指導要領」(平成30年3月告示)「第2章　各学科に共通する各教科」「第8節　外国語」「第2款　各科目」「第4　論理・表現Ⅰ」「1　目標」の一部である。文中の(　①　)～(　⑤　)に当てはまる語句を書きなさい。ただし,同じ番号には同じ語句が入る。

> 英語学習の特質を踏まえ,以下に示す,話すこと[(　①　)],話すこと[発表],書くことの三つの領域(以下この節において「三つの領域」という。)別に設定する目標の実現を目指した指導を通して,第1款の(1)及び(2)に示す資質・能力を(　②　)に育成するとともに,その過程を通して,第1款の(3)に示す資質・能力を育成する。
>
> ― 中　略 ―
>
> (3)　書くこと
>
> ア　日常的な話題について,使用する語句や文,事前の準備などにおいて,多くの(　③　)を活用すれば,基本的な語句や文を用いて,情報や考え,気持ちなどを論理の構成や(　④　)を工夫して文章を書いて伝えることができるようにする。
>
> イ　日常的な話題や(　⑤　)な話題について,使用する語句や文,事前の準備などにおいて,多くの(　③　)を活用すれば,聞いたり読んだりしたことを活用しながら,基本的な語句や文を用いて,意見や主張などを論理の構成や(　④　)を工夫して文章を書いて伝えることができるようにする。

(☆☆☆☆◎◎◎)

解答・解説

【中高共通】

【1】Question 1　③　　Question 2　④　　Question 3　②

〈解説〉問題用紙には設問に対する解答の選択肢のみが印刷されており，2人の会話文及び設問が音声で与えられる問題になっている。放送は2回ある。　Question 1　Cathyの4つ目の発話に着目すると，Cathyの姉または妹に3年前に女の子が生まれて，その子に会うと述べられている。したがって，姪を意味する③が正解。　Question 2　Cathyの2つ目の発話とStaffの3つ目の発話に着目すると，Cathyが予約した飛行機のエコノミーの座席はオーバーブッキング状態で，座席が空いていないと述べられている。したがって，エコノミーの座席が全て埋まっているという④が正解。　Question 3　Cathyの最後の発話に着目すると，Cathyはビジネスクラスの座席でぐっすり寝たいと述べられている。したがって，②が正解。

【2】≪A≫　Question 1　④　　Question 2　②　　Question 3　①
≪B≫　Question 1　①　　Question 2　③　　Question 3　④

〈解説〉【1】と同様に，問題用紙には設問に対する選択肢のみが印刷されており，英文及び設問が音声で与えられる問題である。

≪A≫　Question 1　第2パラグラフの3文目と4文目に対応する記述があり，フィンランドで義務教育1年目にプログラミング教育が行われるのは，インターネットに接続するのは市民の権利であり，ITが生活に不可欠であるためである。 Question 2　第3パラグラフの3文目に対応する記述があり，デンマークの学習プラットフォームによって，教師，子どもそして保護者が学習の進捗状況を共有することができる。 Question 3　第2パラグラフの2文目に対応する記述がある。フィンランドでは教師がどのように教えるかよりも，子どもがどのように学習するかの方が重要である。≪B≫　Question 1　第2パラグラフの1文目に対応する記述がある。ヒンドゥー教徒がガンジス川で沐浴するのは，ガンジス川の水が全ての罪を洗い流してくれると信じられているためである。 Question 2 第2パラグラフの3文目に対応する記述がある。ガンジス川を訪れることで，ヒンドゥー教徒の死生観を学ぶことができる。 Question 3 第4パラグラフの3文目に対応する記述があり，ガンジス川の景色が数百年間は変わっていないと述べられている。

【3】Question 1 ② Question 2 ③ Question 3 ④

〈解説〉【1】及び【2】とは異なり，英文および設問に加えて選択肢も音声で与えられる問題である。 Question 1 第2パラグラフの2文目に対応する記述がある。Keikoの両親は，1年間の海外留学をすることで，日本の大学入試のための勉強ができなくなることを心配している。Question 2 第4パラグラフの3文目と4文目に対応する記述がある。Keikoは，海外留学することで言語だけでなく，国際社会において重要となる，様々な文化に適応する能力を身につけることができるとわかったと述べられている。 選択肢の①も紛らわしいが，入試を受けなくてもよいとまでは述べられていないため不適切である。

Question 3 第3パラグラフの最終文と第5パラグラフの1文目に対応する記述がある。Keikoは担任の先生と会うために両親と一緒に学校に向かっていると述べられており，Keikoの両親は海外留学を認めていることがわかる。

【4】3，5

〈解説〉読み上げられる英文の内容と一致するものを，音声で与えられる選択肢の中から2つ選ぶ問題。まず，第2パラグラフの2文目に，選択肢3と対応する記述がある。猫が水を飲むとき，慣性と重力のバランスが利用されている。次に，第3パラグラフの3文目に，選択肢5と対応する記述がある。猫には口回りだけでなく脚にもひげがあると述べられている。

【5】問1　⑤　　問2　②　　問3　①　　問4　④　　問5　④

〈解説〉問1　英文は「Marieと私がICT事業を立ち上げる前に，私たちは，私たちの責任を詳細に説明した法的拘束力のある契約書を書いた」の意である。legally bindingは「法的拘束力のある」の意味である。

問2　英文は「私たちの会社はEメールやファックスによる全ての問い合わせにすぐ対応するように努めている」の意である。promptlyは「すぐに」の意味である。　問3　英文は「昨年下半期の好業績とは対照的に，今年の上半期はとても芳しくなかった」の意である。今回の文脈でperformanceは「業績」の意味である。　問4　英文は「この地域の住民は，公民館が閉鎖することに対して十分に告知されていなかったと市に苦情を言った」の意である。sufficientは「十分に」の意味である。　問5　英文は「改修工事のため，これから1カ月間は，体育館のトイレの使用が制限される予定だ」の意である。be restrictedは「制限される」の意味である。

【6】問1　②　　問2　⑤　　問3　④

〈解説〉問1　完成した英文はJust before passengers were about to board the plane, it was announced that it would be canceled due to bad weather.であり，be about to doは「まさに～しようとしている」の意である。

問2　完成した英文はThey would not have been able to complete the project without the hard work of their team members.である。カッコの直前にableがあることから，その直後にto不定詞が続くことに着目すればよい。　問3　完成した英文はIn recent years, the shortage of qualified labor has become a serious problem for many small businesses in this town.である。まず，この文の最初にあるIn recent yearsに着目すれば，この文は現在完了形であるため，カッコの直後のbecomeは過去分詞であることがわかる。そのため，hasはカッコ内の最後に位置する。また，与えられた日本語にある「労働者の不足」が主語であることを受けて，the shortage ofの形になることがわかれば，あとは「有能な労働者」をqualified laborとして続ければよい。

【7】問1　③　　問2　②

〈解説〉問1　会話文を全て並べると，F→B→A→E→D→Cの順番になる。まずは，カスタマーセンターからの発話であるFから始まり，その後半にあるCan I help you?を受けて，電話の用件を説明しているBが続く。そして，名前と予約番号を尋ねるAが続き，それを受けて名前を名乗っているEが続き，その後半にあるI don't know the registration number…を受けたDが続く。Dの後半にあるI'll have a staff come up and take a look at it for you right now.を受けたCが最後になる。　問2　会話文を全て並べると，D→E→A→C→B→Fの順番になる。まずは，ベトナム旅行の感想を尋ねているDから始まり，それを受けたEが続く。そして，ベトナムのハノイ支社で勤務しないかと尋ねているAが続き，それを受けて旅行と実際に住むのは異なると答えているCが続く。Cを受けて，ハノイ勤務についてもう少し考えて欲しいと言うB，それを受けたFが続く。

【8】問1　⑤　　問2　③　　問3　④

〈解説〉問1　補充する英文は「自分の経験を通して，もし結果がわからなかったとしても，重要なのは，行動をして常にベストを尽くすということである」の意である。著者がベストを尽くした場面が，第6パラグラフにある初めての野球の試合として描かれていることに着目すればよい。　問2　対応する記述が第3パラグラフの3文目にある。著者の父は「とりあえず1カ月やってみて様子を見てごらん」と言ったことがわかる。　問3　対応する記述が問1で補充した英文と，第8パラグラフの4文目及び6文目にある。野球の経験から，著者は何事にも挑戦してみることが重要だと学んだのである。

【9】問1　③　　問2　③　　問3　③

〈解説〉問1　対応する記述が第4パラグラフの3～5文目にある。カゴやシェルフなどの竹細工品はカンボジアやタイで作られており，その利益の一部が竹細工職人の育成に使われていると述べられている。

問2　対応する記述は第1パラグラフの2文目及び3文目にある。買い物をする際に考慮する点として値段があり，値段を考えずに欲しいものを買い続けていたらすぐに予算がなくなると述べられている。
問3　対応する記述が第3パラグラフの4～6文目にある。フェアトレード商品は少し値段が高いが，それよって農家が持続可能になると述べられている。

【10】問1　②　　問2　④　　問3　④　　問4　⑤
〈解説〉問1　対応する記述が第1パラグラフの1文目にある。良い決定のための選択は，過去の経験の蓄積と未来の可能性に基づいている，と述べられている。 問2　対応する記述が第2パラグラフの4文目及び7文目にある。睡眠不足によって食欲が減退し，私たちの脳が適切な意思決定ができなくなると述べられている。 問3　対応する記述が第5パラグラフの2文目にある。睡眠と判断の関係は個人によって異なると述べられている。 問4　この英文では選択や意思決定をするためには睡眠をはじめとして様々な要因が影響することが述べられている。例えば，第2パラグラフでは睡眠が意思決定に与える影響が述べられており，第4パラグラフでは期待と興奮が睡眠不足の影響を相殺することが述べられている。そして，第5パラグラフの3文目では，私たちの意思決定に影響する様々な要因を認識することが助けになると述べられている。これらを踏まえると正解は5である。

【中学校】

【1】①　視点　　②　思考　　③　文化　　④　他者　　⑤　再構築
〈解説〉出題箇所は，外国語科の目標のうち，「外国語によるコミュニケーションにおける見方・考え方」についての解説の一部である。外国語やその背景にある文化を理解することで他者に配慮したコミュニケーションを行うことが重要とされている。

【2】① やり取り　② 概要　③ 社会的　④ 即興　⑤ まとまり

〈解説〉外国語科における英語の目標と，領域別の目標からの出題である。
① 空欄の直後にある「話すこと[発表]」に着目すれば，正答は「話すこと[やり取り]」であることがわかる。 ② 「読むこと」の目標のうち，項目ウが「文章の要点を捉える」であることに着目すれば，項目イは「文章の『概要』を捉える」と推測できるだろう。なお，「要点を捉える」とは「例えば説明文などのまとまりのある文章を最初から最後まで読み，含まれている複数の情報の中から，書き手が最も伝えたいことは何であるかを判断して捉えること」であり，「概要を捉える」とは「登場人物の行動や心情の変化，全体のあらすじなど，書き手が述べていることの大まかな内容を捉えること」と定義されている。 ③ 「話すこと[発表]」の項目ウとも共通しているが，小学校で身近な事柄や日常生活に関する事柄を扱っているのを受け，中学校では「社会的」な話題を扱うことが求められている。 ④ 小学校における目標を踏まえて，中学校段階では，既習の語句や文を用いて，「即興」で話すことができるようにすることが求められている。
⑤ 空欄の直前にある「事実や自分の考え，気持ちなどを整理し」に着目する。聞き手を踏まえて「まとまりのある」内容を話すことが求められている。

【3】① 知識　② 構造　③ 関連付けて　④ 効率化
⑤ 見通し

〈解説〉①～③ 項目エは文法事項の取扱いに関する記述である。「文法はコミュニケーションを支えるものである」に着目し，文法は知識だけを教え込むものではなく，コミュニケーションを通して気付きを促したり，活用させたりすることが求められていることを踏まえたい。すると，①で求められているのは「知識」の活用であることがわかる。②は空欄直前にある「当該文法事項の規則性」に着目すれば，それと並列されているのは文法知識の一側面であることがわかるため，「構造」が答えとなる。③は前述のように，文法知識はコミュニケーションを支えるものであるから，言語活動と「関連付け」ることが不可欠である。　④　ICTの活用に関する記述である。ICTは個別最適な学びの実現に大きく関わっており，指導の「効率化」が可能になる。
⑤　思考力，判断力，表現力等を高めるための各単元や各時間の指導における学習過程に関する記述である。生徒が学習到達目標を達成できるように，生徒自らが「見通し」を立てて，主体的に学習に取り組めるようにすることが求められている。

【高等学校】

【1】①　論理的　　②　活用　　③　概要　　④　的確　　⑤　解決

〈解説〉外国語科における思考力，判断力，表現力等の内容に関する問題である。小学校で養った自分の考えや気持ちなどを伝え合う基礎的な力と，中学校で養った適切に表現したり伝え合ったりすることができる力を踏まえ，考えなどを形成し，論理的に適切な英語で表現することが求められている。　①　今回の学習指導要領から「論理・表現Ⅰ～Ⅲ」が新設されたことに着目するとよいだろう。　②　中学校の内容に関する記述である。①の直後に「適切な英語で表現する」とあることに着目するとよいだろう。　③　直後にある「要点」に着目するとよい。現行の学習指導要領において，「概要」と「要点」はセットで用いられることが多い。これらの定義については【中学校】【2】の解説で述べているので適宜参考にしてほしい。　④　外国語科の目標に「統合的な言語活動を通して，情報や考えなどを的確に理解したり」とあるのと同様である。　⑤　課題(問題)解決型学習(PBL：project based learning)が推進されていることを踏まえ，「具体的な課題等」の解決を目指すことが重要とされている。

【2】①　I　　②　H　　③　C　　④　B　　⑤　F

〈解説〉教材についての配慮事項に関する問題である。語群が与えられてはいるが，紛らわしい選択肢もあるために慎重に解答を選ぶ必要がある。① 高等学校における外国語科では頻出である「複数の領域を結び付けた『統合的』な言語活動」である。推進されている「技能統合型の言語活動」といった言葉から類推することもできるだろう。
② 空欄直前にある「単元など内容や時間の」に着目すれば，「まとまり」であることがわかるだろう。 ③ 空欄直後にある「事項などを中心とした構成とならないよう十分に留意し」に着目する。従来の文法知識偏重型の授業からの脱却が求められていることから，「文法」(事項)であることがわかる。 ④・⑤ 題材の選択に関する4つの観点に関する記述である。④は多様な考え方や様々な価値観に接することで，公正かつ客観的な「判断力」を養うことが求められている。⑤は「国際理解を深め，国際社会と向き合う」に着目するとよい。日本や世界で起こっていることや話題になっていることについて多面的に考え，「国際協調」の精神を養うことで，平和な共生社会を築いていけるようにすることが求められている。

【3】① やり取り ② 一体的 ③ 支援 ④ 展開 ⑤ 社会的

〈解説〉① 空欄の直後にある「話すこと[発表]」に着目すれば，「話すこと[やり取り]」が正答であることがわかる。 ② 空欄直前にある「第1款の(1)及び(2)に示す資質・能力」が，知識及び技能と思考力，判断力，表現力等であることに着目すればよい。これらを「一体的」に育成することが求められている。 ③～⑤ 書くことの目標である。③は，これが論理・表現Ⅰの目標であることと，前後にある「多くの～を活用すれば」に着目すればよい。論理・表現Ⅰでは「多くの支援」であり，論理・表現Ⅱでは「一定の支援」，そして論理・表現Ⅲでは「支援をほとんど活用しなくても」と，学年が上がるにつれて支援を減らしていくことに留意する。④は空欄直前にある「論理の構成」に着目すればよい。情報や考え，気持ちなどを論理的に伝えるためには，モデルなどを活用して「展開」の仕方を学ぶことが重要とされている。最後に⑤も空欄直前にある「日常的な話題」に着目すればよい。中学校から，日常的な話題に加えて社会的な話題を取り扱うことが求められており，「日常的な話題」と「社会的な話題」はセットで用いられることが多い。

2023年度　実施問題

※福岡市を志望する場合は，【中高共通】の【5】～【11】を解答して下さい。

【中高共通】

【1】次に読まれる英文を聞き，1～3の設問に対する答えとして最も適切なものを，四つの選択肢の中から一つ選びなさい。
(英文及び設問は2回読まれる。)

David : Hello, Sophia. Do you have any plans this Saturday?

Sophia : Hey David. No, I don't have any plans, but why?

David : It looks like it'll rain this Saturday. Would you like to go to the movies?

Sophia : Sure! What kind of movie do you want to see?

David : Well.. I was thinking about watching an action thriller. I like the excitement.
My own life has been quite boring recently. Hahaha.

Sophia : Hahaha. Action movies are ok, but comedies are my favorite.

David : A comedy would be good to watch, too! How about watching that new action comedy film that just opened last Friday? It's also streaming online.

Sophia : Good suggestion! Let's watch it.
Which would you prefer, streaming it online or going to the theater?

David : I'm not sure. I've only been watching movies by streaming them at home recently.
I miss watching movies on the big screen, even though it is expensive and sometimes the theater gets crowded.

Sophia : It does cost a bit, but sometimes you can get the special posters or limited-edition items if you go the movie theater.

David : That's true. I really value limited edition items because I can only buy them then.
So, I guess each choice has its good and bad points. Hmm··· Why don't we try going to the theater in the morning? It will be less crowded than the evening, and tickets are a little cheaper.

Sophia : That's a good idea!

David : Also, we can eat lunch together after watching the movie. There is a recommended café nearby that's been getting really good reviews.

Sophia : That would be very nice.

David : Great! I'll pick you up in my car and we can go together. Is 9am ok?

Sophia : That works for me. I will see you then.

Question 1 : What kind of movie will David and Sophia see this Saturday?

① Adventure

② Action thriller

③ Action comedy

④ Documentary

Question 2 : Why will David and Sophia watch the movie in the morning?

① Theaters are not jammed with people.

② They will get the special posters.

③ They can see movies on a big screen.

④ Movie tickets are more expensive.

Question 3 : How will David and Sophia go to the theater?

① By bus

② By Sophia's car

③ By David's car

④ On foot

(☆☆◎◎◎◎)

【2】次に読まれる英文≪A≫及び英文≪B≫について，それぞれの1～3の設問に対する答えとして最も適切なものを，四つの選択肢の中から一つ選びなさい。
(英文及び設問は2回読まれる。)
≪A≫

"Work-life balance" has become important in recent years. Work-style reform is one of Japan's national policies. It is necessary to ensure a happy and harmonious life for workers. The following social backgrounds contribute to why work-style reforms are being promoted.

One is because there is a shortage of workers due to the declining birthrate and aging population. This causes long and increasing working hours to fill the empty roles. Some people get sick from stress or quit their jobs because of this. It is becoming a common problem in society.

Another is that the number of double-income households is increasing. Instead of being away all day, workers would benefit from an environment where parents can work and raise their children comfortably.

Additionally, the mindset of employees is diversifying. The number of people who highly value community and home life activities, regardless of employment type, is increasing.

New work-styles are being introduced to promote work-style reforms. One example is the flex-time system which allows employees to choose when they start and end work every day, giving them the ability to balance their professional and private schedules more easily.

Another example is teleworking: a system that allows employees to work outside of an office in a location they choose. This helps the employees work while balancing childcare, nursing care, and housework.

Various other systems have been introduced by companies to improve employee work-life balance. Work-life balance is not about having to choose between work and private life, but about creating a harmonious relationship between both.

(253 words)

Question 1 : According to the passage, which statement is not true about the social backgrounds prompting reforms in work-life balance?

① Long working hours have become a problem due to the chronic labor shortage.

② It is favorable to have an environment where people can work while raising children.

③ The number of people who place importance on home and community activities has increased.

④ Increasing double-income households means that people can afford to quit their jobs.

Question 2 : According to the passage, what is an advantage of the flex-time system?

① People can balance their daily private schedules with their work schedules.

② The company decides the starting and finishing times of employees'daily work.

③ Double-income households prevent the declining birthrate and aging population.

④ Workers can work remotely and in a place that is not an office.

Question 3 : According to the passage, which statement is true?

① Work-style reform cannot be done without incorporating a flex-time and telework systems.

② Having an aging population is important to prevent labor shortages.

③ Work-life balance is meant to create a healthy system by harmonizing work and private life.

④ Community and home life activities cause long working hours to happen more frequently.

≪B≫

Since 2020, programming education has been introduced in elementary, junior, and senior high schools. Typically, programming means to make a computer perform an intended operation by giving it instructions in a particular order. However, programming education emphasizes using programming as a tool to develop students' ability to think logically. This is called "programming thinking".

In elementary school, there is no Programming Education class. Instead, the programming element is incorporated into existing subjects such as mathematics and science. In elementary school, developing programmig thinking is the focus of programming education. While students may first experience programming thinking by using a computer, it is also possible to learn it without a computer using a learning method called "unplugged".

In junior high school, students begin taking a Technology and Home Economics course. In addition to creating a computer program, students are required to check, verify, evaluate, improve, and correct their program's operations. It is said that two-way communication between computer and programmer is important. Additionally, a key teaching point in the programming curriculum is "to solve problems in life and in society".

In high school, the main objective in programming class is not to acquire programming skills, but to focus on and understand the mechanism by which information is processed by computers. Furthermore, students must be able to discover and solve problems. This is important in all aspects of life.

By gaining experience in programming thinking in elementary and junior high school, and creating interactive content by programming, students will further deepen their ability to utilize information in high school. In this way, children will acquire basic programming skills, as well as the abilities to think logically and utilize, their knowledge.

(278 words)

Question 1 : According to the passage, what is emphasized in programming education?

① Giving instructions to the computer in order
② Acquiring the ability to think logically
③ Discovering programming skills and knowledge
④ Learning basic programming methods

Question 2 : According to the passage, what is a learning objective of programming classes in junior high school?

① Learning by yourself without using a computer
② Incorporating programming elements into math and science courses.
③ Solving problems in daily life and society
④ Focusing on how information is processed

Question 3 : According to the passage, which statement is true about programming education?

① There are Programming Education classes in elementary schools and junior high schools.
② In all school education, it is the most important to create interactive content in programming.
③ "Unplugged" is not recommended in elementary school programming education.
④ Programming thinking is the ability to think logically, which is developed by learning programming.

(☆☆☆☆◎◎◎◎)

【3】次に読まれる英文を聞き，1～3の設問に対する答えとして最も適切なものを，その後に読まれる四つの選択肢の中から一つ選びなさい。(英文，設問及び選択肢は2回読まれる。)

The aurora is, to put it simply, a light show caused when a flow of electrically charged particles emitted by the sun rushes into the Earth's polar atmosphere and emerges in the sky. The aurora has stirred up our human imagination for a long time. Some say that the supernatural appearance, beauty, and scale of the aurora are not found in other natural phenomena on Earth.

Its name comes from ancient Roman mythology. The goddess Aurora in Roman mythology brought dawn and hope to the creatures on Earth. She drove away the darkness of the night and gave light to the world. Thanks to the goddess Aurora, the dark nights don't last forever, and they give way to morning.

Where does the aurora occur? Many people think that the aurora can only occur in cold regions. However, in fact, the temperature on the ground is not related to the occurrence of the aurora itself. Due to the balance between the solar wind and the Earth's magnetic field, the aurora just happens to appear in the cold polar regions.

As well as seeing the beautiful lights, there are many people around the world who have claimed to hear sound from the aurora. However, it has not been scientifically proven to exist. The University of Helsinki, Finland, hired many subjects to wear blindfolds and study any sounds they heard from the aurora. The subjects allegedly heard sounds which were very similar to the sounds of trees swaying in the wind or the winter clothes they were wearing rubbing together.

(257 words)

Question 1 : According to the passage, what did the goddess Aurora do?

1 She used the magic of light to punish people with dark ideas.

2 She ruled the night and brought it to the faithful people.

3 She ran through the night, giving darkness to some people and light to others.

4 She gave hope and brought the sunrise upon the world.

Question 2 : According to the passage, which sentence correctly describes the generation of the aurora?

1 The solar wind is the necessary element for the generation of the

aurora, but the magnetic field has little effect.

2 The lower the temperature, the greater the influence on the generation of the aurora.

3 The aurora is naturally generated under the influence of the solar wind and magnetic field.

4 The solar temperature and magnetic field are irrelevant to the generation of the aurora.

Question 3 : According to the passage, which sentence correctly describes the experiment by the University of Helsinki?

1 The subjects were given no chance to see the aurora during the experiment.

2 The subjects were not allowed to move while looking at the aurora.

3 The testimony of all the subjects proved that the aurora does not produce sound.

4 The subjects participated in light clothing because winter clothing makes a noise when walking.

(☆☆☆☆◎◎◎)

【4】次に読まれる英文を聞き，英文の内容に合致するものを，その後に読まれる六つの選択肢の中から二つ選びなさい。
(英文及び選択肢は2回読まれる。)

Good morning. Thank you for tuning in to this radio show. This is Judy. Today, I would like to take you on a walk around London.

We are now in front of Buckingham Palace. The Changing of the Guards usually starts at about 11 o'clock, but it seems to be a little late today. Oh, it's starting now. This ritual, in which the current set of guards is replaced by the next set, is accompanied by a performance by the military band. The key to the tightly controlled palace will be handed over to the next guard. This is a well-known ritual in London, so it's a must-see sightseeing event for tourists in London.

Next, let's go to Trafalgar Square, named after the British naval victory in 1805. The landmark of the Square is the Nelson Monument. It is a tall column with a statue of Admiral Nelson at the top, and four lion statues around the foot of the monument. Lions are the national animal of England, and the statues are the work of sculptor Sir Edwin Landseer. This square is visited by more than 30 million tourists annually, and it is a popular site for political speeches and other gatherings.

Next, let's cross the Square to the National Gallery. This is a large museum of European art, with famous paintings by Van Gogh, Picasso and Monet. There are many pictures in here that you might have seen in textbooks. It would take 3-4 hours to take a closer look at all the paintings, but today we are planning to go around a bit faster and stay for an hour, then have a late lunch over at the Sky Garden on the 35th floor of the Walkie Talkie. You can enjoy a delicious lunch for about 20 pounds. From here, you can get a free panoramic view of London. The recommended time for the best view is 30 minutes to an hour before sunset, but it seems that we'll be a little too early today. That's all for today's trip. Tune in tomorrow for the last part of our day out in London. Have a nice afternoon.

(358 words)

1 Judy was late for the Changing of the Guards, so she could not watch the first part of the ritual.
2 The change of personnel ritual is famous and tourists should take a look at it.
3 Below the statue of Admiral Nelson are statues of lions.
4 30 million people give speeches annually in Trafalgar Square.
5 The admission fee for the Sky Garden is 20 pounds and meals cost 35 pounds.
6 The continuation of this journey will take place the day after tomorrow.

(☆☆☆☆◎◎◎)

【5】英文の意味が通るように，(　　)内に入る最も適切なものを選びなさい。

問1　The plans for outdoor events on weekends will be (　　) on the weather.

①　independent　②　reliable　③　continual　④　contingent
⑤　instigated

問2　The water shortage made the people in urban areas (　　) on the use of rainwater whenever possible.

①　target　②　aim　③　focus　④　head　⑤　goal

問3　The university hopes to increase the (　　) of international students by advertising on social media that it offers special scholarships.

①　enrollment　②　annulment　③　clarity　④　stability
⑤　exodus

問4　For most people in the world, smart phones have become a(n) (　　) part of daily life.

①　altruistic　②　indispensable　③　controversial
④　fictitious　⑤　obsolete

問5　It's important to have a few close friends that you can (　　) in when you're in trouble.

①　berate　②　accuse　③　finesse　④　reminisce
⑤　confide

(☆☆☆☆☆◎◎◎◎◎)

【6】次の各問の日本文の意味を表す英文を作るために，(　　)内のA～Eの語句を正しく並べかえたとき，2番目と4番目にくる最も適切な組合せを選びなさい。ただし，組合せの左側を2番目，右側を4番目とする。

問1　幕が上がって司会者がステージに入って来ると，ホールは静けさに包まれた。

A ($_{\text{A}}$over　$_{\text{B}}$the　$_{\text{C}}$hush　$_{\text{D}}$hall　$_{\text{E}}$fell) when the curtain went up and the chairperson stepped onto the stage.

① A－E　② C－A　③ D－A　④ E－B　⑤ E－C

問2　お互いに何年もの間，競い合ってきた後で，その2人のプレーヤーは相互に深い尊敬の念を抱くようになった。

After years ($_A$<u>against</u>　$_B$<u>competing</u>　$_C$<u>one</u>　$_D$<u>another</u>　$_E$<u>of</u>), the two players have developed a deep feeling of mutual respect.

① A－C　② B－C　③ C－B　④ C－E　⑤ D－B

問3　アンケートを集約する最も簡単な方法は，専用のソフトウェアを使うことだ。

The easiest way to ($_A$<u>surveys</u>　$_B$<u>is</u>　$_C$<u>aggregate</u>　$_D$<u>use</u>　$_E$<u>to</u>) dedicated software.

① A－C　② A－E　③ B－A　④ C－B　⑤ E－D

問4　将来どれくらいお金を稼ぐかよりも，自分の興味に基づいて専攻を選ぶ学生たちの方が，いっそう大学生活を楽しむことができると私は思う。

I think that students ($_A$<u>on</u>　$_B$<u>majors</u>　$_C$<u>who</u>　$_D$<u>based</u>　$_E$<u>choose</u>) their interests rather than how much money they might earn in the future can enjoy college more.

① B－D　② C－B　③ D－C　④ E－B　⑤ E－D

(☆☆◎◎◎◎◎)

【7】次の各問のA～Fの英文を二人の会話として意味がつながるように並べかえるとき，2番目と4番目にくる最も適切な組合せを選びなさい。ただし，組合せの左側を2番目，右側を4番目とする。

問1　A : I see. Thank you, Jenny. I will go there tomorrow afternoon.

B : I was thinking of doing the same next year, but I don't know what I should do. Could you give me some advice?

C : I will be free tomorrow afternoon, so I can go with you, if you'd like.

D : Oh, OK. I went to the international studies department of the student services. They gave me a lot of information for studying abroad. You should go there first.

E : Yes, I was in New York for ten months to study architecture.

F : Hi, Jenny. You studied abroad in America last year, right?

① A－B　② B－E　③ C－A　④ D－F　⑤ E－D

問2　A : Yes, they're on a blue leather key chain and there are three keys on it, including my house key.

B : Hello, PIER Department store. This is Matt speaking. May I have your name?

C : Can you describe them?

D : Thank you so much. I'll be there in thirty minutes.

E : Ok, just a moment. Let me check... Yes, we have them. We'll keep them for you at the service counter on the first floor. Please explain the situation to our staff when you arrive.

F : Hi, my name is Jane. I have a question about your lost and found. I think I left my keys on the bench in front of T Café today.

① A－F　② B－E　③ B－F　④ F－A　⑤ F－D

(☆☆☆◎◎◎◎◎)

【8】次の各問の英文を読み，文脈から考えて文中の(　　)に入る最も適切なものを選びなさい。

問1　What kind of physical activity is needed to obtain health benefits?

Walking (　　). Research has shown that walking at a lively pace at least 120 minutes a week can help improve sleep, memory, and the ability to think and learn. It also reduces anxiety symptoms. Walking costs nothing and can be done anytime, just about anywhere.

① is ineffective exercise for maintaining your health

② is a great way to improve or maintain your overall health

③ may help increase your blood pressure

④ for exercise will give you higher stress

⑤ is complicated and one of the most difficult ways to get more active

問2 An internship is a program offered by an employer that provides potential employees with work experience. Generally, there are two types of internships. One is a part-time internship; the other is a full-time one. The main objective of internships for university seniors is to gain a deeper understanding of what it means to work. Students will (　　) through some work experience and meeting people with many different occupations.

① start to think about what they will major in at college
② quit learning about what is important for working
③ have no chance to work in the future
④ be discouraged from working together with co-workers
⑤ discover what they really want to do in the future

問3 Adequate quality sleep is essential for our health and well-being. Why is good quality sleep important? If you have poor quality sleep, no matter how long you sleep, you'll still feel sleepy. How then can we improve our sleep quality? Here are some tips from my personal experiences.

First, create a bedtime routine. Go to bed at about the same time each night and wake up at the same time each morning. Secondly, avoid caffeine which can interfere with your sleep. Lastly, do not use electronic devices at least 30 minutes before bedtime.

Please remember; Having good sleep habits can (　　).

① affect and disrupt your day-to-day life
② make your blood pressure go up
③ help you improve your health and quality of life
④ be the cause of a broad spectrum of diseases
⑤ harm every organ of the body

問4 There are computers which you can wear on your wrist, arm, or head such as smart watches or smart glasses. We used to see items like these in anime, but they're finally becoming a reality. They are the result of great progress in (　　), such as CPUs and memory units. These wearable devices have a wide range of uses, for example, receiving and checking emails and messages posted on social media, monitoring heart rate, and recording hours slept. We can choose a device according to our needs.

① increasing the size of cellphones

② years of watching anime

③ delaying technological innovation in Japan

④ the miniaturization of computer components

⑤ a scientific decline of robotics

問5 What is needed to achieve a major goal in a business or sports team?

Sharing a vision with people in the team is the first step for it. By doing this, everybody in the team can understand where they all should be headed. There are some small goals necessary for reaching the final goal, so people have to divide roles in the team and decide who will do what, by when. Then, each person can take responsibility and have a sense of purpose in the mission. It is also important for people to evaluate what they have done in the short term and evaluate and improve the way to do their job.

(　　) makes a successful team.

① The lack of mutual understanding among teammates

② Having individual, divergent goals

③ Sticking to traditional practices

④ Having everyone play the same role

⑤ Repeating the cycle of focus and improvement

(☆☆☆◎◎◎◎◎)

【9】次の英文を読んで，以下の問に答えなさい。

Have you ever heard the word “serendipity” ?

The (A) about Alexander Fleming accidentally discovering penicillin is very famous around the world. In the early 1920s, Fleming tried various fungicides on bacteria and white blood cells. While observing the Petri dish, a drop of tears fell on the bacterial incubator. A day later, he examined the dish and noticed that there were no bacteria around where the tears fell. As he continued his experiments, one day he noticed that one of the dishes in which the bacteria were cultivated had (B) spaces where no microorganisms were growing. When he looked at them closely, there was mold in the center. Mold spores were somehow mixed into the dish. This one coincidence was the next big discovery that saved millions of lives. His willingness to research encouraged his experiments, even though he had made countless mistakes by the time he got there.

Archimedes' bathtub, Newton's apples, and Watt's steaming kettles may certainly be myths curated by fans for future generations. However, in each of these cases, it is the diligent minds of sientists and inventors that have turned the (C) phenomena into new means understanding.

"Serendipity" means something good happening by chance. It is important to always strive for awareness of many issues so that (D).

問1 Choose the most appropriate word from the following that will fit in (A) in the sentence.

① despair
② suspicion
③ compassion
④ uniformity
⑤ anecdote

問2 Choose the most appropriate word from the following that will fit in (B) in the sentence.

① concentric
② desirable
③ relaxing
④ formidable
⑤ capricious

問3 Choose the most appropriate word from the following that will fit in (C) in the sentence.

① optimum
② mundane
③ placid
④ versatile
⑤ vicious

問4 Choose the most appropriate phrase from the following that will fit in (D) in the sentence.

① you may be able to convert brief moments of chance into inspiration and excellent results
② you can express your feelings honestly and you can be positive
③ you will be able to turn abstract ideas into concrete events and make yourself understood
④ you can be fair to all and be a world-famous person like Alexander Fleming
⑤ you will be able to discover bacteria that are useful for human health from many types of microorganisms

(☆☆☆☆☆◎◎◎◎◎)

【10】次の英文を読んで，以下の問に答えなさい。

Many people have heard about “The Super Bowl”. It is the annual champion ship game of the National Football League. Then, how about “The Japan Bowl” ? Is it also the name of an NFL game?

The National Japan Bowl Tournament is one of the best Japanese language contests in the United States, celebrating its 30th anniversary this year. Every spring, the Japan-America Society of Washington DC invites 200 of the best Japanese language learners from American high schools to Washington, DC to take part in a tournament. Since 2020, the Japan Bowl has been held online as “The Digital Japan Bowl”.

The Japan Bowl was established in 1992. Contestants compete with their knowledge of Japanese language and culture, and it is a competition to measure the progress of Japanese learners throughout the US. The first Japan Bowl Tournament was a (A) tournament just for Washington, DC. After that, high schools around the United States began to participate in the tournament and, within a few years, it developed into the grand-scale tournament that it is today.

One of the unique features of the Japan Bowl is that it assesses not only language, but also knowledge of Japanese culture, society, daily life, history, geography, and even current affairs. This is because, when a student chooses to study Japanese, they are also inherently expressing interest in learning about the language's origin country. Contestants are divided according to their level of Japanese proficiency and compete in teams of three.

The Japan Bowl is unlike a general exam and more like a quiz game. Contestants are asked questions and consult with their team members to answer within a limited time. Questions are delivered in both Japanese and English about (B). The participating students spend a lot of time preparing for the Japan Bowl through autonomous learning and collaborative learning. By forming a team, they can <u>foster</u> cooperation skills, and by studying the topics, they can broaden their horizons in other academic fields. The Japan Bowl aims to encourage participants to always be ambitious and acquire Japanese communication skills and cultural knowledge.

Most of the Japan Bowl contestants continue to study about Japan after entering university and wish to study abroad in Japan. (C), the students who participate in the Japan Bowl hope to have a "connection with Japan" through business, academics, arts, public services, etc. in the future. No matter what path the students take, the knowledge and skills they cultivate at the Japan Bowl will be a great step toward becoming future leaders in US-Japan relations.

問1 According to the passage, which of the following is true about the Japan Bowl?

① The Japan Bowl is a national championship game of high school football in the United States and has a longer history than the Super Bowl.

② The Japan Bowl used to be an in-person contest, but in the last few years, it has been held online.

③ The Japan Bowl is organized by the Japan-America Society of Washington DC and it is held during the summer vacation.

④ The Japan Bowl is a competition between schools and students get excited in cheering for their school.

⑤ The Japan Bowl has been getting popular worldwide and more and more junior and senior high schools from overseas participate in it.

問2 Choose the most appropriate combination of words and phrases to fill in (A), (B), and(C).

① A regional　B a wide range of topics
　C In addition

② A national　B historical social issues
　C Nevertheless

③ A small　B a few highly technical subjects
　C By contrast

④ A state scale　B a limited number of themes
　C In short

⑤ A worldwide　B political problems Japan faces
　C Furthermore

問3 Choose the most appropriate word to replace <u>foster</u>.

① nurture　② contemplate　③ restrain　④ condemn
⑤ administer

問4 According to the passage, which of the following is true about contestants of the Japan Bowl?

① Contestants are strictly required to have knowledge of the Japanese language and they need to pass a Japanese proficiency test.

② No matter how well contestants can speak Japanese, they are divided by grade and state to participate in the Japan Bowl.

③ Contestants are expected to have a good command of Japanese and are encouraged to compete alone to become a champion.

④ Contestants put in a lot of hours to prepare for the Japan Bowl and they need to submit a report of their study time.

⑤ Almost all of the Japan Bowl contestants have an ambition to live or study in Japan after graduating from high school.

(☆☆☆☆☆◎◎◎◎◎)

【11】次の英文を読んで，以下の問に答えなさい。

Penguins spend a lot of time grouped together when they are huddling on the ice or keeping their eggs warm. The penguins' flock has no specific leader or boss. If the flock is in danger, the penguins can escape together by following the one that detected the danger earliest. It is a characteristic of their collectivism to follow the "first one" rather than the "strong one".

This habit is demonstrated when penguins, who normally spend time on land, must enter the ocean to catch fish. When hunting, individuals form a platoon and take collective action to corral and catch fish. However, because of their strong tendency to stay in a group, they will remain together on the ice until one penguin makes s move. After the first bird breaks rank and jumps in, the rest of the birds will follow suit and dive into the sea one after another.

It is not easy to be the first penguin into the sea. Terrifying predators such as orcas, sea lions, and fur seals may be lurking under the water. The penguin that jumps in first－despite the danger to its life－shows their peers that the sea is safe and enables the other birds. To be the first penguin is very risky, but taking action early is also a tactical advantage to get ahead of the rest of the flock and catch more fish.

High risk and high return is also a strong motivator in human society. In the business world, this brave "first" refers to the founders of pioneer companies that challenge areas that no one has ever set foot in. These professionals drive innovation and take courageous first steps into new niches. Some Japanese organizations call these businesses "First Penguin" companies.

Aspiring to be an entrepreneur is very popular in young Americans because students have been taught from a young age to aim to be the first penguins, not to follow the crowd. In the 1980s, when the Internet was in development, who could have imagined that it would make such a fundamental difference in society and become an integral part of people's lives? At that time, the first penguins believed in themselves, took risks, and jumped into the sea of opportunity. They created what grew to become a global IT mega-structure with top-level market capitalization which dominates most of modern industry.

We need someone to take the lead when we start something new. Given that social progress is the result of many first penguins taking on new businesses without fear of risk, their courage is highly regarded. To improve our society, we want people to be able to act like first penguins.

問1　According to the passage, which of the following is true about the behavior of penguins?

① Penguins get away from danger under the direction of their strong leader.

② Each individual acts differently, except for when catching fish in the sea.

③ Penguins spend a long time underwater and hatch their eggs there.

④ Penguins tend to follow the penguin that takes action first.

⑤ Penguins sometimes break their rules selfishly and put the flock in danger.

問2　Choose the most appropriate phrase that describes "First Penguin" companies.

① companies which expand businesses extensively

② companies which protect marine lives

③ companies which spearhead novel projects

④ companies which distribute processed marine products

⑤ companies which deceive people

問3 Choose the most appropriate phrase to replace entrepreneur.

① business venturer ② legal bureaucrat

③ software developer ④ cultural anthropologist

⑤ resident butler

問4 According to the passage, which of the following is true?

① Most Japanese people prefer the idea of high risk and high return to the idea of being consistent in performance.

② Innovation emerges when someone is brave and invests in something new regardless of the risks.

③ In America, students have been taught the idea that people who stick out too much get punished.

④ Several decades ago, people were sure that they would have more convenient lives using information technology.

⑤ Modern global companies have been passing down their traditions, which has made them successful.

(☆☆☆☆☆◎◎◎◎◎)

【中学校】

【1】次の文は，「中学校学習指導要領解説　外国語編」(平成29年文部科学省)「第1章　総説」「2　外国語科改訂の趣旨と要点」「(1)　改訂の趣旨」の一部である。次の(　①　)~(　⑤　)に当てはまる語句を書きなさい。ただし，同じ番号には同じ語句が入る。

> 今回の外国語科の改訂に当たっては，中央教育審議会答申を踏まえ，次のような，これまでの成果と課題等を踏まえた改善を図った。
>
> ―中略―
>
> ・一方，授業では依然として，文法・語彙等の(　①　)がどれだ

け身に付いたかという点に重点が置かれ，外国語によるコミュニケーション能力の育成を意識した取組，特に「(　②　)」及び「書くこと」などの言語活動が適切に行われていないことや「やり取り」・「(　③　)」を意識した言語活動が十分ではないこと，読んだことについて意見を述べ合うなど，複数の領域を(　④　)した言語活動が十分に行われていないことなどの課題がある。また，生徒の英語力の面では，習得した(　①　)や(　⑤　)を生かし，コミュニケーションを行う目的や場面，状況等に応じて自分の考えや気持ちなどを適切に表現することなどに課題がある。

(☆☆☆◎◎◎)

【2】次の文は，「中学校学習指導要領」(平成29年3月告示)「第2章　各教科」「第9節　外国語」「第2　各言語の目標及び内容等」の一部である。次の(　①　)～(　⑤　)に当てはまる語句を書きなさい。

第2　各言語の目標及び内容等

英語

1　目標

英語学習の特質を踏まえ，以下に示す，聞くこと，読むこと，話すこと[やり取り]，話すこと[発表]，書くことの五つの領域別に設定する目標の実現を目指した指導を通して，第1の(1)及び(2)に示す資質・能力を一体的に育成するとともに，その過程を通して，第1の(3)に示す資質・能力を育成する。

(1)　聞くこと

ア　はっきりと話されれば，日常的な話題について，必要な(　①　)を聞き取ることができるようにする。

イ　はっきりと話されれば，日常的な話題について，話の(　②　)を捉えることができるようにする。

ウ　はっきりと話されれば，社会的な話題について，短い説明の(　③　)を捉えることができるようにする。

－中略－

(3)　話すこと[やり取り]

ア　関心のある事柄について，簡単な語句や文を用いて即興で伝え合うことができるようにする。

イ　日常的な話題について，事実や自分の考え，気持ちなどを(　④　)し，簡単な語句や文を用いて伝えたり，相手からの質問に答えたりすることができるようにする。

ウ　社会的な話題に関して聞いたり読んだりしたことについて，考えたことや感じたこと，その(　⑤　)などを，簡単な語句や文を用いて述べ合うことができるようにする。

(☆☆☆◎◎◎◎◎)

【3】次の文は，「中学校学習指導要領」(平成29年3月告示)「第2章　各教科」「第9節　外国語」「第2　各言語の目標及び内容等」「英語」「3　指導計画の作成と内容の取扱い」の一部である。次の(　①　)～(　⑤　)に当てはまる語句を書きなさい。

3　指導計画の作成と内容の取扱い

－中略－

(3)　教材については，次の事項に留意するものとする。

ア　教材は，聞くこと，読むこと，話すこと[やり取り]，話すこと[発表]，書くことなどのコミュニケーションを図る資質・能力を総合的に育成するため，1に示す五つの領域別の目標と2に示す内容との関係について，(　①　)など内容や時間のまとまりごとに各教材の中で明確に示すとともに，実際の言語の使用場面や言語の働きに十分配慮した題材を取り上げること。

イ　英語を使用している人々を中心とする世界の人々や日本人の日常生活，風俗習慣，物語，地理，歴史，(　②　)，自然科学などに関するものの中から，生徒の発達の段階や興味・関心に即して適切な題材を効果的に取り上げるものとし，次の観点に配慮すること。

(ア)　(　③　)な考え方に対する理解を深めさせ，公正な判断力を養い豊かな心情を育てるのに役立つこと。

(イ)　我が国の文化や，英語の背景にある文化に対する関心を高め，理解を深めようとする(　④　)を養うのに役立つこと。

(ウ)　広い視野から(　⑤　)を深め，国際社会と向き合うことが求められている我が国の一員としての自覚を高めるとともに，国際協調の精神を養うのに役立つこと。

(☆☆☆◎◎◎)

【高等学校】

【1】次の文は，「高等学校学習指導要領」(平成30年3月告示)「第2章　各学科に共通する各教科」「第8節　外国語」「第3款　英語に関する各科目にわたる指導計画の作成と内容の取扱い」の一部である。文中の(　①　)～(　⑤　)に当てはまる語句を書きなさい。

1　指導計画の作成に当たっては，小学校や中学校における指導との(　①　)に留意しながら，次の事項に配慮するものとする。

－中略－

(4)　多様な生徒の実態に応じ，生徒の(　②　)に配慮しながら，年次ごと及び科目ごとの目標を適切に定め，学校が定める卒業までの指導計画を通して十分に段階を踏みながら，外国語科の目標の実現を図るようにすること。

(5)　実際に英語を使用して自分自身の考えを伝え合うなどの言語活動を行う際は，(　③　)の語句や文構造，文法事項などの学習内容を繰り返し指導し定着を図ること。

－中略－

(8)　言語活動で扱う題材は，生徒の興味・関心に合ったものとし，国語科や地理歴史科，理科など，他の教科等で学習した内容と関連付けるなどして，英語を用いて(　④　)を図る力を育成する工夫をすること。

－中略－

(10)　指導計画の作成や授業の実施に当たっては，ネイティブ・スピーカーや英語が堪能な(　⑤　)などの協力を得る等，指導体制の充実を図るとともに，指導方法の工夫を行うこと。

(☆☆☆◎◎◎)

【2】次の文は，「高等学校学習指導要領解説　外国語編　英語編」(平成30年文部科学省)「第2章　外国語科の各科目」「第6節　論理・表現Ⅱ」「2　内容」の一部である。文中の(　①　)～(　⑤　)に当てはまる語句を書きなさい。

エ　書くこと

(ア)　学校外での生活や地域社会などの日常的な話題について，必要に応じて，使用する語句や文，文章例が示されたり，準備のための一定の時間が確保されたりする状況で，情報や考え，気持ちなどを適切な理由や根拠とともに複数の段落を用いて詳しく書いて伝える活動。また，書いた内容を読み合い，(　①　)をしたり，意見や感想を伝え合ったりする活動。

－中略－

ここでは，「論理・表現Ⅰ」で扱った一つの段落の文章を書く段階から，複数の段階から成る文章を書く段階になることから，論理の構成や展開，使用する表現などが多様になることが考えられる。論理の構成や展開においては，理由や根拠の示し方に留意しながら，(　②　)を明らかにしたり，(　③　)を行ったりすることにより，読み手に分かりやすい構成や展開にすることが大切である。例えば，主張の根拠となる具体例を分類して列挙したり，複数の具体例の相違点や類似点を比較したり，主張の理由について(　④　)を示しながら述べたりするような複数の段落を書くことが考えられる。

また，主張をどのように展開するか，主張を支持する理由や根拠が適切か，主張に(　⑤　)があるかなどの点についても指導することも大切である。

(☆☆☆◎◎◎)

【3】次の文は，「高等学校学習指導要領解説　外国語編　英語編」(平成30年文部科学省)「第1章　総説」「第3節　外国語科の目標」の一部である。文中の(　①　)～(　⑤　)に当てはまる語句を書きなさい。また，文中の〔　㋐　〕～〔　㋔　〕に当てはまる語句を以下の語群から一つずつ選んで記号で答えなさい。

(3)　外国語の背景にある文化に対する理解を深め，聞き手，読み手，話し手，書き手に配慮しながら，主体的，自律的に外国語を用いてコミュニケーションを図ろうとする態度を養う。

(3)は，外国語科における「どのように(　①　)や世界と関わり，よりよい人生を送るか」という「学びに向かう力，人間性等」

の〔　㋐　〕に関わる目標として掲げたものである。

－中略－

外国語教育における「学びに向かう力，人間性等」は，生徒が言語活動に主体的・自律的に取り組むことが外国語によるコミュニケーションを図る資質・能力を身に付ける上で不可欠であるため，極めて重要な観点である。「知識及び技能」を実際のコミュニケーションの場面において活用し，考えを形成・(　②　)させ，話したり書いたりして表現することを繰り返すことで，生徒に〔　㋑　〕が生まれ，主体的・自律的に学習に取り組む態度が一層向上するため，「知識及び技能」及び「思考力，判断力，表現力等」と「学びに向かう力，人間性等」は不可分に結び付いている。生徒が興味をもって取り組める言語活動を〔　㋒　〕に取り入れたり，(　③　)活動を工夫したりするなど，様々な手立てを通して生徒の主体的・自律的に学習に取り組む態度の育成を目指した指導をすることが大切である。

－中略－

「聞き手，読み手，話し手，書き手に配慮しながら」については，(2)でも述べたとおり，例えば「話すこと」や「聞くこと」の活動であれば，相手の(　④　)を確かめながら話したり，相手が言ったことを〔　㋓　〕に受け止める言葉を返しながら聞いたりすることなどが考えられる。

－中略－

また高等学校では，中学校における「主体的」に加え「自律的にコミュニケーションを図ろうとする態度」としている。これは，外国語科の特性として，目標を達成するための言語活動において他者とのコミュニケーションが必要とされるが，学習内容等が(　⑤　)・複雑化する高等学校においては，授業等において言語活動を通して実際にコミュニケーションを図るだけでなく，それらのコミュニケーションを通して自分にはどのような力が足りないか，どのような学習が更に必要かなどを自ら考え，それぞれが授業での言語活動を充実させるための努力を〔　㋔　〕でも続けようとするより自律的な態度が一層強く求められることと関連している。

《語群》

A　授業外	B　形成	C　特別活動	D　喜び	E　共感的
F　段階的	G　意図的	H　涵養	I　積極的	J　自信

(☆☆☆◎◎◎)

解答・解説

【中高共通】

【1】Question 1　③　　Question 2　①　　Question 3　③

〈解説〉男女の対話と設問を2回聞き，印刷されている4つの選択肢から適切な答えを選ぶ問題。　Question 1　Davidはan action thriller，Sophiaはcomedyがそれぞれ好きであり，折衷案としてHow about watching that new action comedy film that just opened last Friday?と述べられている。　Question 2　映画館に朝に行くことを提案した直後にはIt will be less crowded than the evening, and tickets are a little cheaper.と述べているので，crowdedをjammedで言い換えている①が適切。　Question 3　映画館へ行く方法についてI'll pick you up in my car and we can go together.と，Davidが車を出してくれることを述べている。

【2】≪A≫　Question 1　④　　Question 2　①　　Question 3　③
≪B≫　Question 1　②　　Question 2　③　　Question 3　④

〈解説〉2つのモノローグと設問を2回聞き，印刷されている4つの選択肢から適切な答えを選ぶ問題。なお，1つの英文につき3つの設問がある。

≪A≫　ワークライフバランスが推進される5つの背景(少子高齢化，共働き，家庭を重視する傾向，フレックスタイム制，テレワーク)について述べた英文である。　≪A≫　Question 1　英文で述べられている5つの背景について正しくないものを選ぶ問題。double-income householdsは，父親も母親も働くことであるから，④のquit their jobs「仕事を辞める」は不適切。　Question 2　フレックスタイム制のメリットはallows employees to choose when they start and end work every day, giving them the ability to balance their professional and private schedules more easilyと述べられている。よって，①「仕事とプライベートのバランスを取りやすい」が適切。　Question 3　ワークライフバランスは，about creating a harmonious relationship between both(work and private life)と述べられているため，③「仕事とプライベートライフの調和により健康的なシステムをつくること」が適切。　①　フレックスタイム制とテレワークは新しいワークスタイルの例として示されているが，ワークライフバランスに必須であることは述べられていない。　②　高齢化が労働力不足を改善することは述べられていない。　④　地域や家庭での活動が長時間労働につながることは述べられていない。
≪B≫　小中高におけるプログラミング教育について述べた英文である。　Question 1　プログラミング教育で重視されていることについてはprogramming education emphasizes using programming as a tool to develop students' ability to think logicallyと述べられている。よって，②「論理的な思考力を身に付ける」が適切。　Question 2　中学校でのプログラミング授業の目標についてはa key teaching point in the programming curriculum is "to solve problems in life and in society" と述べられている。よって，③「日常生活と社会生活における課題解決」が適切。　Question 3　①　プログラミング教育は，小学校と中学校ではなく，中学校と高校で行われていることから不適切。　②　インタラクティブな(双方向性の)コンテンツは中学校で重要とされているため，in all school educationの部分が不適切。　③　本文では，小学校では，コンピュータを使用しない方法(unplugged)が可能であると述べられていることと矛盾するため不適切。

【3】Question 1　4　　Question 2　3　　Question 3　1

〈解説〉オーロラについて述べたモノローグ(257 words)と3つの設問を2回聞き，4つの選択肢から適切な答えを1つ選ぶ問題。なお，選択肢は印刷されていない。　Question 1　ローマ神話における女神Auroraが行ったことは，brought dawn and hope to the creatures on Earth，drove away the darkness of the night and gave light to the worldと述べられている。よって，4「世界に希望を与え日の出をもたらした」が適切。　Question 2　オーロラが発生する原因について，本文ではDue to the balance between the solar wind and the Earth's magnetic fieldと述べられている。これらのことから，3「太陽風と磁場の影響下で自然に発生する」が適切。Question 3　the University of Helsinkiの実験について，本文ではhired many subjects to wear blindfolds and study any sounds they heard from the auroraと述べられており，被験者に目隠し状態でオーロラの音を聞く実験を行っている。このことから，1「実験中，被験者はオーロラを見る機会を与えられなかった」が適切。

【4】2，3

〈解説〉モノローグと6つの選択肢を2回聞き，本文の内容と合致するものを2つ選ぶ問題。なお，選択肢は印刷されていない。内容はロンドンの散歩をコンセプトにしたラジオ番組である。バッキンガム宮殿の衛兵の交代，トラファルガー広場のネルソン提督とライオンの像，ナショナルギャラリーの絵画，ウォーキー・トーキーの愛称で知られる高層ビルの35階にあるスカイガーデンでのランチを紹介している。

1　レポーターのJudyが遅れたのではなく，衛兵の交代時間がいつもよりも遅れたが，Judyは交代式を見ることができたため不適切。

2　バッキンガム宮殿の衛兵の交代式は有名であり，観光客に見ることを勧めているため適切。　3　トラファルガー広場のネルソン提督像の足元には4体のライオンの像があることが述べられているため適切。 4 トラファルガー広場には年間3000万人の観光客が訪れると述べられているが，3000万人が演説をするとは述べられていないため不適切。 5 本文では，スカイガーデンは35階にあり昼食は20ポンドと述べられている。また，スカイガーデンの入園料金については触れられていない。よって不適切。 6 Tune in tomorrow for the last part of our day out in London.と述べられており，明日，放送の続きがあることがわかる。よって，the day after tomorrowが不適切。

【5】問1 ④ 問2 ③ 問3 ① 問4 ② 問5 ⑤

〈解説〉問1 reliable「信頼できる」，continual「繰り返される，連続した」の2つは限定用法，be independent from A「Aから独立している」，be contingent on A「A次第の」，be instigated to do「～するようにそそのかされる」の3つは叙述用法の形容詞である。 問2 「都市部での水不足により雨水の使用に注目が集まることとなった」という文意である。targetとaimは他動詞であるため，後続のonが不適切。headは両方であるが自動詞ではoffやforを伴う。goalは名詞のみであるため，使役動詞makeが選択する原形不定詞として不適切。 問3 enrollment「入学」，annulment「取り消し，無効」，clarity「明快さ」，stability「安定」，exodus「大移動」。大学が特別奨学金をSNSで広告して増やすものして適切なのは留学生の入学である。 問4 altruistic「利他主義の」，indispensable「必要不可欠な」，controversial「物議を醸す」，fictitious「偽りの，架空の」，obsolete「時代遅れの」。 問5 berate A for B「AをBのことで叱責する」，accuse A of B「AをBのことで告発する，非難する」，finesse A「策略を用いてAを切り抜ける」，reminisce about A「Aの思い出話をする」，confide in A「Aに秘密を打ち明ける，Aを信頼する」。

【6】問1 ④ 問2 ② 問3 ② 問4 ⑤

〈解説〉問1 正しい順番はhush fell over the hallである。a hush fell over A「Aが静まり返る」。hushは「静けさ，沈黙」という意味の名詞であり，

fallおよびoverとコロケーションをなす。　問2　正しい順番はof competing against one anotherである。compete against/with A「Aと競争する」。one anotherはeach otherと同じ意味であるが，いくらか堅い言い方で，書き言葉で使われることが多い。　問3　正しい順番はaggregate surveys is to useである。aggregate A「Aを集める」。なお，主動詞は主語the easiest wayが単数であるためisとなる。　問4　正しい順番はwho choose majors based onである。関係代名詞whoを使って先行詞studentsを修飾している。

【7】問1　⑤　　問2　④

〈解説〉問1　正しい順番はF→E→B→D→A→Cである。アメリカへ10カ月の間留学に行っていたJennyに，来年留学に行こうとしているが何をしていいかわからずにアドバイスを求めるという会話である。会話の順番を並べ替える際には疑問文や代名詞に着目するとよい。今回はBとFが疑問文を表し，the sameやgo thereなどが使われている。これらを手がかりに，直前の文で何が置き換わっているかを確認することで並べ替えていく。　問2　正しい順番はB→F→C→A→E→Dである。電話で忘れ物について問い合わせているJaneとPIER百貨店のMattの会話である。忘れ物をした際，その特徴を述べることとなるため，鍵の特徴を述べるAが会話の中心となる。コミュニケーションの場面や目的などを把握すると解きやすくなる。

【8】問1　②　　問2　⑤　　問3　③　　問4　④　　問5　⑤

〈解説〉問1　空所の次の文では，ウォーキングが睡眠や記憶の質を向上させ，お金もかからないなどのメリットが記述されていることから，ウォーキングが健康によいことを述べている②が適切。他の選択肢は非効果的，血圧の上昇，ストレス，難しいなどのネガティブな内容であるため不適切。　問2　大学生の上級生は，インターンシップを経験することで，働くことの意味を深く理解することができる。空所の前後では仕事に関するポジティブなことが述べられているため，空所でも将来本当にやりたいことがわかるようになるというポジティブな⑤が適切。①は仕事に関係のない内容であり，他の選択肢はネガティブな内容であることから不適切。　問3　良質な睡眠をとることは健康にとって重要であることを述べている。空所の前の段落では良質な睡眠のために取る方法を3つ述べている。空所のある文では睡眠習慣を身に付けることの重要性を強調していることから，ポジティブな③が適切。Please rememberで始まっていることから，上述の内容を踏まえて覚えておいてほしいことの要約を述べていると推測できる。
問4　ウェアラブルコンピュータについて述べている。これらの進化はコンピュータの小型化によるものである。　問5　ビジネスやスポーツのチームで目標を達成する際に重要なことについて述べている。空所はチームとして成功するために何をするかが入るため，第2パラグラフの内容をまとめている⑤が適切。②を選んでしまう人がいるかもしれないが，②では個別に小さな目標を立てることが述べられており，大きな共通目標を立てることと矛盾するため不適切。

【9】問1　⑤　　問2　①　　問3　②　　問4　①

〈解説〉空所に当てはまる語句を選択肢から選ぶ問題。　問1　despair「絶望」，suspicion「疑い」，compassion「憐れみ」，uniformity「均一性」，anecdote「逸話」。空所の後にはAlexander Flemingが様々な防カビ剤を細菌と白血球に対して調査していたエピソードが述べられている。
問2　ペトリ皿の上で細菌を培養していたが，微生物が全くいないスペースを発見した。このスペースは涙のしずくが垂れた箇所であることから，concentric「同心円の」スペースであることがわかる。desirable「望ましい」，relaxing「ホッとする」，formidable「手に負えない，強力な」，capricious「気まぐれな，不安定な」。　問3　アルキメデスの浴槽(浮力の原理)，ニュートンのリンゴ(万有引力の法則)などは作り話であるが，これらに共通するのは科学者や発明家が(　　)な現象を理解の方法へと変える勤勉な精神である，と述べられている。このことを具体的に示す例が，第2段落に述べられている。アレクサンダー・フレミングは，細胞培養皿の中に涙のしずくがたまたま落ちたことがきっかけで，細菌の繁殖を抑制する成分を発見したこと，また，細胞培養皿の中のカビが，のちのペニシリンの発見につながったことが述べられている。よって，偉大な発見のきっかけは，ごくありふれた現象が偶然起こったことであったとわかる。このことから，mundane「日常の，ありふれた」が適切。optimum「最善の」，placid「落ち着いた，穏やかな」，versatile「多芸の，用途の広い」，vicious「残忍な，悪意のある」。　問4　serendipity「予期することなく大きな発見をすること」に関する逸話を通して，この英文が伝えたいのは，様々な問題に注意を払うことで，大きな成果を上げることができるということである。この内容に合致するのは，①「一瞬のチャンスをインスピレーションと素晴らしい成果に変えることができるかもしれない」である。　②　誠実さやポジティブな感情などは述べられていない。　③　抽象的なことから具体的なことへという順番が逆である。④　誰に対しても公明正大で，著名人になれることとは無関係である。⑤　多くの微生物の中から人類の健康に役立つバクテリアを発見することは，本文中の逸話の一例であり，メインテーマとは異なる。

【10】問1　②　　問2　①　　問3　①　　問4　⑤

〈解説〉問1　The Japan Bowlについて述べているものとして適切なものを選ぶ問題。　①　The Japan Bowlは，日本語や文化などを問うクイズ大会と述べられていることから，high school footballの部分が不適切。②　2020年からの大会がオンラインで開催され，The Digital Japan Bowlと名付けられていることと一致するので適切。　③　春に開催されることから，the summer vacationの部分が不適切。　④　学校間で競うことは述べられていないため不適切。　⑤　The Japan Bowlの対象はアメリカの高校生であるため，worldwide，junior high schoolの部分が不適切。　問2　空所Aの前後では1992年に始まったThe Japan Bowlは最初，ワシントンのみで行われていたが，数年で全国レベルにまで拡大したことが述べられている。ワシントンという一つの地域に限定されていることから，regionalが適切。空所Bの前の段落で，The Japan Bowlでは，日本語だけでなく，日本文化，日常生活，地理や時事問題などまで問われると述べられている。幅広い分野の問題に解答することとなることから，a wide range of topicsが適切。空所Cの前後ではThe Japan Bowlに参加した高校生が将来に日本に留学したり，大学でも日本の言語や文化について学び続けたりすることが述べられている。このことから，空所Cは情報を付け加えるIn additionが適切。　問3　下線部foster A「Aを育成する，促進する」の意味として適切なものは，nurture A「Aを育てる」である。fosterの意味を知らなくても，3人のチームを作ることで，協力する能力を「育成する」ことであると推測できる。contemplate A「Aを意図する，熟考する」，restrain A「Aを抑制する」，condemn A for B「AをBのことで責める」，administer A「Aを管理する，運営する」。　問4　Japan Bowlについて正しい記述を選ぶ問題。　①　日本語熟達度テストに合格していなければならないことは述べられていない。　②　学年や参加する州によって区分されることは述べられていない。　③　1人で大会に参加するわけではなく，3人のチームを作ることとなる。　④　学習時間を報告する必要があることは述べられていない。　⑤　本文中にMost of the Japan Bowl contestants continue to study about Japan after entering university and wish to study abroad in Japan.と述べられていることから，「The Japan Bowl出場者のほとんどは，高校卒業後に日本で暮らしたり留学したりすることを熱望している」は正しい。

【11】問1　④　　問2　③　　問3　①　　問4　②

〈解説〉ペンギンの習性を例に，ビジネスにおいてニッチを最初に開拓するリスクとリターンについて述べた読解問題。　問1　ペンギンの習性についての適切な記述を選ぶ問題。ペンギンは陸上で群れて行動しており，危険を最初に察知して行動した個体に続くこととなる。そのため，他の動物のように強いオスが群を率いるわけではない。このことを適切に表しているのは，④「ペンギンは最初に行動したペンギンに続く傾向がある」である。　問2　First Penguinとは最初にリスクを負いながらも他のペンギンよりも魚を多く捕まえることができるペンギンで，群れの中で最初に海に飛び込む個体のことを指す。この名前を冠する会社は周りで提供されていないサービスや製品を新しく作る企業であると推測できる。このことを適切に表しているのは，③「斬新なプロジェクトを率先する企業」である。　①の文中のexpand Aは「Aを拡大する」，③のspearhead Aは「Aの先頭に立つ」，④のdistribute Aは「Aを分配する」，⑤のdeceive Aは「Aを騙す」。　問3　下線部entrepreneur「起業家，興業主」の意味として適切なのはbusiness venturer「ビジネスのベンチャー起業主」。legal bureaucratは「法務官僚」，software developerは「ソフトウェアの開発者」，cultural anthropologistは「文化人類学者」，resident butlerは「住み込みの執事」。問4　英文に適切な記述を選ぶ問題。　①　日本人が業績の安定よりハイリスク・ハイリターンを好むという記述はない。　②　最終段落より，「危険を顧みず勇気をもって新しい何かに投資することから改革が生れる」は正しい。　③　アメリカの学生はstick out too much「目立ちすぎる」ことで罰せられるとは本文には述べられていない。逆に，アメリカ人は若いころから，ファーストペンギンになるよう教えられると述べられている。　④　本文では，1980年代にインターネットが登場した際，それによって社会や生活が大きく変わることを誰が想像できただろうか，と述べられている。したがって，people were sureの部分が不適切。　⑤　伝統を次の世代に引き継がせることは，ファーストペンギンになることと反するため不適切。

【中学校】

【1】①　知識　　②　話すこと　　③　即興性　　④　統合　　⑤　経験

〈解説〉平成29(2017)年改訂の学習指導要領から，従来1つの領域であった「話すこと」は，ディベートやディスカッションなどの「話すこと〔やり取り〕」と，スピーチやプレゼンテーションなどの「話すこと

〔発表〕」の2つの領域に分けられた。従来は読むことを中心とした受容技能の指導が行われてきたが，現在は話すことや書くことの発表技能の指導に注目が集まり，従来行われてきた日本語での解説を中心に据えた文法訳読式から，ペアやグループでのタスクに基づくFocus on Formへと授業の方向性が移ってきた。例えば，話すことについては，原稿などを用意せずにその場での即興的なやり取りが重視され，また，相手からの電子メールを「読み」，返事を「書く」ことのように，技能統合型学習にも注目が集まっている。

【2】① 情報 ② 概要 ③ 要点 ④ 整理 ⑤ 理由

〈解説〉聞くことの目標である日常的な話題の「必要な情報」とは，話されていることの全てを聞き取るのではなく，自分の置かれた状況などから判断することを意味している。「話の概要を捉える」とは，一語一語など特定の部分にのみとらわれたりすることなく，全体としてどのような話なのかを捉えることである。社会的な話題に関しては，話し手が伝えようとする最も重要なことは何であるかを判断して捉えることが求められている。話すことを「整理」するとは，聞き手が理解しやすいように伝える項目を精選したり適切な順序に並べ替えたりするなど，話す内容をまとめてコミュニケーションの見通しを立てることを意味している。

【3】① 単元 ② 伝統文化 ③ 多様 ④ 態度 ⑤ 国際理解

〈解説〉出題の項目アでは「英語を用いて何ができるようになるか」という観点から，ある単元において，どの領域のどの目標に焦点を当てた指導をするとよいかを明らかにし，その目標を実現するためにどのような言語活動を行い，どのような言語材料を活用するのか適切に関連づけ，各教材の中で明示することを意味している。項目イの「伝統文化」とは，昔から伝えられてきた風習・制度・思想・技術・芸術などを示している。外国の伝統文化について知るだけでなく，自国の伝統文化について外国の人々に発信できる素養を培うことも必要である。項目(ア)の「多様な考え方」は，英語を使用している人々をはじめ，世界の様々な人々の多様な考え方や行動の仕方である。これらについて知ることができる教材の選択が大切であることを示している。項目(イ)が示す態度とは，英語の学習を通して，日本の文化と，英語の背景にある文化の共通点や相違点を知り，それらに関心を持ち，理解を深めようとする態度を指している。項目(ウ)は，外国の文化や考え方などについて受け身的に学ぶだけでなく，日本の文化や日本人の考え方を積極的に外国の人々に知らせることで，国際理解を深めることを指す。

【高等学校】

【1】① 接続　② 学習負担　③ 既習　④ 課題解決
⑤ 地域人材

〈解説〉指導計画の作成にあたっては，小学校および中学校における指導との接続に留意することとなる。項目(4)の配慮事項は，高等学校の外国語科の目標の実現を図るため，各学校における生徒の発達の段階と実情を踏まえ，年次ごと・科目ごとの目標を適切に定めることの必要性を述べたものである。高等学校の場合は，中学校での既習事項を実際のコミュニケーションに運用できる力を十分に身に付けていない生徒から，留学・進学などの目的に応じて高い英語力を目指す生徒まで，多様性が見られる。生徒の実態をよく把握した上で，その学習上の負担に一層考慮する必要があることを示している。項目(5)の配慮事項である既習の語彙や文構造などは，高等学校においては，意味のある文脈でのコミュニケーションの中で繰り返し活用することで定着を図るようにすることが重要である。項目(8)の配慮事項と関連し，他の科目との関連付けとして，授業実践の研究会などでは調理実習や修学旅行の計画などを英語で行うなど創意工夫された発表を聞くことができる。項目(10)の配慮事項にある地域人材は，海外姉妹校とのやりとりを行う際などに協力を得られることがあるだろう。

【2】① 質疑応答 ② 論点 ③ 順序付け ④ 因果関係
⑤ 一貫性

〈解説〉「論理・表現Ⅱ」では，発表技能を中心に批判的・論理的思考を用いた課題解決型タスクが扱われる。ここでは，自分で文章を書き，書いたものをクラスで互いに読み合い，それに基づいたスピーキング活動に繋がるように，技能が統合されている。論理の構成や展開で重要となるのは，論点を明確にすることと，読み手にわかりやすいように書くことを順序づけて考えることである。主張の一貫性に関しては，書く内容がバラバラにならないように留意すること，代名詞や談話標識を活用して文・パラグラフ同士の結束性を高めることなどが挙げられる。

【3】① 社会 ② 深化 ③ 自己表現 ④ 理解 ⑤ 高度化 ㋐ H ㋑ J ㋒ F ㋓ E ㋔ A

〈解説〉空所となっている語句は学習指導要領の中でも特に重要である。特に「形成・深化」や「(人間性や精神の)涵養」，「主体的・自律的」といった用語は教育の目的と関わる用語であるため，確実に押さえておきたい。

2022年度　実施問題

※福岡市を志望する場合は，【中高共通】の【5】～【10】を解答して下さい。

【中高共通】

【1】次に読まれる英文を聞き，1～3の設問に対する答えとして最も適切なものを，四つの選択肢の中から一つ選びなさい。
(英文及び設問は2回読まれる。)

Host　　: Hello. Thank you for calling the Farmhouse restaurant. How may I help you?

Customer : Hello. I'd like to make a reservation for a party of five. Friday, July 13th at 7:30 pm. Is a table by the window overlooking the lake available? We'd like to watch the sunset.

Host　　: Let me check. Uh, I'm sorry but we don't have anything available in that seating area.

Customer : How about the following day?

Host　　: Yes, a table is available. May I have a name, please?

Customer : Emily Jones.

Host　　: Thank you.

Customer : Do you offer special dinner courses?

Host　　: Yes, we offer a Southern BBQ course and an all-you-can-eat buffet. The buffet is 35 dollars per person. Drinks are 3 dollars extra per person.

Customer : I see. Then I'd like to reserve 5 buffet meals and 5 drinks, please. Do you do anything special for birthdays?

Host　　: Yes, you can pre-order the double chocolate deluxe cake and have the staff sing "Happy Birthday". Each person will have to pay 2 dollars more.

Customer : That sounds great. I'd like to add that.

Host : Okay. Ms.Jones, I've made a reservation for Saturday, July 14th at 7:30 pm with 5 buffet meals, drinks, and the special birthday service.

Customer : Great. Thank you.

Host : My pleasure.

Question 1 : What is the reason for this phone call?

① To arrange for a hotel concierge.
② To ask about local attractions.
③ To make a dinner reservation.
④ To complain about a lack of allergy menu items.

Question 2 : Why did Emily want a table by the window?

① Because she wanted to feel fresh air.
② Because she wanted to watch the sunset.
③ Because she did not like crowded spaces.
④ Because she wanted to get a tan.

Question 3 : How much will each person have to pay in total?

① 35 dollars.
② 38 dollars.
③ 40 dollars.
④ 42 dollars.

(☆☆◎◎◎◎)

【2】次に読まれる英文≪A≫及び英文≪B≫について，それぞれの1～3の設問に対する答えとして最も適切なものを，四つの選択肢の中から一つ選びなさい。

(英文及び設問は2回読まれる。)

≪A≫

Hello, I'm Kazuki Sato. I'll tell you about SDGs, Sustainable Development Goals. They were created at the summit of the United Nations six years ago. They were made for the good of the earth, all people around the world, and the future.

There are 17 SDGs. They are various goals to solve problems concerning society, the economy, and the environment. When I learned about SDGs, I was especially shocked by problems in developing countries. I learned that hundreds of millions of people don't have enough food and millions of children die before they reach 5 years old. SDGs 1 and 2 are goals to end poverty and hunger issues and SDG 3 is a goal to promote good health and well-being for all people. I also learned that some organizations and doctors from Fukuoka have supported some developing countries for a long time. Some have been developing agriculture for these developing countries. Others have been promoting medical support and teaching better manufacturing skills.

I think making a sustainable world is a mission for all people. We can't achieve SDGs without the cooperation of everyone. We should do what we can.

Question 1 :　According to the passage, what is the purpose of SDGs?

① To adopt various opinions in the summit of the United Nations.

② To reduce the problems of only some developing countries.

③ To support participants in a summit of the United Nations.

④ To solve problems concerning society, the economy, and the environment.

Question2 :　According to the passage, why was the speaker shocked?

① Because he learned a great number of people don't have enough food.

② Because he had to give up his dream of working abroad.

③ Because he couldn't promote medical support and manufacturing skills.

④ Because he noticed that he couldn't make a sustainable world.

Question3 : According to the passage, which statement is NOT true?

① SDGs were created in the summit of the United Nations six years ago.

② The speaker has been teaching agriculture and manufacturing skills.

③ Some doctors from Fukuoka have supported developing countries.

④ SDG 3 is a goal to encourage good health and well-being for all people.

≪B≫

ALTs, Assistant Language Teachers, play an important role at schools in Japan. Some of them are members of the JET Program. The JET Program, the Japan Exchange and Teaching Program, aims to promote international exchange at the local level through fostering ties between primarily Japanese youth and people of other cultures. A secondary goal is to enhance foreign language education in Japan. The objectives of the Program are achieved by offering JET Program participants the opportunity to serve in local authorities, as well as in elementary, junior high, and senior high schools throughout the country.

The Program is conducted by the Ministry of Internal Affairs and Communication, the Ministry of Foreign Affairs, and the Ministry of Education, Culture, Sports, Science, and Technology, in cooperation with local authorities which appoint participants to places of work.

The Program started in 1987 with the cooperation of the governments of participating countries. In 2019, there were over 5000 participants on the Program from 57 countries. Since the Program has achieved an excellent reputation over the last 34 years, it is of great importance that this reputation be maintained. Participants are invited to Japan as honored representatives of their countries. As such, they are expected to perform enthusiastically in all their activities, especially those concerning the promotion of mutual understanding between the nations. It is therefore desirable for participants to be adaptable, be mentally and physically capable of performing work duties, and have a deep interest in Japan.

Question 1 : According to the passage, what is the purpose of the JET Program?

① To offer participants the opportunity to serve in local authorities.

② To promote international exchange and enhance foreign language education.

③ To make participants train new Japanese Teachers of English.

④ To enable foreigners to spend time leisurely in Japan while earning money.

Question 2 : According to the passage, what are JET Program participants expected to do?

① To work at the Ministry of Education, Culture, Sports, Science, and Technology.

② To maintain an excellent reputation as an ALT all over the world.

③ To promote mutual understanding between nations.

④ To have an interest in mental and physical education.

Question 3 : According to the passage, which statement is true about the JET Program?

① It aims to boost English education in high schools and universities.

② Only one ministry in Japan is responsible for implementing the JET Program.

③ It is important for JET Program participants to have a teacher's license.

④ It is desirable for participants to have a deep interest in Japan.

(☆☆◎◎◎◎)

【3】次に読まれる英文を聞き，1～3の設問に対する答えとして最も適切なものを，その後に読まれる四つの選択肢の中から一つ選びなさい。
(英文，設問及び選択肢は2回読まれる。)

The origins and meaning of the song “Auld Lang Syne” are not familiar to most people, although the song is known to millions around the globe. If you are in Japan, you might associate it with graduation ceremonies. The words are in fact a poem written in 1788 by Scottish poet Robert Burns and the associated tune is a traditional folk melody. Burns is considered to be the national poet of Scotland and is the focus of tremendous admiration and affection. While he wrote on occasion in English, he is well acknowledged for writing in the characteristic Scots language and has had a great influence on Scottish literature.

“Auld Lang Syne” is perhaps Burns'most well-known piece, though it is believed that the lines partially originated from old Scottish folk songs rather than being written by Burns himself. It soon became a national Scottish custom to celebrate the New Year with this song, and then the song spread universally as Scottish people went to live abroad. Only the first verse and chorus are familiar to most people, but there are, in fact, five verses. The last verse talks about “giving your hand to a friend” and people often sing that part, crossing their arms and shaking hands with the person either side of them.

“Auld Lang Syne” can roughly translate as “for old time's sake” and is a kindly call to remember the good times and treasure old friendships and bonds. Therefore, the song has gained its popularity as it suits occasions such as saying goodbye to the past year or giving a toast at weddings. Robert Burns died at the age of 37 but his poem is immortal.

Question 1 :　According to the passage, what is true about Robert Burns?

1　Robert Burns wrote both the lyrics and melody of the song “Auld Lang Syne”.

2　Robert Burns is admired and loved as the national poet of Scotland.

3　Most of Robert Burns'works were produced almost exclusively in English.

4　The works of Robert Burns had a huge influence on Scottish music afterwards.

Question 2 :　According to the passage, what is true about the song "Auld Lang Syne" ?

1　Some parts of the song's lyrics may have come from old folk songs of Scotland.

2　The song consists of five verses and they are all well-known to most people.

3　Immigrants abroad started singing the song, and then it became famous in Scotland.

4　Singing the song at graduation ceremonies in Japan triggered its popularity in the world.

Question 3 :　According to the passage, what is the most appropriate explanation ofthe song "Auld Lang Syne" ?

1　The song talks about saying goodbye to your home country and starting over in a new one.

2　The last verse talks about old customs of Scotland such as crossing arms with friends.

3　The phrase "Auld Lang Syne" roughly means "not to dwell on the past" and encourages us to have courage to move on.

4　The phrase "Auld Lang Syne" means something like "for the old times" and encourages us to treasure the bonds with old friends.

(☆☆☆◎◎◎◎)

【4】次に読まれる英文を聞き，英文の内容に合致するものを，その後に読まれる六つの選択肢の中から二つ選びなさい。

(英文及び選択肢は2回読まれる。)

It is believed that the proportion of land occupied by cities is increasing, and the number of people moving to cities is steadily growing as well. Forests and farmland are being replaced by cities. People in cities spend more of their time inside and less of their time around nature. This affects how they feel and even think. For example, people living near parks have less stress. Researchers say that a simple walk in nature makes people happier. Another study shows that part of the brain involved with negative thinking is less active after walking through nature. People who walked through an urban area near a highway did not get the same effect. Being in nature actually influences the way the brain works.

It seems that the natural world is connected to our human nature. In every culture, people choose to look at pictures of nature. In fact, simply looking at nature affects us positively. Some researchers showed that after being in nature, the length of office workers'concentration was improved. Also, people in hospital who had a view of a tree had shorter hospital stays and reported less pain than those whose window faced buildings. These examples show that nature can greatly affect us.

1 The number of people moving closer to nature, such as forests or parks, is growing.

2 The world's forests and farmland have been growing in the last decade.

3 Even in cities, people who live near the parks are said to have lower stress levels than those who don't.

4 People think less negatively after walking through either cities or nature.

5 Our human nature seems to be positively influenced by the natural world and simply having a view of nature can be beneficial.

6 Making a connection to nature made patients in hospital feel more pain.

(☆☆☆◎◎◎◎)

【5】英文の意味が通るように，(　　)内に入る最も適切なものを選びなさい。

問1　Customers (　　) this bakery because the staff is very friendly.

①　vandalize　②　patronize　③　harmonize　④　sympathize
⑤　emphasize

問2　The travel agent will let us know by e-mail when our travel dates have been (　　).

①　confronted　②　condemned　③　concluded
④　confirmed　⑤　concentrated

問3　The house has only (　　) historical value itself but its garden is supposed to date back to the eighteenth century.

①　insignificant　②　inapplicable　③　innate　④　inanimate
⑤　inconceivable

問4　Last year, my aunt took me on a sightseeing tour of the city's most (　　) monuments.

①　fictitious　②　conscript　③　ambiguous　④　illustrious
⑤　industrious

問5　This type of engine is not used in this motorbike now; it has been (　　) for over 70 years.

①　fashionable　②　absolute　③　resolute　④　obtuse
⑤　obsolete

(☆☆☆◎◎◎◎)

【6】次の各問の日本文の意味を表す英文を作るために，(　　)内のA～Eの語句を正しく並べかえたとき，2番目と4番目にくる最も適切な組合せを選びなさい。ただし，組合せの左側を2番目，右側を4番目とする。

問1　日本語を学んでいる外国人が日本にやってくる主な理由は，日本語だけが話されている環境に身を置くことである。

The main ($_A$Japanese $_B$foreigners $_C$reason $_D$learning $_E$why) come to Japan is to experience the place where only Japanese is spoken.

① B－A　② B－D　③ C－A　④ E－B　⑤ E－D

問2　話し手はスピーチをする前に自分の考えをまとめ，すべての文章を暗記しようとしないことが重要だ。

It is important that ($_A$ideas $_B$the $_C$organize $_D$speakers $_E$their) before presenting a speech and try not to memorize full sentences.

① A－B　② C－B　③ D－B　④ D－E　⑤ E－A

問3　結果がすべてではない。目的を達成するまでの過程を大切にしなければならない。

The result is not everything. The process of ($_A$be $_B$goal $_C$the $_D$achieving $_E$must) valued.

① C－B　② C－E　③ D－A　④ D－C　⑤ E－A

問4　今までに私が観た映画の中で，これほど感銘を受けたものはない。

Of all the movies I have seen so far, no other movie ($_A$much $_B$moved $_C$so $_D$has $_E$me) as this one.

① B－C　② B－D　③ C－A　④ C－E　⑤ D－C

(☆☆◎◎◎◎)

【7】次の各問のA～Fの英文を二人の会話として意味がつながるように並べかえるとき，2番目と4番目にくる最も適切な組合せを選びなさい。ただし，組合せの左側を2番目，右側を4番目とする。

問1　A : But we've been waiting at least twenty minutes. Is there some trouble with the bus? When is our appointment with the customers?

B : It's one ten now. So a bus should come very soon.

C : That would be better.

D : Right. I hope there will be one soon, but if not let's take a taxi.

E : According to this time-table, there's a bus every twelve minutes to South Town. Do you know what time it is now?

F : We'll meet them at two o'clock, so I think we have to be at Green Station by one fifty.

① A－B　② A－D　③ B－F　④ E－A　⑤ F－C

問2 A : No problem. Why did you want to have an interview with me?

B : I would like to talk about how American policy has evolved over the past twelve years.

C : Actually I'm studying American foreign policy, so meeting and asking a diplomat like you seemed like a good idea for my research.

D : OK. I've been a diplomat for 26 years, so I think I can talk about that.

E : Thank you so much for accepting my interview request, Mr.Brown.

F : I see. So what do you want to talk about?

① A－B　② A－F　③ D－B　④ E－A　⑤ F－B

(☆☆◎◎◎◎)

【8】次の各問の英文を読み，文脈から考えて文中の(　　)に入る最も適切なものを選びなさい。

問1 For many people, mornings are difficult, but handling them effectively can be important in getting your day started well. A good morning routine, for example getting up at fixed time, drinking some green tea, checking the news, and so on, (　　). I think establishing your own routine is important. If you have a good morning routine, you might achieve more in your day. Please find your own great morning routine.

① will negatively impact the rest of the day
② is more beneficial for your body than for your heart
③ makes us selfish people who bother others
④ can positively affect your performance
⑤ seems to improve your computer literacy

問2 (　　), if we try to learn humbly when we make mistakes. We can't achieve success without failure. Many successful people had many mistakes. As Thomas A. Edison said, "I have not failed. I've just found 10,000 ways that won't work." We all are challengers, and we might fail when we start to do something. If so, we should check where we made the first mistake, and try it over and over again until we break through.

① Success is the only thing that brings us happiness
② We all fail in our challenges
③ Failure teaches us a lot of things
④ There is no meaning in the mistakes in our life
⑤ Life is filled with unexpected situations

問3 What is a true leader? Most people think that a leader is a person who is at the top of some organization. That's true actually, but I think everybody can be a true leader. First of all, most of the true leaders I've met think simply, ( ). They try to find the true value of things and can abandon the things they don't need for achieving the goal. Another point is that they speak great words which encourage people around them even in difficult situations.

① because they are pessimistic
② because they know where they are heading
③ because they lose the way to the goal
④ because they have a big support system
⑤ because they don't have enough energy to think

問4 Technology impacts our daily life in many ways. It brings a big change to our lifestyle. Ten years ago, in Japan, it was normal to pay in cash when we bought something. But now we have many ways to pay, like with credit cards, mobile wallets, and QR codes. ( ) because we don't need to carry any coins or count them when paying at the cash register. But we must be cautious. We should be aware of some hazards of a cashless society, such as overspending and security issues.

① Cash payment is easier
② Mobile wallets and QR codes are complicated
③ Electronic payment is convenient
④ Cyber security is not a threat

⑤　Fewer of us use electronic payment

問5　Have you ever heard of the sharing economy? It is an economic system that consists of lending and borrowing idle assets owned by individuals via the Internet. Lenders earn income by utilizing idle assets. Borrowers (　　). Now in Japan, there are many sharing systems for cars, bicycles, empty spaces, human resources, and so on. They are made possible by matching. As sharing systems spread in Japan, it will be possible to solve various issues that the region faces.

①　can use them without owning the item
②　are unavailable in Japan
③　lend the items they own for free
④　do not require an Internet connection
⑤　are prohibited from paying for them

(☆☆☆◎◎◎◎)

【9】次の英文を読んで，以下の問に答えなさい。

What kind of homework did you procrastinate most when you were a student? A simple math drill or a creative art project? Even though the answer should depend on each individual's preference, for many, it is essay writing assignments. One of the reasons students procrastinate writing assignments lies in the feeling called "writer's block" .

A writer's block is the feeling of being unable to write. It is different from writer's cramp, which is stiffness of the hand caused by writing for a long time. Three different kinds of block have been diagnosed: physical, procedural and psychological. Physical blocks occur when (　A　). Procedural blocks occur when (　B　). Psychological blocks occur when (　C　).

One of the main difficulties in writing for native speakers of English is the process of "getting started" . [　①　] A questionnaire was sent to students at a university in England and one in Canada by some researchers. One of the questions was 'What do you like least about writing?' "Writing the first paragraph" was the most common response. ② It is not an exaggeration to say that almost every respondent experienced some kind of writer's block. If writing the first paragraph presents difficulties for native speakers of English, the problem for non-native speakers of English must be at least as great. ③ A survey conducted by another researcher confirmed this.

Various suggestions have been made to overcome the problem of "getting started" in writing. One fairly common one is to begin by simply jotting down ideas or notes on paper-(D), to get what you want to say down on paper as quickly as possible. ④ At this stage it does not matter if sentences are incomplete.

The next suggestion is to review the writing that you worked on in the past. Looking over your own work, which should give you a certain sense of confidence, is a good way to set your mind in your writing. ⑤ Moreover, it should present you with a great opportunity to brainstorm the main idea you are going to tackle. Restructuring in your mind the concept or notion which used to be of importance to you should bring to mind some topics which are of importance to you now.

問1 Choose the most appropriate combination to fill in (A), (B), and (C).

① A ウ B イ C ア
② A ウ B ア C エ
③ A エ B イ C ア
④ A エ B ウ C イ
⑤ A イ B ア C エ

ア the writer cannot decide what to write next

イ the writer has a specific topic to write about and is ready to start writing

ウ the writer is tired and it just becomes too much of an effort to continue

エ the words should come, and could come, but the writer cannot let the words appear on the paper

問2 Choose the most appropriate transition for (D).

① in other words ② hence ③ in fact

④ on the contrary ⑤ in addition

問3 Put the following sentence in the correct placement in the passage from [①], [②], [③], [④], and [⑤].

Editing, polishing, changing, resequencing, and the like can be left until later.

問4 According to the passage, which of the following statements is true?

① Students prefer the writing assignment most because it reflects each individual's perspective.

② Respondents of a questionnaire said they most enjoyed writing the first paragraph.

③ The problem of getting started in writing is unique to native speakers of English.

④ By making complete sentences, ideas become clearer and the writing starts to flow.

⑤ Reviewing your past work offers you a good chance to brainstorm your ideas.

(☆☆☆◎◎◎◎)

【10】次の英文を読んで，以下の問に答えなさい。

Our daily life is a series of choices. It can be difficult to make a decision when faced with an issue, even if you gather information thoroughly and (A) about it. When we lose our way in work or life, or when we encounter any (B), we sometimes intuitively choose which path to take and how to act. Intuition is a result of repeated thoughts where the answer suddenly flashes in your head like (C). Intuition cannot be born from nothing, but it behaves unpredictably.

Among the various types of people, people (D) likely have a keen intuition that seizes opportunities. For example, in a soccer game, it often happens that a striker who is good at scoring goals manages to be in the right place at the right time. If the striker were uncertain and their decision was delayed by even a second, they wouldn't be able to score a goal. They have a high level of intuition.

It is said that successful people have better intuition in many areas in business and life. For example, wise entrepreneurs have a keen intuition and listen to their inner voice to take action so that they can compete with others even if there are downs in business. The more we improve our intuition, the better we can make important choices and the more we can achieve great results in our work or hobbies.

There are plenty of ways to train your intuition. One way is to take on a lot of challenges and gain a lot of experience. The more trials you make, the more your intuition will improve. Even if you fail, take time to reflect and think about ways to improve your judgement. Another way is to train the right side of your brain. The human brain is divided into a right side and a left side which govern different fields: "inspiration and design" and "logic and language" respectively. In order to train your intuition, you need to improve the work of the right side of your brain. One way to do this is by playing different games. This could be sports, board games, or challenging video games. To become successful at playing different games, you must train yourself to find the best move at the best time. It requires creativity and flexible thinking, so games are helpful for developing the right side of your brain, and subsequently your intuition.

You don't need to be a great athlete or business owner to achieve highly. If you can improve your intuition over time, good decisions will come to you and bring you success.

問1 Choose the most appropriate combination of words and phrases to fill in (A), (B), and (C).

①	A	think deeply	B	obstacles	C	a lightbulb
②	A	do research	B	routes	C	overflowing wate
③	A	take action	B	dangers	C	a movie screen
④	A	read reluctantly	B	distress	C	a memory
⑤	A	care so much	B	old friends	C	the blue sky

問2　Choose the most appropriate phrase to fill in (　D　).

① who act cautiously
② who think excessively
③ who do things spontaneously
④ who lack professional knowledge
⑤ who behave politely

問3　According to the passage, what is a function of the left side of the brain?

① It handles art.
② It is credited with imagination.
③ It has a creative and less organized way of thinking.
④ It is connected to logic.
⑤ It deals with people's feelings.

問4　According to the passage, which of the following statements is true?

① If we think over and over again, we can easily reach desirable outcomes.
② We can clearly and easily notice when intuition is going to work.
③ Great achievement often comes from good decisions based on improved intuition.
④ Athletes and entrepreneurs have the highest intuition among all people.
⑤ The only way to be successful in our life is to train our right brain.

(☆☆☆◎◎◎◎)

【11】次の英文を読んで，以下の問に答えなさい。

Maria Montessori was born in Italy in 1870. She studied hard even though the education of girls was not as advanced as it is today. She was eventually accepted to study at the medical department at the University of Rome, and she became the first woman in Italy to receive her PhD in medicine. Despite sexist discrimination against her, she got a job as a doctor at a mental hospital. Patients in the mental hospital at that time were given no therapeutic treatment. One day, in this desperate workplace, she noticed a toddler with intellectual disabilities playing constantly with bread crumbs that had fallen to the floor. She carefully observed the infant's actions, discovering that she was seeking sensory stimuli. She became convinced that by stimulating the senses, even children with intellectual disabilities could improve their intelligence and have similar education to children without disabilities.

Montessori shocked the Italian education and medical communities when she explored this idea and worked with the children in the hospital with intellectual disabilities. She gave them intelligence tests which resulted in their intelligence scores surpassing those of children outside the hospital at the time. Upon seeing these results, she believed that her methods could be applied to the education of all children. In 1907, Montessori opened her first "Children's House" for the children of the San Lorenzo district of Rome. The children in the Children's House, who at first were rampaging in the classroom and could not concentrate at all, were introduced to Montessori's sensory teaching tools and gradually became calmer, more skilled, and controlled themselves (A) autonomously. Having made these great achievements, Montessori re-entered the University of Rome, devoted herself to the study of philosophy, physiology, and psychiatry, and later established what is called the Montessori method in education.

The premise of the Montessori method is the existence of "self-educational ability": that children have the ability to raise themselves. Children will acquire various abilities by repeatedly working on the activity of their choice until they are satisfied. Even if a skill isn't taught to the child directly, seeing others attempt the skill and being in an environment where they can be actively involved results in the child assimilating and learning the skill independently. In an environment where this inherent power can be fully exerted and freedom is guaranteed, children will grow up while voluntarily repeating beneficial activities and develop their own independence and autonomy.

Known not only as an educator but also as a pioneer in women's social advancement, Montessori worked around the world to promote peace, equality, and education. Her teaching method was shared worldwide and was praised by educational professionals of many countries. She was even nominated for the Nobel Peace Prize three times for her achievements. Even now, more than 100 years later, her method is supported worldwide and it is said that Montessori practice gardens currently exist in more than 140 countries around the world. Maria Montessori's teaching method has had a profound impact on the world and, regardless of time and culture, its influence has been continually recognized all over the world to the present day.

問1　According to the passage, what led Montessori to believe her teaching methods could benefit all children?

① She proved that playing constantly with bread crumbs will increase children's intelligence.

② She was the first woman to receive a scholarship to study for a PhD and go back to university.

③ After opening "Children's House", she did research by giving the children intelligence tests.

④ Children she worked with in the hospital got good scores in intelligence tests.

⑤ Her influence inspired the implementation of therapeutic treatment in the mental hospital.

問2　Choose the most appropriate word or phrase to replace (　A　).

①　of their own will　　②　diligently　　③　as a group

④　loosely　　⑤　strictly

問3　According to the passage, what is the idea behind the Montessori method?

①　Children should be involved with as many teachers as possible and take in strict guidance from them.

②　Special learning plans for each child are indispensable for educating them and they should be revised according to their performance.

③　Children have the ability to memorize a lot of information once they hear it and retain it for a long time.

④　Children need to choose their learning style from the advice of their teachers and continue to study until they reach their own goal.

⑤　When provided with various activities, children will practice them out of their own natural interest and learn skills by themselves.

問4　According to the passage, which of the following statements is true?

①　In the nineteenth century, Italy was the leading country for women's education.

②　In the mental hospital, Montessori gave therapeutic treatment to the adult patients.

③　Due to her colleague's support, Montessori found the importance of stimulating children's senses.

④　After successful results in the Children's House, Montessori pursued further education about the mind and body.

⑤　Montessori became famous as an educator as well as a social leader, and won three Nobel Peace Prizes for her work.

(☆☆☆◎◎◎◎)

【中学校】

【1】次の文は，「中学校学習指導要領解説　外国語編」(平成29年文部科学省)「第1章　総説」「2　外国語科改訂の趣旨と要点」「(1)　改訂の趣旨」の一部である。次の①～⑥に当てはまる語句を書きなさい。ただし，同じ番号には同じ語句が入る。

> 今回の外国語科の改訂に当たっては，中央教育審議会答申を踏まえ，次のような，これまでの成果と課題等を踏まえた改善を図った。
> ・グローバル化が急速に進展する中で，外国語によるコミュニケーション能力は，これまでのように一部の業種や職種だけでなく，生涯にわたる様々な場面で必要とされることが想定され，その能力の向上が課題となっている。
> ・平成20年改訂の学習指導要領は，小・中・高等学校で一貫した外国語教育を実施することにより，外国語を通じて，言語や(　①　)に対する理解を深め，積極的に外国語を用いてコミュニケーションを図ろうとする(　②　)や，情報や考えなどを的確に理解したり適切に伝えたりする力を身に付けさせることを目標として掲げ，「聞くこと」，「話すこと」，「読むこと」，「書くこと」などを総合的に育成することをねらいとして改訂され，様々な取組を通じて指導の充実が図られてきた。
> ・しかし，学年が上がるにつれて児童生徒の(　③　)に課題が生じるといった状況や，学校種間の(　④　)が十分とは言えず，進級や進学をした後に，それまでの学習内容や指導方法等を発展的に生かすことができないといった状況も見られている。
> ・中学校においては，小学校における(　⑤　)の成果として，英語で積極的にコミュニケーションを図ろうとする(　②　)が育成され，「聞くこと」及び「話すこと」の活動を行うことに慣れているといった変容が生徒に見られること等も踏まえ，授業における教師の英語使用や生徒の英語による(　⑥　)の割合

などが改善されてきている。

(☆☆☆◎◎◎◎)

【2】次の文は,「中学校学習指導要領」(平成29年3月告示)「第2章　各教科」「第9節　外国語」「第2　各言語の目標及び内容等」の一部である。次の①~⑤に当てはまる語句を書きなさい。

第2　各言語の目標及び内容等

英語

1　目標

英語学習の特質を踏まえ,以下に示す,聞くこと,読むこと,話すこと[やり取り],話すこと[発表],書くことの五つの領域別に設定する目標の実現を目指した指導を通して,第1の(1)及び(2)に示す資質・能力を一体的に育成するとともに,その過程を通して,第1の(3)に示す資質・能力を育成する。

—中略—

(2)　読むこと

ア　日常的な話題について,簡単な語句や文で書かれたものから必要な(　①　)を読み取ることができるようにする。

イ　日常的な話題について,簡単な語句や文で書かれた短い文章の(　②　)を捉えることができるようにする。

ウ　社会的な話題について,簡単な語句や文で書かれた短い文章の(　③　)を捉えることができるようにする。

—中略—

(5)　書くこと

ア　(　④　)のある事柄について,簡単な語句や文を用いて正確に書くことができるようにする。

イ　日常的な話題について,事実や自分の考え,気持ちなどを整理し,簡単な語句や文を用いてまとまりのある文章を書くことができるようにする。
ウ　社会的な話題に関して聞いたり読んだりしたことについて，考えたことや感じたこと，その(　⑤　)などを，簡単な語句や文を用いて書くことができるようにする。

(☆☆☆◎◎◎◎)

【3】次の文は，「中学校学習指導要領」(平成29年3月告示)「第2章　各教科」「第9節　外国語」「第2　各言語の目標及び内容等」「英語」「3　指導計画の作成と内容の取扱い」の一部である。次の①～④に当てはまる語句を書きなさい。

(1)　指導計画の作成に当たっては，小学校や高等学校における指導との接続に留意しながら，次の事項に配慮するものとする。
ア　(　①　)など内容や時間のまとまりを見通して，その中で育む資質・能力の育成に向けて，生徒の主体的・対話的で深い学びの実現を図るようにすること。その際，具体的な課題等を設定し，生徒が外国語によるコミュニケーションにおける見方・考え方を働かせながら，コミュニケーションの目的や場面，状況などを意識して活動を行い，英語の(　②　)や語彙，表現，文法の知識を五つの領域における実際のコミュニケーションにおいて活用する学習の充実を図ること。

—中略—

ウ　実際に英語を使用して互いの考えや気持ちを伝え合うなどの言語活動を行う際は，2の(1)に示す言語材料について理解したり練習したりするための指導を必要に応じて行うこと。また，小学校第3学年から第6学年までに扱った簡単な語句や基本的な表現などの学習内容を(　③　)指導し定着を図ること。

—中略—

オ　言語活動で扱う題材は，生徒の興味・関心に合ったものとし，国語科や理科，音楽科など，他の教科等で学習したことを活用したり，学校行事で扱う内容と(　④　)たりするなどの工夫をすること。

(☆☆☆◎◎◎◎)

【高等学校】

【1】次の文は，「高等学校学習指導要領」(平成30年3月告示)「第2章　各学科に共通する各教科」「第8節　外国語」「第3款　英語に関する各科目にわたる指導計画の作成と内容の取扱い」の一部である。文中の①～⑤に当てはまる語句を書きなさい。ただし，同じ番号には，同じ語句が入る。

2　内容の取扱いに当たっては，次の事項に配慮するものとする。

(1)　単に英語を日本語に，又は日本語を英語に置き換えるような指導とならないよう，各科目の内容の(1)に示す言語材料については，(　①　)のある文脈でのコミュニケーションの中で繰り返し触れることを通して指導すること。また，生徒の発達の段階に応じて，聞いたり読んだりすることを通して(　①　)を理解できるように指導すべき事項と，話したり書いたりして表現できるように指導すべき事項とがあることに留意すること。

—中略—

(7)　生徒が(　②　)する機会を増やすとともに，他者と(　③　)する力を育成するため，ペア・ワーク，グループ・ワークなどの学習形態について適宜工夫すること。その際，他者とコミュニケーションを行うことに課題がある生徒については，個々の生徒の特性に応じて指導内容や指導方法を工夫すること。
(8)　生徒が身に付けるべき資質・能力や生徒の実態，教材の内容などに応じて，視聴覚教材やコンピュータ，情報通信ネットワーク，教育機器などを有効活用し，生徒の興味・関心をより高めるとともに，英語による情報の(　④　)に慣れさせるために，キーボードを使って英文を入力するなどの活動を効果的に取り入れることにより，指導の(　⑤　)や言語活動の更なる充実を図るようにすること。

(☆☆☆☆◎◎◎◎)

【2】次の文は，「高等学校学習指導要領」(平成30年3月告示)「第2章　各学科に共通する各教科」「第8節　外国語」「第2款　各科目」「第1　英語コミュニケーションⅠ」「1　目標」の一部である。文中の①～⑤に当てはまる語句を書きなさい。ただし，同じ番号には，同じ語句が入る。

(1)　聞くこと
ア　日常的な話題について，話される速さや，使用される語句や文，(　①　)などにおいて，多くの(　②　)を活用すれば，必要な情報を聞き取り，話し手の意図を把握することができるようにする。
イ　社会的な話題について，話される速さや，使用される語句や文，(　①　)などにおいて，多くの(　②　)を活用すれば，必要な情報を聞き取り，概要や要点を目的に応じて捉えることができるようにする。

―中略―

(3)　話すこと[やり取り]
ア　日常的な話題について，使用する語句や文，(　③　)の展開などにおいて，多くの(　②　)を活用すれば，基本的な語句や文を用いて，情報や考え，気持ちなどを話して伝え合うやり取りを続けることができるようにする。

イ　社会的な話題について，使用する語句や文，(　③　)の展開などにおいて，多くの(　②　)を活用すれば，聞いたり読んだりしたことを基に，基本的な語句や文を用いて，情報や考え，気持ちなどを(　④　)に注意して話して伝え合うことができるようにする。

(4)　話すこと[発表]

ア　日常的な話題について，使用する語句や文，事前の(　⑤　)などにおいて，多くの(　②　)を活用すれば，基本的な語句や文を用いて，情報や考え，気持ちなどを(　④　)に注意して話して伝えることができるようにする。

イ　社会的な話題について，使用する語句や文，事前の(　⑤　)などにおいて，多くの(　②　)を活用すれば，聞いたり読んだりしたことを基に，基本的な語句や文を用いて，情報や考え，気持ちなどを(　④　)に注意して話して伝えることができるようにする。

(☆☆☆◎◎◎)

【3】次の文は，「高等学校学習指導要領解説　外国語編　英語編」(平成30年文部科学省)「第1部　外国語編」「第3章　各科目にわたる指導計画の作成と内容の取扱い」「第3節　教材についての配慮事項」の一部である。文中の①～⑧に当てはまる語句を以下の語群から一つずつ選んで記号で答えなさい。

3　教材については，次の事項に留意するものとする。

(1)　教材は，五つの領域別の言語活動及び複数の領域を結び付けた(　①　)な言語活動を通してコミュニケーションを図る資質・能力を総合的に育成するため，各科目の五つの領域別の目標と2に示す内容との関係について，(　②　)など内容や時間のまとまりごとに各教材の中で明確に示すとともに，実際の言語の(　③　)や言語の働きに十分に配慮した題材を取り上げること。

―中略―

(2)　英語を使用している人々を中心とする世界の人々や日本人の日常生活，風俗習慣，物語，地理，歴史，伝統文化，自然科学などに関するものの中から，生徒の発達の段階や興味・関心に即して適切な題材を効果的に取り上げるものとし，次の観点に配慮すること。

―中略―

このように，教材の選定に当たっては，生徒の発達の段階，興味・関心について十分に配慮しながら，英語の目標に照らして適切であり，(　④　)に応じた言語材料で構成されているような適切な題材を(　⑤　)をもたせて取り上げるように配慮する必要がある。

以下に題材の選択に関する四つの観点が示されている。

(ア)　(　⑥　)考え方に対する理解を深めさせ，(　⑦　)判断力を養い豊かな心情を育てるのに役立つこと。

―中略―

(ウ)　社会がグローバル化する中で，広い(　⑧　)から国際理解を深め，国際社会と向き合うことが求められている我が国の一員としての自覚を高めるとともに，国際協調の精神を養うのに役立つこと。

―中略―

(エ) 人間，社会，自然などについての考えを深めるのに役立つこと。

《語群》

A	授業	B	単元	C	視野	D	知識
E	使用場面	F	活用方法	G	構造	H	学習段階
I	習熟度	J	ゆとり	K	変化	L	能動的
M	統合的	N	道徳的	O	冷静な	P	公正な
Q	一貫した	R	多様な				

(☆☆☆◎◎◎)

解答・解説

【中高共通】

【1】Question 1　③　　Question 2　②　　Question 3　③

〈解説〉対話文を聞いて，3つの設問に選択肢で答える四択問題。対話文と設問は2度放送される。　Question 1　Emilyは，5人分のディナーを予約するため，レストランに電話した。　Question 2　夕日を見たいから，湖を見渡せる窓際の席を予約したいと言っている。

0Question 3　1人当たり食事が35ドル，飲み物が3ドル，ケーキ2ドルを計算して解答する。

【2】≪A≫　Question 1　④　　Question 2　①　　Question 3　②

≪B≫　Question 1　②　　Question 2　③　　Question 3　④

〈解説〉200～250語程度の2つのパッセージを聞いて，それぞれ3つの設問に選択肢で答える四択問題。放送は2度ある。　≪A≫　Question 3は，パッセージの内容に合致しない答えを選ぶ内容不一致問題であるので，聞き間違えないようにしたい。トピックはSDGsで，その目的や目標の詳細を聞き取る。　≪B≫　トピックはJET program(語学指導等を行う外国青年招致事業)で，その目的やプログラム参加者に求められていることを聞き取る。特に難解なスクリプトではないが，全体を把握すべき内容一致(不一致)問題が含まれている。

【3】Question 1　②　　Question 2　①　　Question 3　④

〈解説〉280語程度のパッセージを聞き，3つの設問について，読み上げられる4つの選択肢から正答を選ぶ形式。放送は2度あるものの，文字情報がなく，聞き取らなければならない選択肢の英文量が多い。受験者間で差がつく問題になると思われる。トピックは，日本では「蛍の光」の原曲として知られるスコットランドの民謡Auld Lang Syneについてである。設問は，「(作詞者の)Robert Burnsについて正しいものはどれか」，「Auld Lang Syneの歌について正しいものはどれか」，「Auld Lang Syneの歌について最も適切な説明はどれか」。聞き取るべき内容が多く，問われる内容も細かいので，メモを素早く取りながら聞くことが大切である。

【4】③，⑤

〈解説〉200語程度のパッセージを聞いて，6つの選択肢の中から，内容に合致するものを2つ選ぶ形式。放送は2度あるが，【3】と同様に，文字情報がなく，選択肢は長めである。聞き逃さないように集中しなければならない。パッセージのトピックは，自然に触れることの大切さについてであり，特に難解なものではない。1度目の放送時にできるだけ多くの誤肢を取り除き，2度目の放送時には聞き逃したところを確認する。

【5】問1　②　　問2　④　　問3　①　　問4　④　　問5　⑤

〈解説〉問1「スタッフがとても親切なので，客はこのパン屋をひいきにしている」。patronize～「～をひいきにする」。　問2「旅行の日程が確定すると，旅行会社がメールで知らせてくれる」。confirm～「～を確認する」。　問3「その家は歴史的には取るに足らない価値しかないが，庭は18世紀のものと推定される」。insignificant「重要でない，些細な」。　問4「昨年，叔母(伯母)は，私を街の最もすばらしい遺跡の観光ツアーに連れて行ってくれた」。illustrious「著名な，輝かしい」。問5「この種のエンジンは今ではオートバイに使われていない。それは70年以上も前にすたれてしまった」。obsolete「使われなくなった，時代遅れの」。

【6】問1　⑤　　問2　④　　問3　②　　問4　①

〈解説〉問1　整序すると，reason why foreigners learning Japaneseとなる。問2　整序すると，the speakers organize their ideasとなる。　問3　整序すると，achieving the goal must beとなる。　問4　整序すると，has moved me so muchとなる。

【7】問1　③　　問2　②

〈解説〉問1　顧客との約束がある会社員とその同僚がバスを待っている場面。E→B→A→F→D→Cとなる。　問2　インタビューを承諾したMr. Brownとインタビュアーの会話。E→A→C→F→B→Dとなる。

【8】問1　④　　問2　③　　問3　②　　問4　③　　問5　①

〈解説〉問1　モーニングルーティーンを確立することを勧める内容。よいモーニングルーティーンは，④「あなたのパフォーマンスにプラスに影響する」。　問2　失敗を恐れず，成功するまで何度でもチャレンジすることを説く文。失敗した時に謙虚に学ぼうとすれば，③「失敗は私たちに多くのことを教えてくれる」。　問3　真のリーダー像について述べている文。まず，私が今までに会ったリーダーのほとんどは，②「目指す場所を知っているので」シンプルに考える。　問4　トピックは支払方法の多様化。③「電子決済は便利である」。なぜなら硬貨を持ち歩いたり，レジの支払いで勘定したりしなくてよいからだ。

問5　シェアリングエコノミーについての説明。貸し手は遊休資産を利用して収入を得る。借り手は，①「物を所有せずにそれらを利用することができる」。

【9】問1　②　　問2　①　　問3　④　　問4　⑤
〈解説〉問1　writer's block「書けないという感情」の3つの種類，physical block(身体的ブロック)，procedural block(手順ブロック)，psychological block(心理的ブロック)が，どのような場合に起きるかを考える。イの「書き手が書こうとする特別なトピックを持ち，書き始める準備ができている」は明らかに誤りだと判断できる。　問2　空所を含む段落では，「書き始める」という困難を克服するための提案の1つが示されている。空所前のjot down「～をさっとメモに書く」を空所後では，別な表現で言い換えている。よって空所には，①のin other words「言い換えると」が入る。　問3　挿入文は「編集したり，推敲したり，変更したり，並べ直したりなどは，後回しにできる」。④の位置に挿入すると，続く文で「この段階では，文章が不完全でもかまわない」と述べているため，意味がスムーズにつながる。　問4　最終段落参照。⑤「過去の作品を見直すと，あなたの考えを引き出すよい機会となる」が正しい。

【10】問1　①　　問2　③　　問3　④　　問4　③
〈解説〉問1　不適な選択肢を除きながら，正解にたどり着くことができる。Aでは，read reluctantly「仕方なく本を読む」，Bでは，old friends「旧友」などが，明らかに消去できる。　A「問題に直面した時，たとえ完璧に情報を集め，それについて深く考えても，決断するのは難しい」。　B「仕事や人生で道に迷った時，または障害に遭遇した時に，私たちは直感的にどちらの道に進むか，どのように行動するかを選択する」。　C「直感とは度重なる思考の結果で，そこでは答えが電球のように頭にひらめくのだ」。　問2　好機をとらえる鋭い直感力を持っているのはどのような人か。空所後の文で，「得点するのが上手いス

トライカーは何とかして適時に適所にいようとする」と述べていることから，③「自発的に物事をする」人。　問3　左脳の働きについて書かれている第4段落6文目を参照。左脳はlogicとlanguageを司る。問4　第3段落の最終文に「直感力を磨けば磨くほど，重要な選択をよりよくすることができ，仕事や趣味において素晴らしい結果が得られる」とある。よって，③「素晴らしい成功は，磨かれた直感力に基づく的確な決定にしばしば由来する」が正しい。

【11】問1　④　　問2　①　　問3　⑤　　問4　④
〈解説〉問1　設問は「Montessoriはなぜ自分の指導法がすべての子どもたちのためになると信じたのか」。第2段落の2，3文目参照。④「彼女が病院で携わっていた子どもたちが知能テストでよいスコアをとったから」が正しい。　問2　autonomously「自律的に」に置き換えられるのは，①のof one's own will「自分の意志で，自主的に」。　問3　設問は「Montessori教育法の背景にある考えは何か」。第3段落2文目及び3文目参照。Montessori教育法の前提は自己教育能力の存在である。よって，⑤「様々な活動が提供されれば，子どもは自身の興味に基づきそれらを実践し，自身でスキルを身に付ける」が正しい。　問4　第2段落最終文参照。Montessoriは，ローマ大学に再入学して哲学，生理学，精神医学の研究に没頭し，のちにいわゆるモンテッソーリ教育法を確立した。よって，④「Children's Houseで成果を挙げたあと，Montessoriは心と身体に関する教育をさらに追求した」が正しい。

【中学校】

【1】①　文化　　②　態度　　③　学習意欲　　④　接続　　⑤　外国語活動　　⑥　言語活動
〈解説〉「改訂の趣旨」及び「改訂の要点」については，改訂の基となった平成28年12月21日答申「幼稚園，小学校，中学校，高等学校及び特別支援学校の学習指導要領等の改善及び必要な方策等について(答申)」(中教審第197)を参照しながら，理解を深めておいてほしい。平成29年

3月告示の中学校学習指導要領では，外国語教育を通じて育成を目指す資質・能力全体を貫く軸として，他者とのコミュニケーションの基盤を形成する観点を重視しつつ，他の側面(創造的思考，感性・情緒等)からも育成を目指す資質・能力が明確となるよう整理されている。

【2】① 情報　② 概要　③ 要点　④ 関心　⑤ 理由

〈解説〉中学校段階での「読むこと」の領域では，日常的な話題について書かれたものから情報を読み取り，概要を捉えるという段階を経て，社会で起こっている出来事や問題に関する文章を読み，大切な部分を捉える力を身に付けさせることを目標としている。文章全体の大まかな内容を把握するのではなく，文章から複数の情報を取り出し，どの情報がその説明の中で最も重要であるかを判断することに留意する必要がある。「書くこと」では，文構造や文法事項を正しく用いて正しい語順で文を構成し，伝えたいことについての情報を正確に捉え，整理したり確認したりしながら書けるようにすることを目標としている。自分の関心のある事柄から，日常的な話題を経て，最終的には，広く国内外で起こっている出来事や問題に関わる話題について自分の意見や感想をもち，その内容をまとめて書く力を身に付けさせることが大切である。

【3】① 単元　② 音声　③ 繰り返し　④ 関連付け

〈解説〉ア　外国語科の指導計画の作成に当たり，生徒の主体的・対話的で深い学びの実現を目指した授業改善を進めることとし，外国語科の特質に応じて，効果的な学習が展開できるように配慮すべき内容を示したものである。　ウ　中学校第1学年においては，特に，生徒が在籍していた小学校において，どのような時間割編成，指導体制によって授業が行われているかを把握することにより，中学校への円滑な接続を図ることが必要である。　オ　生徒が，主体的に英語を用いてコミュニケーションを図ろうとする態度を養うには，生徒の発達の段階や知的好奇心を踏まえ，言語活動への積極的参加を促せるよう工夫する必要がある。題材には，他教科等でこれまで学んできた，あるいは現在学んでいることを積極的に活用するなど，教科等間で学びのつながりや広がりがあるものとなるよう工夫が求められる。

【高等学校】

【1】① 意味　② 発話　③ 協働　④ 発信　⑤ 効率化

〈解説〉(1) この配慮事項は，言語材料の指導に当たって，知識を実際のコミュニケーションにおいて活用できる技能が身に付くよう指導することが必要であることを述べている。生徒の発達の段階や学習の目的を踏まえ，それぞれの言語材料をどの程度まで習得させる必要があるのかを見極めることが大切である。 (7) 生徒の様々な個性や特性を把握した上で，指導に効果的と考えられる学習形態を柔軟に選択することが求められている。特にペア・ワークやグループ・ワークにおいては，「生徒が発話する機会」を増やしたり「他者と協働する力を育成」したりすることができるような工夫が必要であり，様々な形態のコミュニケーションを通して，互いに学び合える環境を整備していくことが重要である。 (8) コンピュータや情報通信ネットワークを使うことによって，生徒が主体的に世界と関わっていこうとする態度を育成することができる。教育機器は外国語科の指導にとって大切な役目を果たすものである。生徒が，社会生活においてコンピュータ上でやり取りをする機会が今後さらに増えることなどを考慮し，教育機器の効果的な活用を工夫していくことが重要である。

【2】① 情報量　② 支援　③ 対話　④ 論理性　⑤ 準備

〈解説〉「英語コミュニケーションⅠ」は，中学校における学習を踏まえた上で，5つの領域別の言語活動と複数の領域を結び付けた統合的な言語活動を通し，5つの領域を総合的に扱うことを重視する必履修科目として設定された。更に高等学校学習指導要領解説外国語編・英語編(平成30年7月)の巻末には，資料として，高等学校「外国語の目標」の科目段階別一覧表及び高等学校「外国語の言語活動の例」の科目段階別一覧表が収められている。出題の「英語コミュニケーションⅠ」と同Ⅱ，同Ⅲを比較対照し，段階別にどのように目標や活動内容が変化するかを，併せて確認されたい。

【3】① M　② B　③ E　④ H　⑤ K　⑥ R
⑦ P　⑧ C

〈解説〉教材は，情報や考えなどを的確に理解したり適切に表現したり伝え合ったりするコミュニケーションを図る資質・能力を育成するために，適切なものを選定する必要がある。ある単元において，どの領域のどの目標に焦点を当てた指導をするとよいかを明らかにした上で，その目標を実現するためにどのような言語活動を行うのか，その際どういった言語材料を活用するのかを適切に関連付けることが必要である。さらに，題材については，例えば，領域別の言語活動を共通の題材で関連させたり，複数の単元を通して一つの題材について，日常的な話題から徐々に社会的な話題に広げ，言語活動の中で生徒が思考，判断，表現する過程を深めたりするなどの工夫も考えられる。

2021年度　実施問題

※福岡市を志望する場合は，【中高共通】の【5】～【10】を解答して下さい。

【中高共通】

【1】次に読まれる英文を聞き，1～3の設問に対する答として最も適切なものを，四つの選択肢の中から一つ選びなさい。
(英文及び設問は2回読まれる。)

Staff : Thank you for calling the Hawaii Travel Agency. Can I help you?
Eric : Yes. I am hoping to book a tour.
Do you have any tours available on The Big Island tomorrow?
Staff : Yes. Our travel agency has many of them.
Is there something in particular you'd like to see?
Eric : Well, I want to see a waterfall.
Staff : I recommend Akaka Falls. You'll see a rainbow if you're lucky.
Eric : Really? Is it difficult to get there?
Staff : Not really. Where are you staying?
Eric : The Hilo Ocean Resort.
Staff : In that case we can pick you up at your hotel. Then we'll drive you to the falls.
Eric : That sounds good.
Staff : Great. We offer many opportunities to see Hawaii's fantastic ecological diversity.
We have half-day and full-day tours.
Which would you prefer?
Eric : A full－day tour. How much is it?
Staff : It's 55 dollars per person, including the entry fee for Akaka Falls and a lunch.

Eric : Oh, we won't need a lunch; we'll bring our own.

Staff : O.K. Without lunch, the cost per person will be 10 dollars less.

Eric : That's perfect. Can I make a reservation now?

Staff : Absolutely. May I have your names?

Eric : My name is Eric Green. My wife is Nancy Green.

Staff : All right. Anything else I can help you with?

Eric : I think that's all...Oh, I almost forgot. What time does the tour start?

Staff : We'll pick you up at 9:30 a.m.

Eric : Thanks.

Staff : Anything else?

Eric : No, thank you.

Staff : Okay. We look forward to seeing you tomorrow.

(237 words)

Question 1: What was Eric's reason for calling the Hawaii Travel Agency?

① Ordering a book.

② Booking a tour.

③ Confirming an appointment.

④ Taking an order.

Question 2: Why did the staff recommend that Eric see Akaka Falls?

① Because Eric may have a chance to see a rainbow at Akaka Falls.

② Because Eric may see wild animals of all species up close safely.

③ Because Eric can discover delicious snacks made from locally-sourced ingredients.

④ Because Eric can climb the waterfall with the tour guide.

Question 3: How much will Eric and his wife have to pay in total to join the tour?

① 45 dollars.

② 55 dollars.

③　90 dollars.

④　110 dollars.

(☆☆◎◎◎◎)

【2】次に読まれる英文≪A≫及び英文≪B≫について，それぞれの1～3の設問に対する答として最も適切なものを，四つの選択肢の中から一つ選びなさい。

(英文及び設問は2回読まれる。)

≪A≫

Hello, my name is Mary. Let me tell you about my research on the pros and cons of telecommuting.

Telecommuting is a work arrangement in which an employee works outside of an office, often working from home or a nearby location, such as a coffee shop or a library. In surveys regarding job satisfaction and turnover rates, employers and employees prefer this style to the traditional office environment. Employees can avoid a long commute to the office and save valuable time. Most companies with telecommuting report that it raises employee productivity and helps lower company expenses. As equipment, real estate, and rental fees are reduced, more employees can be hired and employee turnover rates remain low.

Further, employees note the biggest benefit of telecommuting is that the commute itself is removed, saving time and money. Balancing work and family obligations becomes easier, and daily costs such as lunch and spending money on one's wardrobe can largely be reduced.

While most employers and employees are optimistic about telecommuting, some companies feel otherwise. These employers feel uncomfortable with the inability to regularly contact employees face-to-face. Companies also note worker's compensation insurance becomes a tough issue when employees are not in the office.

In conclusion, in order for telecommuting to be successful, it's clear that some company policies will need to be updated.

(217 words)

Question 1: According to the passage, what is the largest benefit of telecommuting employees?

① Employers can undergo a major life change like relocating to another place.

② Employers can easily evaluate and supervise employees' performance.

③ Employees cut down on expenses for office facilities and utilities.

④ Employees reduce commuting time and improve their performance.

Question 2: According to the passage, why are some employers uncomfortable with telecommuting?

① Because employees can lessen travel time and the stress of commuting.

② Because employers can focus better on their tasks with fewer disruptions.

③ Because employers cannot contact their employees regularly in face-to-face conversation.

④ Because working from home is a lonely venture that may subject employees to stress.

Question 3: According to the passage, which statement is true?

① Some researchers say telecommuting can be good for a person's health.

② The best working place for a telecommuting employee is a public place such as a coffee shop or a library.

③ Companies are creating clearer policies for worker's compensation.

④ Supervising employees who work from home can be a challenge for managers.

≪B≫

It seems to me that more and more people live alone now than any other time in history because of the changing of their lifestyles and their philosophies. I looked at the website and learned that 30 percent of all households of our city contain a single occupant. I wondered whether the decision to live alone is a cultural reason or an economic one. Which do you think is true?

I thought that metropolises in the US like New York or Washington had the largest population of people living alone because of their self-reliance and culture of individualism. But, according to one survey, households with a single dweller make up more than half of Paris, the rate tops 60 percent in Stockholm, while the rate in Washington is just around half of households there. The reason is said to be that living alone is largely seen as promoting freedom, personal control, and selfrealization, which are all prized aspects of our modern world. So the decision is not made by cultural nor economic reason.

Another research has shown the surprising fact that living alone can make it easier to be social, contrary to my belief. Single people have more free time to engage in social activities because they have fewer family obligations. Compared with those who are married, single people are more likely to spend time with friends and neighbors, go to restaurants, and attend classes and lectures open to community members.

(241 words)

Question 1 : According to the passage, what did the speaker find on the website?

① The percentage of households having one person in the speaker's city.

② The percentage of people who live alone in the speaker's city.

③ The percentage of households having one person in the speaker's country.

④ The percentage of people who live alone in the speaker's country.

Question 2 : According to the passage, which city has the highest rate of single dwellers?

① Washington.
② Paris.
③ Stockholm.
④ New York.

Question 3 : According to the passage, what is the surprising fact about the research?
① Single people have more time to contact their family members.
② Single people have more time to engage in indoor activities alone.
③ Single people have more time to spend on social activities with various people.
④ Single people have more time to decide according to their cultural philosophy.

(☆☆◎◎◎◎)

【3】次に読まれる英文を聞き，1～3の設問に対する答として最も適切なものを，そのあとに読まれる四つの選択肢の中から一つ選びなさい。
(英文，設問及び選択肢は2回読まれる。)

Global warming is a serious issue to us, to those living in modern times. Nobody denies this. If you study the history of our planet, you will see that there were times in the past when the climate was much warmer than we anticipated.

Around 1000 years ago, for example, the climate at that time was rather warm, so it is sometimes called the "Medieval Warm Period." In Europe, the Vikings we're said to be able to sail in the ocean unhindered by ice and to discover Greenland and some other northern islands. In Japan, one study shows that the temperature during the Heian Era was relatively high, according to the style of the architecture of palaces of the aristocracy. There were only roofs and see-through screens with few walls in the mansion, so the rooms had good ventilation. There were a few ponds around the mansion as well, so when the wind blew over the ponds, the air would get a bit cooler, making the mansion cooler. Another study says that the growth rings of trees show good evidence of the warmth of that time, Without any electric air conditioners, the people used many methods to make their life more comfortable in summer, regardless of the severe cold in winter.

(211 words)

Question 1 : According to the passage, what is true about the "Medieval Warm Period" ?

1 It was so warm that dinosaurs could swim in the ocean.

2 It was so warm that some tribes couldn't go out from Greenland.

3 It is said that the Vikings worried about global warming.

4 It is said that the Vikings could sail in the northern ocean.

Question 2 : According to the passage, why did the people in the Heian Era make ponds around the mansion?

1 Because bathing there made them cooler.

2 Because they wanted to make the air cooler.

3 Because they wanted to grow plants to feel cooler.

4 Because the sight of the ponds made them feel cooler.

Question 3 : According to the passage, what shows the warmth of the Heian Era?

1 The sea level of the ocean.

2 The growth rings of the trees.

3 The temperature of the ponds.

4 An electric thermometer.

(☆☆☆◎◎◎◎)

【4】次に読まれる英文を聞き，英文の内容に合致するものを，そのあとに読まれる六つの選択肢の中から二つ選びなさい。
(英文及び選択肢は2回読まれる。)

Welcome to our workshop. All of you here must be interested in working as a high school teacher in Pram City. I think it is a good choice for you. I'm going to tell you some of the features of the public high schools of our city.

There are two important features.

One is the wide variety. There are 10 different kinds of high schools in our city. Each of them has several kinds of courses to meet the students' career planning. They range from highly academic schools where you can prepare to enter the top national universities or other famous universities abroad, to professional vocational schools where you can acquire many qualifications or licenses for your future job. Moreover, each classroom has adequate ICT devices with an electronic blackboard, a document camera, a projector and a screen. Each teacher will be distributed a tablet PC for teaching in their classrooms, so surely their classes should be fascinating!

The other feature is the highly professional skills our teachers have. In addition to the ICT environments, the teachers are also offered opportunities to take seminars and lessons as a job in order to improve their teaching skills. You can take their excellent lessons and classes every day.

The reform of working conditions and styles has been highly achieved in our city. There have been fewer teachers who work overtime than the national average, and teachers have good supporting staff or clerks to help them concentrate on teaching. So please send your application to us. Let's work together!!

(261 words)

1　This is a workshop for those who want to teach at high school.

2　The purpose of the workshop is to show the demerits of working as teachers.

3　Some high schools in Pram City that prepare students for Universities abroad have only a single course.

4　The teachers should bring their own private PC to use ICT in the classrooms.

5　It is a kind of the teachers' job to take seminars for their improvement.

6　More teachers in Pram City work overtime than those in other parts of the country.

(☆☆☆◎◎◎◎)

【5】英文の意味が通るように，(　　) 内に入る最も適切なものを選びなさい。

問1　The store is always crowded. Many people are (　　) through some items.

①　reflecting　②　browsing　③　paying　④　producing
⑤　raising

問2　The company wanted me to send an academic (　　).

①　transcript　②　prescription　③　script　④　subscript
⑤　subtitle

問3　Only a few members were selected to play an important role (　　) the new administration.

①　down　②　upon　③　along　④　under　⑤　between

問4　For the (　　) of me, I can't remember what my teacher told me then.

①　purpose　②　life　③　body　④　feeling　⑤　dislike

問5　The data showed a vast (　　) in the number of students belonging to various sports clubs at the high school.

①　decrease　②　area　③　opportunity　④　feature
⑤　victory

(☆☆☆◎◎◎◎)

【6】次の各問の日本文の意味を表す英文を作るために，(　　)内のA～Eの語句を正しく並べかえたとき，2番目と4番目にくる最も適切な組合せを選びなさい。ただし，組合せの左側を2番目，右側を4番目とする。

問1　企業は，金融やコンピュータ・プログラミングの専門的な知識と秀でたコミュニケーション能力を備えている社員を探しています。

Companies are looking for ($_{A}$specialized $_{B}$employees $_{C}$possess $_{D}$who $_{E}$knowledge) in finance and computer programming, and excellent communication skills.

① A－C　② A－E　③ D－A　④ D－C
⑤ E－B

問2　プラスティックゴミを減らそうとする私たちの努力が実った。

Our efforts to ($_{A}$successful $_{B}$plastic garbage $_{C}$proven $_{D}$reduce $_{E}$have).

① A－C　② B－C　③ B－E　④ C－A　⑤ C－E

問3　都市部での無料駐車などの所有者が得られる特権を考慮すれば，電気自動車の増加はそんなに驚くことではない。

The increase of electric vehicles is no surprise ($_{A}$the benefits $_{B}$given $_{C}$their owners $_{D}$considering $_{E}$to), including free parking in cities.

① A－B　② A－E　③ C－B　④ E－A　⑤ E－C

問4　じっくり時間をかけて適切に英字新聞を読むことはあなたの語彙を増やすことに役に立つ。

Taking the time to read the newspaper in English ($_{A}$you $_{B}$to $_{C}$help $_{D}$properly $_{E}$will) increase your vocabulary.

① B－D　② B－E　③ C－A　④ C－B　⑤ E－A

(☆☆◎◎◎◎)

【7】次の各問のA～Fの英文を二人の会話として意味がつながるように並べかえるとき，2番目と4番目にくる最も適切な組合せを選びなさい。ただし，組合せの左側を2番目，右側を4番目とする。

問1　A : Thank you so much. I am a freshman and I move into the dorm today. Can I get my dorm key at the student hall?

B : No problem. I hope you move in smoothly.

C : Excuse me, could you tell me how to get to the student hall?

D : That is extremely helpful. Thanks again.

E : Yes, you might have to sign up there. There should be student volunteers in front of the student hall. They can show you where to unload your things.

F : Well, go straight down Aloma Street and turn left onto Gilbert Avenue. The student hall is on the right.

① A−C　② A−D　③ C−A　④ F−B　⑤ F−E

問2　A : It is fingered citron. In Japanese we call it “bushukan”, because it looks like the hands of Buddha.

B : Oh really? I want to eat it.

C : No, I don’t. Actually, I have never tried it, but I heard it tastes like oranges.

D : I have never seen this fruit before. What is this?

E : It has little pulp, so you would do better to make marmalade from its peel than to eat it.

F : Wow, the hands of Buddha? Do you know what it tastes like?

① A−C　② A−E　③ D−F　④ D−B　⑤ F−A

(☆☆◎◎◎◎)

【8】次の各問の英文を読み，文脈から考えて文中の(　　)に入る最も適切なものを選びなさい。

問1　Which do you like better, printed books or e-books? Recently e-book readers have greatly increased. One of the benefits is that we can carry many books anywhere because they are light weight. It is (　　). Another big benefit is that we can save our time going to the bookstore to buy them. On the other hand, printed books hold memories. Each time you read a book you invest your time in the story, which creates enjoyable memories.

① fun to share printed books with friends

② bad for our health to look at the screen’s blue light for a long time

③ uncomfortable not to bring printed books

④ not necessary to carry several printed books when we travel somewhere

⑤ inconvenient to download thousands of books on the Internet

問2　Employers offer an educational opportunity to students who are called interns for a certain period of time. This is called an "internship program". An internship can either be paid or voluntary. Of course, the former one is more competitive. What is the difference between an internship and a part-time job? A part-time job has tasks that are decided to some extent. So to speak, the main purpose is to earn money. Alternatively, the purpose of an internship is (　　).

① to give students opportunities to do an interview on the Internet
② to test out a career and find out what kind of skills you have
③ to send the resume first to some companies
④ to prepare some questions that you want to ask the interviewer
⑤ to consult with your college career center

問3　How do you improve your English skills during busy times? There are many ways that it can be integrated into your day. I would like to share with you a few of them that seem the most effective. The first is to listen to an English radio program or podcast for just ten minutes every day. If you can, please take notes about words and sentences which you could not understand and then listen to it again. The second is to try and keep a short English diary. An English diary will help you to (　　). As a result, you could improve your ability to express what you want to say in English.

① be able to manage your own schedule
② increase the amount of familiar words that you often use in everyday life
③ reduce your stress level for your health
④ remember what your favorite things are
⑤ gain knowledge and skills for various teaching methods

問4　The number of international students in Japan in 2019 was 312,214. The country that had the largest number of international students who came to Japan was China with 124,436 students. This was followed by Vietnam with 73,389 students and Nepal with 26,308 students. Asian countries accounted for the top five countries. Every year most of the international students must study Japanese (　　) because most classes are taught in Japanese.

① along with other subjects
② in spite of other languages
③ even if they do not register for any classes
④ after they go back to their home country
⑤ even though they do not hear it in class

問5 Traditional Japanese houses have a soft mat floor called *tatami*. It is a cultural practice unique to Japan. *Tatami* can have (　　) because of rush, which is a raw material for *tatami* mats. The biggest advantage of rush is maintaining clean air. The rush also has relaxing properties because of its composition. That is why most Japanese people feel comfortable sitting or lying on it.

① changed our lifestyles all over the world
② about 40% of light pass through it
③ a positive effect on our body and mind
④ the added ability to amplify sound
⑤ functions which make us irritated

(☆☆☆◎◎◎◎)

【9】次の英文を読んで，あとの問に答えなさい。

I like red. I like it so much that whenever possible I prefer to use red objects. For example, my wallet, key chains, and diary are all red! This love of red runs so deep that when my son was younger, I would often dress him up in something red too. Although I had never before considered my (A)<u>predilection</u>, there came a chance to the other day.

I had gone out shopping with my son. While perusing some stationery, I unconsciously reached out to inspect some red pieces. All of a sudden my son said, “Doesn’t red make you uneasy? I feel uncomfortable around so much red stuff." We discussed colors we like and eventually promised to learn how colors affect us.

We read several books and gathered information from various websites. We discovered that each color inspires unique reactions in people which differ depending on the person's culture.

Before discussing these effects, let's consider how humans recognize colors. To identify a color, light is necessary. Did you know that white light contains all colors? [Z]

With that in mind let's look at feelings our own culture has toward some specific colors.

Black : a symbol of evil and death, presents as slim and also luxurious
White : associated with weddings, angels, purity, cleanliness, and innocence
Red : evoking strong emotion, excitement, aggression, love, comfort, and energy
Blue : promotes calm, serene, tranquil, sad, and industrious feelings; hinders appetite
Green : represents nature and health yet also jealousy; calming and improves reading
Yellow : perceived as hale, warm, energetic, catchy, as well as frustrating and fatiguing

Thinking about these characteristics and effects aids in choosing which color best suits a certain situation. For example, when on a diet, it may be better to use blue dishes instead of red ones. Right now, I'm debating which color I should choose for the curtain of my son's room. He needs to study hard and memorize many things for his exams. I am turning these things over in my mind while I make my decision.

As for me personally, now I understand why I like red. The color red gives me positive feelings and energy. On the other hand, it impacts my son differently. It causes his heart to beat faster, which makes him feel uneasy.

What color do you prefer? When shopping, which color do you $_{\text{(B)}}$ gravitate toward? Maybe next time you will think about colors and their qualities before you buy something.

問1 Put the following five sentences in order in [Z]. Choose the most appropriate one from ① to ⑤ that shows the right order.

(a) It's these wavelengths which are caught by our eyes.

(b) Our brain recognizes the color based on the brain's memories.

(c) As a result, only certain wavelengths of light are reflected back.

(d) When light hits an object, certain energies of light are absorbed.

(e) They are transmitted to our brain and then translated as colors.

① (a)→(c)→(d)→(b)→(e) ② (d)→(b)→(c)→(a)→(e)

③ (d)→(c)→(a)→(e)→(b) ④ (e)→(d)→(c)→(a)→(b)

⑤ (e)→(b)→(c)→(a)→(d)

問2 According to the passage, which color should the author choose for the curtain of her son's room?

① black or green ② white or red ③ green or yellow

④ blue or green ⑤ red or yellow

問3 Choose the most appropriate word to replace (A).

① definition ② fondness ③ disinclination ④ bias

⑤ weakness

問4 Choose the most appropriate word to replace (B).

① head ② graze ③ observe ④ recognize

⑤ ignore

(☆☆☆◎◎◎◎)

【10】次の英文を読んで，あとの問に答えなさい。

Do you eat breakfast every morning? If not, why?

Most people acknowledge that eating breakfast is a good idea. Despite this, many people don't understand the real reason why it is important. The science behind breakfast deals with the relationship between the brain, the body and glucose. Human brains use glucose as their source of energy. When a person wakes up, their body doesn't have enough available glucose to kick start the brain. Therefore, without breakfast, even if the body is moving, the brain lacks the energy required to function properly. By eating breakfast, humans take in glucose, which enables their bodies and brains to become fully active. This heightened level of activity in turn (　A　) the ability to concentrate and perform actions.

Therefore, breakfast greatly improves humans' ability to focus and function throughout the day. Yet many people still don't eat breakfast regularly. In fact, several studies are conducted each year on this very topic.

Starting at the top, Japanese government ministries carry out regular studies about young people and their breakfast habits. According to research from the Ministry of Agriculture, Forestry, and Fisheries in 2018, 5.5% of sixth graders and 8.0% of ninth graders did not eat breakfast. In 2016, the same ministry investigated the percentage of university students who did not eat breakfast and the reasons they skipped it. In that study, 59% of university students answered that they ate breakfast almost every day, 23.6% of them answered that they ate breakfast two to five days a week, and 17.4% of them responded that they seldom ate breakfast. The top reason for them to have skipped breakfast was that they preferred sleeping longer rather than spending that same time eating breakfast. The second most common reason was that they did not have time for breakfast as it took too much time for them to get ready before they went out.

As for information regarding the long-term effects of eating breakfast, another interesting report was published in 2018. In it, researchers tried to uncover the reason why skipping breakfast shows positive (　B　) with increased occurrence of obesity and type-2 diabetes. They discovered that missing breakfast disrupts bodies' biological clocks. This results in stress on the metabolic system which pressures it to store more fat.

This means the common idea that breakfast is good for one's health has been scientifically supported by research front the government and other sources. In response to such information, the Japanese government has tried to (C) the rate of meal-skipping among its citizens. It uses advertising to show the benefits of eating breakfast. These advertisements urge people to eat breakfast more regularly. Now that you too have read about such research and government efforts, will you wake up early tomorrow and greet the new day with a nice, healthy breakfast?

問1 Choose the most appropriate combination of words to fill in (A), (B) and (C).

①	A lowers	B changes	C cut
②	A promotes	B feelings	C keep
③	A reduces	B connections	C increase
④	A raises	B attitudes	C focus
⑤	A elevates	B correlations	C reduce

問2 According to the passage, what is one main reason for university students to skip breakfast?

① It's expensive.

② Cooking is difficult.

③ They drink coffee instead.

④ To increase sleeping time.

⑤ Because of dieting.

問3 According to the passage, which of the following statements is true?

① Having coffee is physically and mentally enough to start a day.

② About 40% of university students skipped breakfast two or more days in a week in 2016.

③ By eating breakfast, humans take in almost a third of the energy which they use in a day.

④ Breakfast should follow our biological clock and be eaten at the same time every day.

⑤ The author of this article does not eat breakfast every morning.

問4 What is the main topic of this passage?

① Morning routines of university students.

② Government research on humans' biological clocks.

③ The importance of not missing breakfast.

④ Obesity and diabetes among young people.

⑤ Comparing generations and their glucose requirements.

(☆☆☆◎◎◎◎)

【11】次の英文を読んで，あとの問に答えなさい。

What is a teacher's responsibility to students? Or, to think of the question more simply, what should teachers teach?

The simplest answer to this question is knowledge, and the simplest definition of knowledge is subject matter. Elementary school teachers teach a broad range of subjects to students, and junior and senior high school teachers teach one specific subject exclusively. For example history teachers discuss what transpired a decade, a century, or even many millennia ago. They require students to memorize and discuss such information. Math teachers on the other hand may explain subtraction, geometric figures, or algebraic formulae. (A) Regardless of the subject though, teachers all undeniably teach subject matter.

However, when humans interact with the world, what mental tools do they use? (B) Whenever a person receives information, in other words any time a person interacts with the world, the person performs a process. They comprehend the information, determine its reliability, form an opinion, predict the outcomes of various responses, and finally react based on perceived risks and benefits. The first step of this process often requires linguistic knowledge to understand information. (C) On the other hand, the latter steps require critical thinking, understanding of social interaction, and a level of selfconfidence necessary for taking action. If these are the things which are indispensable for living in the world, shouldn't teachers be teaching these in addition to pure academic knowledge?

[Y], teachers are aware of this and already devote themselves to teaching such non-academic skills to students. Knowledge drives student education, but think about social interactions. School etiquette is practiced at schools around the world. The rules applied to students provide them with moral education. (D) The regimen of school as well as the act of graduating itself gives students confidence. Teachers have always provided not just knowledge but also experience that students need in order to be able to interact meaningfully in the world.

In this modern era though, the world is changing both more dramatically and more rapidly than ever before, so what should teachers today teach their students? (E) In this ever-changing world, adults need to teach themselves new technologies, new social norms, and new professions. That is how they stay connected, stay employed, and put food on the table. It follows that the most valuable skill today, in addition to those already being taught, is the ability to teach oneself. Therefore, an ideal teacher, while teaching various kinds of knowledge and skills, should also provide motivation for self-learning, explain methods to do it, and help students learn to teach themselves. By introducing these things, a teacher shows students how to adapt to the modern world. Teachers too must adapt and teach this new skill, as it is what will prepare students for the new world and the new professions that will appear after they graduate from school.

As the old saying goes, "[Z]"

問1 Choose the most appropriate transition for [Y].

① Henceforth　② Actually　③ Putting that aside

④ For example　⑤ Counter to this idea

問2 Put the following sentence in the correct placement in the passage from (A) to (E).

This teaches them how humans act and react towards each other.

問3　According to the passage, which of the following statements is untrue?

①　Teachers already teach more than pure academic knowledge.

②　The world did not change in the past like it is changing now.

③　Thorough knowledge of subject matter is enough to live in the world.

④　Self-confidence is a part of education that can be gained at school.

⑤　One of the most valuable skills in modern society is self-teaching.

問4　Choose the most appropriate saying to put in [　Z　].

①　A penny saved is a penny earned

②　You can't make an omelet without breaking a few eggs

③　You can lead a horse to water, but you can't make him drink

④　If you're not part of the solution, you are part of the problem

⑤　Give a man a fish; you feed him for a day. Teach a man to fish, and you feed him for a lifetime

(☆☆☆◎◎◎◎)

【中学校】

【1】次の文は,「中学校学習指導要領解説　外国語編」(平成29年文部科学省)「第1章　総説」「2　外国語科改訂の趣旨と要点」「(2)　改訂の要点」の一部である。次の①～④に当てはまる語句を書きなさい。

> 中央教育審議会答申を踏まえ，目標及び内容等に関して，次のような改善を図った。
>
> — 中　略 —
>
> ・互いの考えや気持ちなどを伝え合う対話的な言語活動を一層重視する観点から,「話すこと[やり取り]」の領域を設定するとともに，言語の(　①　)や言語の働きを適切に取り上げ，語，文法事項などの言語材料と言語活動とを効果的に関連付けて指導することとするなどの改善・充実を図った。
>
> — 中　略 —
>
> ・小・中学校の(　②　)を重視するとともに，学びの連続性を意識した指導をするために，指導計画の作成に当たっては，語

彙，表現などを異なる場面の中で繰り返し活用することによって，生徒が自分の考えなどを表現する力を高めることなどを明記した。
・言語材料については，発達の段階に応じて，生徒が受容するものと(　③　)するものとがあることに留意して指導することを明記した。
・授業は英語で行うことを(　④　)とすることを新たに規定した。

— 省 略 —

(☆☆☆◎◎◎◎)

【2】次の文は，「中学校学習指導要領」(平成29年3月告示)「第2章　各教科」「第9節　外国語」「第2　各言語の目標及び内容等」「1　目標」の一部である。次の①～⑤に当てはまる語句を書きなさい。

第2　各言語の目標及び内容等
　英語
1　目標
　英語学習の特質を踏まえ，以下に示す，聞くこと，読むこと，話すこと[やり取り]，話すこと[発表]，書くことの五つの領域別に設定する目標の実現を目指した指導を通して，第1の(1)及び(2)に示す資質・能力を一体的に育成するとともに，その過程を通して，第1の(3)に示す資質・能力を育成する。
(1)　聞くこと
　ア　はっきりと話されれば，日常的な話題について，(　①　)情報を聞き取ることができるようにする。
　イ　はっきりと話されれば，日常的な話題について，話の(　②　)を捉えることができるようにする。
　ウ　はっきりと話されれば，社会的な話題について，短い説明の(　③　)を捉えることができるようにする。

― 中　略 ―

(4)　話すこと[発表]

ア　関心のある事柄について，簡単な語句や文を用いて(　④　)で話すことができるようにする。

イ　日常的な話題について，事実や自分の考え，気持ちなどを整理し，簡単な語句や文を用いてまとまりのある内容を話すことができるようにする。

ウ　社会的な話題に関して聞いたり読んだりしたことについて，考えたことや感じたこと，その(　⑤　)などを，簡単な語句や文を用いて話すことができるようにする。

― 省　略 ―

(☆☆☆◎◎◎◎)

【3】次の文は，「中学校学習指導要領」(平成29年3月告示)「第2章　各教科」「第9節　外国語」「第2　各言語の目標及び内容等」「2　内容」の一部である。次の①～⑥に当てはまる語句を書きなさい。

(1)　英語の特徴やきまりに関する事項

実際に英語を用いた言語活動を通して，小学校学習指導要領第2章第10節外国語第2の2の(1)及び次に示す言語材料のうち，1に示す五つの領域別の目標を達成するのにふさわしいものについて理解するとともに，言語材料と言語活動とを効果的に関連付け，実際のコミュニケーションにおいて活用できる(　①　)を身に付けることができるよう指導する。

― 中　略 ―

エ　文，文構造及び文法事項

小学校学習指導要領第2章第10節外国語第2の2の(1)のエ及び次に示す事項について，(　②　)のある文脈でのコミュニケーションの中で繰り返し触れることを通して活用すること。

— 中 略 —

(2) 情報を整理しながら考えなどを形成し，英語で表現したり，伝え合ったりすることに関する事項

具体的な課題等を設定し，コミュニケーションを行う(③)や(④)，状況などに応じて，情報を整理しながら考えなどを形成し，これらを(⑤)に表現することを通して，次の事項を身に付けることができるよう指導する。

— 中 略 —

イ 日常的な話題や社会的な話題について，英語を聞いたり読んだりして得られた情報や表現を，(⑥)したり抽出したりするなどして活用し，話したり書いたりして事実や自分の考え，気持ちなどを表現すること。

— 省 略 —

(☆☆☆◎◎◎◎)

【高等学校】

【1】次の文は，「高等学校学習指導要領」(平成30年3月告示)「第2章 各学科に共通する各教科」「第8節 外国語」「第3款 英語に関する各科目にわたる指導計画の作成と内容の取扱い」の一部である。文中の①～⑤に当てはまる語句を書きなさい。

1 指導計画の作成に当たっては，小学校や中学校における指導との(①)に留意しながら，次の事項に配慮するものとする。

(1) 単元など内容や時間の(②)を見通して，その中で育む資質・能力の育成に向けて，生徒の主体的・対話的で深い学びの実現を図るようにすること。

— 中 略 —

(7) 言語能力の向上を図る観点から，言語活動などにおいて(③)科と連携を図り，指導の効果を高めるとともに，

日本語と英語の語彙や表現，論理の展開などの違いや共通点に気付かせ，その背景にある歴史や(　④　)，習慣などに対する理解が深められるよう工夫をすること。

— 中　略 —

(9)　障害のある生徒などについては，学習活動を行う場合に生じる困難さに応じた指導内容や指導方法の工夫を計画的，(　⑤　)的に行うこと。

(☆☆☆☆◎◎◎◎)

【2】次の表は，「小学校，中学校，高等学校及び特別支援学校等における児童生徒の学習評価及び指導要録の改善等について(通知)」(平成31年3月29日付30文科初第1845号)に示されている「別紙　5」「各教科等の評価の観点及びその趣旨(高等学校及び特別支援学校高等部)」「1-1.高等学校及び特別支援学校(視覚障害，聴覚障害，肢体不自由又は病弱)における各学科に共通する各教科・科目の学習の記録」の一部である。文中の①～⑤に当てはまる語句を書きなさい。ただし，同じ番号には，同じ語句が入る。

教科	観　点	趣　旨
外国語	知識・(　①　)	・外国語の音声や語彙，表現，文法，言語の働きなどについて理解を深めている。 ・外国語についての音声や語彙，表現，文法，言語の働きなどの知識を，聞くこと，読むこと，話すこと，書くことによる実際のコミュニケーションにおいて，(　②　)や(　③　)，状況などに応じて適切に活用できる(　①　)を身に付けている。
	思考・判断・表現	コミュニケーションを行う(　②　)や(　③　)，状況などに応じて，日常的な話題や社会的な話題について，外国語で情報や考えなどの(　④　)や(　⑤　)，詳細，話し手や書き手の意図などを的確に理解したり，これらを活用して適切に表現したり伝え合ったりしている。

(☆☆☆◎◎◎)

【3】次の文は,「高等学校学習指導要領解説　外国語編　英語編」(平成30年文部科学省)「第2章　外国語科の各科目」「第5節　論理・表現Ⅰ」「2　内容」の一部である。文中の1～8に当てはまる語句を下の語群から一つずつ選んで記号で答えなさい。ただし，同じ番号には，同じ記号が入る。

> 情報や考え，気持ちなどを適切な理由や根拠とともに話して伝える活動としては，例えば，次のように段階的な手順を踏みながら，実際の発表につなげるよう指導することが考えられる。
>
> ①　扱う話題について自分の意見や主張を整理して何について話すかを決める。
> ②　自分の意見や主張に(　1　)をもたせるための理由や根拠を考えた上で，発表のためのこ(　2　)を作る。
> ③　発表する際に活用できる表現などを，発表内容や形態に応じた(　3　)となる映像を見るなどして学ぶ
> ④　発表のためのメモや原稿などを準備する。
> ⑤　発表の仕方に注意しながら発表の練習を行う。
>
> ここでの活動は，扱う話題について(　4　)でディスカッションをした後，クラス全体に(　4　)での話合いの概要を報告するような「話すこと[やり取り]」における活動と結び付けることもできる。
>
> また，発表した後に，生徒同士が，内容や発表の仕方についてどのような点がよかったかなどの感想や意見を伝え合うことも効果的である。
>
> 実際の活動においては，一つのペアで行った活動を(　5　)を変えて複数回行うなど，異なる相手に何度も話す機会を作るような指導も大切である。繰り返し話すことで，自分の伝え方のよい点や改善点は何か，どのように話すと聞き手にとって分かりやすくなるのかなどについて，生徒が自分の伝え方を(　6　)

に振り返ることが可能になる。そのような振り返りが，生徒が自ら異なる語句や文を使って言い換えをしてみたり，話の(7)や進め方を工夫したりするような(8)な学びや自律的な学習へとつながっていくと考えられる。

《語群》

A	アウトライン	B	教員	C	協働的	D	構成
E	グループ	F	客観的	G	資質能力	H	台詞
I	説得力	J	タイトル	K	発表	L	背景知識
M	パートナー	N	主体的	O	モデル		

(☆☆☆◎◎◎)

解答・解説

【中高共通】

【1】Question1　②　　Question2　①　　Question3　③

〈解説〉237 wordsの対話文を聞いて，3つの英問に選択肢で答える形式。放送は2度流れる。旅行会社に男性がツアーの予約の電話をする場面での対話。Question1，2は，会話文からそのまま解答できる素直な質問となっている。Question3は，計算して解答する問題。1人当たりの旅行代金は入場料と昼食込みで55ドルだが，昼食は不要だと言っているので，それより10ドル安くなる。よって，2人分の料金は，45〔ドル〕×2＝90〔ドル〕。

【2】≪A≫　Question1　④　　Question2　③　　Question3　④

≪B≫　Question1　①　　Question2　③　　Question3　③

〈解説〉Aは217 words，Bは241 wordsのスピーチを聞いて，それぞれ3つの英問に選択肢で答える形式。特に難解なスクリプトではないが，スピーチ全体やパラグラフ全体を把握すべき問いが含まれている。放送は2度流れる。 ≪A≫ トピックは在宅勤務で，その利点や不便な点を聞き取ることが求められている。 ≪B≫ トピックは単身世帯の増加についてで，単身世帯の割合が最も高い都市名や，リサーチ結果の内容が問われている。

【3】Question1 4 Question2 2 Question3 2

〈解説〉211wordsの英文と，3つの英問を聞いて，読みあげられる選択肢で答える形式。放送は2度あるが，文字情報がなく，読まれる英文量も多い。トピックは過去に起きた気候変動で，中世の温暖期の人々の暮らしについて問われている。1度目は全体の流れを把握し，設問や選択肢を簡単にメモできるとよい。設問を把握した後の2度目は，答えを再確認するつもりで聞くこと。

【4】1，5 (順不同)

〈解説〉261wordsの英文を聞いて，内容に合致するものを，読み上げられる選択肢の中から2つ選ぶ形式。【3】と同様，放送は2度あるが，文字情報はない。ワークショップで，ある都市のいくつかの公立高等学校の特徴についての説明を聞いているという場面設定である。6択問題であり，各選択肢の英文も長めなので，英文量が多い。1度目にできるだけ多くの誤肢を取り除き，2度目の放送で聞き逃したところを確認する。

【5】問1 ② 問2 ① 問3 ④ 問4 ② 問5 ①

〈解説〉問1 browse through～「～を見て回る」。 問2 academic transcript「成績証明書」。 問3 under the new administration「新体制の下」。 問4 for the life of me「どんなに必死に努力しても，どうしても」。 問5 decrease in the number of～「～の数の減少」。

【6】問1　③　　問2　②　　問3　②　　問4　⑤

〈解説〉問1　整序すると，employees who possess specialized knowledgeとなる。　問2　整序すると，reduce plastic garbage have proven successfulとなる。prove successful「成功だとわかる」。　問3　整序すると，considering the benefits given to their ownersとなる。considering～「～を考慮すれば」。　問4　整序すると，properly will help you toとなる。

【7】問1　⑤　　問2　①

〈解説〉問1　入寮しようとしている新入生と案内をする人の会話。どちらのせりふかを区別しながら，話の流れをつくる。C→F→A→E→D→Bとなる。　問2　仏手柑を初めて見たという相手に名前の由来や味について説明し，果肉が少ないので食べるよりマーマレードを作るように勧めている。D→A→F→C→B→Eとなる。

【8】問1　④　　問2　②　　問3　②　　問4　①　　問5　③

〈解説〉問1　空所には，e-bookの利点である「どこにでも持ち運べる」を更に詳しく述べている「どこかに旅行するとき，数冊の印刷された本を持ち運ぶ必要がない」が適切。　問2　internshipとpart-time jobの違いを述べているので，「インターンシップの目的は仕事を実際に試し，自分がどのようなスキルを持っているのかを見つけだすことである」となる。　問3　空所には，英語のスキルを上達させるため日記を書くことがどのように役立つか述べている，「日常生活でしばしば使うなじみのある単語量を増やす」が適切。　問4　空所後「たいていの授業は日本語で教えられるので」という理由に合致する主節の文は「毎年ほとんどの留学生は他の教科とともに日本語を勉強しなければならない」。　問5　畳の原料のイグサの効果を述べている文。「身体によい影響を与える」が適切。

【9】問1　③　　問2　④　　問3　②　　問4　①

〈解説〉問1　空所には，「人間がいかに色を認識するのか」の説明となる順に文を整序する。(d)「光が物体に当たると，光のエネルギーが吸収される」→(c)「結果，ある光の波長が反射する」→(a)「私たちの目にとらえられるのはこれらの波長である」→(e)「それらは私たちの脳に転送され色として変換される」→(b)「私たちの脳は脳の記憶に基づいた色を認識する」。　問2　質問は「筆者は息子の部屋のカーテンを何色にすべきか」。第6段落の4文目参照。息子は一生懸命勉強し，試験のために多くのことを覚えなければならないとある。青の説明中の「穏やかで，落ち着いた，静かな，悲しげな，勤勉な感情を促進する」と緑の説明中の「穏やかで，読解が向上する」から青か緑と判断できる。　問3　筆者は赤い色が大好きであると述べている。predilection「偏愛，好み」に置き換えられるのは，fondness「好み」。
問4　gravitate toward～「～の方に引き付けられる」に置き換えられるのは，head to ward～「～の方を向く」。

【10】問1　⑤　　問2　④　　問3　②　　問4　③
〈解説〉問1　空所Aを含む文意は「この増大した活動レベルが，次に集中したり行動を起こしたりする能力を高める」となると考えられる。よって選択肢①と③は不適。空所Bを含む文意は「その中で，研究者たちはなぜ朝食を抜くことが肥満や2型糖尿病の発生と正の相関関係を示すのかという理由を明らかにしようとした」。positive correlation「正の相関関係」。空所Cを含む文意は「このような情報に応じて，日本政府は市民の食事を抜く割合を減らそうとしてきた」。　問2　第4段落の最後から2文目参照。学生が朝食を抜く一番の理由は朝食を食べるのに時間を費やすより，長く寝ていたいから。　問3　第4段落の3，4文目参照。2016年には，23.6％の学生が週に2回から5回朝食をとる。即ち週に2回以上朝食を抜いた。17.4％の学生がほとんど食べない。よって選択肢②は「大学生の約40％が2016年には，週に2回以上朝食を抜いた」が適切。　問4　筆者は，朝食を食べることの大切さについて述べている。よって，③「朝食を食べ損ねないことの重要性」が適切。

【11】問1　②　　問2　D　　問3　③　　問4　⑤

〈解説〉問1　空所Yの前の文意は「これら(信頼性を特定したり，意見を形成したりするなどの過程)が世の中で生きていく上で必要不可欠であれば，単なる学問的知識に加えて教師はこれらを教えるべきではないのか」。空所Yの直後の文意は「教師はこのことに気づき，すでに生徒にそのような非学問的スキルを教えることに専念している」。2文をつなぐには，actually「実は」が適切。　問2　挿入文の文意は「これは，人間がいかに行動し，互いに対して反応するかを彼らに教える」なので，これ(This)と彼ら(them)が具体的に何を指すか考えながら空所A～Eを検討する。空所Dの直前の文「生徒たちに適用されるルールは彼らにモラル教育を提供する」に注目すると，Thisがモラル教育，themが生徒たちを指すことがわかり，Dに挿入すれば自然な流れとなる。問3　第3段落で筆者は，世の中で生きていく上で，単なる学問的知識だけでなくクリティカルシンキングなどが必要だと述べている。よって，③「教科に関わる深い知識があれば世の中で生きるのに十分である」が誤り。　問4　第5段落で筆者は，(様々な知識や技能を教える一方で)セルフラーニングのモチベーションを生徒に与え，方法を説明し，その手助けをするのが理想的な教師であるとまとめている。よって，最後の段落に入ることわざとして，⑤「人に魚をあげれば，彼を一日食べさせられる。人に魚の釣り方を教えれば，彼を一生食べさせられる(生きる術を教えよ)」が適切。他のことわざは，①「1ペニーの節約は1ペニーの儲け(塵も積もれば山となる)」，②「卵を割らなくては，オムレツは作れない(まかぬ種は生えぬ／虎穴に入らずんば，虎子を得ず)」，③「馬を水辺に連れていくことはできるが，水を飲ませることはできない(やる気のない人はどんなに指導しようとしてもだめだ)」，④「もしあなたが解決の一部でなければ，あなたは問題の一部である(問題を改善しようと行動しない人が問題である)」。

【中学校】

【1】① 使用場面 ② 接続 ③ 発信 ④ 基本

〈解説〉出題箇所以外にも，総説におけるキーワードとして「主体的・対話的で深い学び」，「カリキュラム・マネジメント」などを押さえておきたい。 ① 外国語科の英語における内容については，小学校や高等学校における学習内容との接続の観点も踏まえて改善された。なお，今回は出題されなかったが，本項では取り扱う語数の改訂についても記述がある。小学校で学習する600～700語に加え，現行の「1200語程度」の語から，五つの領域別の目標を達成するための言語活動に必要な「1600～1800語程度」の語に改訂されたことを覚えておくこと。 ②～④ 外国語科の英語における指導計画の作成と内容の取扱いについて図られた改善点である。

【2】① 必要な ② 概要 ③ 要点 ④ 即興 ⑤ 理由

〈解説〉学習指導要領について，今回出題の「第2 各言語の目標及び内容等」の「1 目標」，前出の「2 内容」，また，今回は出題がなかったが「3 指導計画の作成と内容の取扱い」については，空所記述式で解答できるようにしておくことは必須である。なお，本問の「(1) 聞くこと」の項目ウでは，項目ア・イと異なり，聞き取る対象が「日常的な話題」ではなく「社会的な話題」であることに注意しよう。小学校の外国語科では「日常生活に関する身近で簡単な事柄」のみを取り上げるのに対し，中学校では広く日常的な話題から社会的な話題まで扱うことに留意する必要がある。同様に，「(4) 話すこと[発表]」の項目ア～ウは，小学校の外国語科で取り上げるのが「日常生活に関する身近で簡単な事柄」などであるのに対し，中学校では「関心のある事柄」から「日常的な話題」や「社会的な話題」へと広がっていく。そして，社会的な話題に対する自分なりの意見や感想を，理由や自分が学んだこと，経験したことの例示などとともに表現することが求められることに注意しよう。

【3】① 技能　② 意味　③ 目的　④ 場面　⑤ 論理的
⑥ 選択

〈解説〉今回出題された「(1)　英語の特徴や決まりに関する事項」,「(2)　情報を整理しながら考えなどを形成し，英語で表現したり，伝え合ったりすることに関する事項」以外に,「(3)　言語活動及び言語の働きに関する事項」からの出題も多いので，解答できるように準備をしておく必要がある。

【高等学校】

【1】① 接続　② まとまり　③ 国語　④ 文化　⑤ 組織

〈解説〉本項では，指導計画の作成に当たり，小・中・高等学校を通じた領域別の目標の設定という観点を踏まえ，小学校や中学校における指導との接続に留意した上で配慮すべき事項を示している。対策をしていないと②，⑤などは解答に迷うかもしれない。例年，記述式で出題されることを踏まえて，キーワードが再生できるまで読み込んでおこう。

【2】① 技能　② 目的　③ 場面　④ 概要　⑤ 要点

〈解説〉文部科学省の資料にはできるだけ目を通しておくことが望ましい。外国語の評価の観点としては，出題の「知識・技能」,「思考・判断・表現」の他に「主体的に学習に取り組む態度」があり,「外国語の背景にある文化に対する理解を深め，聞き手，読み手，話し手，書き手に配慮しながら，主体的，自律的に外国語を用いてコミュニケーションを図ろうとしている」ことが大切である。

【3】1 I　2 A　3 O　4 E　5 M　6 F　7 D
8 N

〈解説〉出題箇所である「情報や考え，気持ちなどを適切な理由や根拠とともに話して伝える活動」は,「2　内容」の「(3)　言語活動及び言語の働きに関する事項　①　言語活動に関する事項」の「イ　話すこと

[発表]　(ア)」の解説文の一部である。選択式問題なので，解答はさほど困難ではないと思われる。「高等学校学習指導要領解説　外国語編 英語編」(平成30年7月　文部科学省)はかなり厚い冊子であるが，細かいところも含め全頁に目を通しておくのが理想である。また，同書の高等学校「外国語科の目標」の科目段階別一覧表や，「言語活動」の科目段階別一覧表などを上手く利用したい。

2020年度　実施問題

【中高共通】

【1】次に読まれる英文を聞き，1～3の設問に対する答として最も適切なものを，四つの選択肢の中から一つ選びなさい。
(英文及び設問は2回読まれる。)

Receptionist : Hello. Thank you for calling the Hawaii International Hotel.
George Brown : Hello. I'd like a room for two nights for two people.
Do you have any rooms available tomorrow?
Receptionist : Just a moment, please. Let me check. Would you like one or two beds?
George Brown : Two, please.
Receptionist : We have one vacancy, but it's a smoking room.
George Brown : That's fine. What's the cost?
Receptionist : It's 95 dollars per person, per night.
George Brown : That's perfect. I'll take it.
Receptionist : Wonderful. What time do you expect to check-in?
George Brown : About five.
Receptionist : Okay. May I have your names?
George Brown : My name is George Brown. My wife's name is Maria.
Receptionist : All right. I've reserved a room for two under George Brown for tomorrow, September 15th, for two nights.
George Brown : Great, thanks. Is there internet in the room?
Receptionist : Absolutely.
George Brown : That's convenient. Oh, I almost forgot. Could you recommend any restaurants in the area?
I'm planning a surprise birthday party for my wife.

Receptionist : That's great. There are many good restaurants around the hotel, but I recommend Café La Tour. It's been popular these days.

George Brown : Sounds good. I'm looking forward to surprising her. Thanks.

Receptionist : Can I help you with anything else?

George Brown : No, thank you.

Receptionist : We look forward to seeing you tomorrow. Thank you for choosing our hotel. (198 words)

Question 1: What is the reason for this phone call?

① Booking a hotel
② Reserving a restaurant
③ Scheduling a meeting
④ Confirming an appointment

Question 2: How much will George Brown and his wife have to pay to stay at the Hawaii International Hotel?

① 95 dollars
② 190 dollars
③ 285 dollars
④ 380 dollars

Question 3: Why did George ask the receptionist if there are good restaurants near the hotel?

① Because he likes to take pictures of food.
② Because he and his wife want to have a fancy dinner.
③ Because he is planning a birthday party for his wife.
④ Because he wants to celebrate his birthday with a nice meal.

(☆☆◎◎◎◎◎)

【2】次に読まれる英文≪A≫及び英文≪B≫について，それぞれの1～3の設問に対する答として最も適切なものを，四つの選択肢の中から一つ選びなさい。

(英文及び設問は2回読まれる。)

≪A≫

Hello. My name is Jack. Let me tell you about my research on how sugar affects our bodies.

Sugar was seen as a treasure for a long time. Originally it was a luxury good that was only eaten by the upper echelon of society, but people have discovered ways of producing it in large quantities. Sugar has since become a common food in the human diet. Now it has the advantages of being comparatively cheap, easily digestible, rich in energy and useful for flavoring various foods.

However, sugar also has many disadvantages. The most serious disadvantage of sugar is its adverse effect on our health. For example, despite giving energy, sugar does not provide enough nourishment. It may give food an attractive flavor, like in cakes or ice cream, but it tends to replace less tasty food items that would give more nutritional value to our diet, like fresh fruit or vegetable snacks. Furthermore, excessive consumption of sugar may cause serious ailments, such as heart problems, diabetes, obesity, or even tooth decay.

According to available scientific research, cavities are becoming more prevalent in all people, from the very young to the very old. Due to the high consumption of sugar these days, dental health has become a serious issue. High consumption of sugar can also lead to diabetes caused by obesity, as our bodies cannot manage large amounts of sugar.

In order to maintain a healthy lifestyle, we must keep in mind that we should limit the amount of sugar we consume. Thank you for listening.

(256 words)

Question 1: According to the passage, why has sugar become a common food in the human diet?

① Sugar can help people to lower their stress by calming their nerves.

② People noticed that sugar has more nourishment than vegetables.

③ People have discovered more ways of quickly producing sugar in large amounts.

④ People like to have luxury goods, like sugar, to show their status.

Question 2: According to the passage, what advantage does sugar offer us?

① Sugar can help us to maintain a healthy lifestyle.

② Sugar may encourage increased energy in our bodies.

③ Consumption of sugar can cure serious ailments.

④ Tooth decay may decrease all over the world.

Question 3: According to the passage, which statement is true?

① Sugar continues to be a treasured item for consumption by the wealthy.

② Overconsumption of sugar is the best way to improve our health.

③ Sugar is a kind of medicine for people all around the world.

④ Limiting our consumption of sugar is necessary to keep us healthy.

≪B≫

Some people believe that large parts of the brain go unused while only small sections are activated, or that the brain is only 10 percent active during rest and becomes more active during consciousness. Experiments have disproven these theories by revealing that most parts of the brain are active almost all the time, which results in the fact that the brain accounts for a mere three percent of the body's weight but consumes twenty percent of the body's energy.

The human brain consists of three parts. The largest portion is called the "cerebral neocortex". It performs most of all cognitive functions like understanding, reasoning, memorizing, calculation, and so on. Another part is called the "motor cortex", which is responsible for motor functions, such as the coordination of movement and balance. The final part, which is called the "brainstem", is engaged in involuntary functions like breathing. The majority of the energy consumed by the brain enables millions of neurons in these three parts to interact with each other. Researchers argue that these interactions make all of the brain's higher functions possible.

It seems to be an accepted idea that, at any given moment, not all of the brain's regions are simultaneously activated. However, brain researchers have shown that, like the body's muscles, most of it is active over a 24-hour period; even in sleep, some areas of the brain are actively functioning.

(231 words)

Question 1: According to the passage, what can be said about the brain, compared to the other parts of the body?

① Only 10% of it is active when you are sleeping.

② It is the only active part of the body when you are at rest.

③ It accounts for around 10% of the body's weight.

④ It uses a lot of energy for its weight.

Question 2: According to the passage, what is the "cerebral neocortex"?

① It is the part that doesn't perform when you are at rest.

② It is the part that is relating to cognition.

③ It is the part that makes the other parts of the body move physically.

④ It is the part that reflexively moves the other parts of the body.

Question 3: According to the passage, what have brain researchers proved?

① The brain likes the body's muscles when it is active.

② Most parts of the brain will stop functioning in sleep.

③ The brain and the muscles are active throughout the day and night.

④ The brain keeps activated, but muscles don't when you are sleeping.

(☆☆◎◎◎◎◎)

【3】次に読まれる英文を聞き，1～3の設問に対する答として最も適切なものを，そのあとに読まれる四つの選択肢の中から一つ選びなさい。(英文，設問及び選択肢は2回読まれる。)

When I was a small child, I was afraid of the dark. I remember lying in bed and the lights going down. Then my fear would grow bigger and bigger, and I couldn't help thinking that monsters would come from the darkness, or from behind a curtain, while I was left alone in my bedroom. I was under the impression this was normal in every country, but I found out that wasn't the case when I made a friend from a different culture.

Naomi, who became one of my best friends, grew up in a culture where the main parental goal is to integrate children into the household and society. In this culture, babies are held close at hand, even during the night. Therefore, she didn't understand the philosophy at first that, in our society which values independence and self-reliance, babies and children sleep alone. The ways parents treat children while they are very young have major effects on how they turn out as adults.

How parents let their children sleep can have an impact on moral values, too. People in our society believe it is morally "correct" for infants to sleep alone and thus learn to be independent. We view child-parent co-sleeping as psychologically unhealthy. Those in co-sleeping cultures such as Naomi's country see our practice of placing an infant alone as wrong, inclined to regard it as child neglect. Most parents in both cultures believe that only their moral structures are correct. (244 words)

Question 1: According to the passage, why was the speaker afraid at night?

No. 1 Because his parents told him scary stories.

No. 2 Because he was made to sleep without his parents by his side.

No. 3 Because he was made to sleep behind the curtain.

No. 4 Because his parents kept holding his hand all through the night.

Question 2: According to the passage, why do babies sleep together with their parents in Naomi's culture?

No. 1 Because in Naomi's culture, parents think this is right.

No. 2 Because in Naomi's culture, parents neglect their children.

No. 3 Because in Naomi's culture, this encourages independence.

No. 4 Because in Naomi's culture, families have only one bedroom.

Question 3: According to the passage, what can a family's sleeping arrangement affect?

No.1　A child's sense of direction.

No.2　A child's sense of beauty.

No.3　A child's sense of humor.

No.4　A child's sense of morality.

(☆☆☆☆◎◎◎◎◎)

【4】次に読まれる英文を聞き，英文の内容に合致するものを，そのあとに読まれる六つの選択肢の中から二つ選びなさい。

(英文及び選択肢は2回読まれる。)

This is a Beach City Radio program: traffic information and weather forecast. Traffic seems to be a bit more congested for this morning's commuters, as it is the beginning of the month today. First off, construction in the East Park District began at 7:00 am this morning. The alternative route from Richmond to Beach City is Route 3, but it is backed up. It will probably take an hour and a half to get there. To make driving conditions even worse, an accident involving three cars occurred early this morning on North Street between central Richmond and Route 3. The traffic around this area is almost stopped. There is a detour via Millennium Bridge and South Street to Beach City. As more commuters are expected to choose this alternative, it will probably take two hours to get there.

Now for today's weather forecast. A low pressure system is approaching from the west. It is sunny in the morning but will become overcast in the afternoon. Slight showers are expected in some areas of the coastal region tonight, so if you come home late in the evening, I'd recommend bringing a foldable umbrella with you. A day time high of 25 degrees Celsius is expected, almost the same as yesterday, but strong winds from the north are expected, so it will feel cooler than the actual temperature.

That's it. Have a good day!

(232 words)

No.1　This broadcast is on air at the end of the day.
No.2　There is less traffic than is usually expected in this region.
No.3　Route 3 was experiencing heavy traffic conditions when this broadcast aired.
No.4　There was a traffic accident on South Street.
No.5　The weather is expected to get worse during the day.
No.6　It is expected to be as warm and calm as yesterday.

(☆☆☆☆◎◎◎◎)

【5】英文の意味が通るように，(　　) 内に入る最も適切なものを選びなさい。

問1　You cannot park your car here, sir. The sign over there says that this area is a towaway (　　).

① lap　② meter　③ spirit　④ zone　⑤ park

問2　If your address on the form is incorrect, please (　　) with a red pen and print the correct address below.

① make it up　② mix it up　③ cross it out
④ turn it on　⑤ hold it up

問3　It was (　　) of you not to drive home during rush hour. Traffic was backed up on the freeway for over five kilometers.

① gullible　② sensible　③ artificial　④ coarse
⑤ indigenous

問4　The motorcycle had been kept in a garage and well-maintained over the past 20 years, so in spite of its age, it was in (　　) condition.

① mint　② prolific　③ sordid　④ frail
⑤ ragged

問5　As I walked down the street, the wind blew and (　　) the fallen leaves at my feet.

① croaked　② sizzled　③ nibbled　④ gargled
⑤ rustled

(☆☆☆☆◎◎◎◎◎)

【6】次の各問の日本文の意味を表す英文を作るために，(　　)内のA～Eの語句を正しく並べかえるとき，2番目と4番目にくる最も適切な組合せを選びなさい。

ただし，組合せの左側を2番目，右側を4番目とする。なお，文頭にくる語も小文字で表している。

問1　トムの会社は手頃な価格で顧客に衣類を提供している。

Tom's company ($_{A}$with $_{B}$customers $_{C}$provides $_{D}$at reasonable prices $_{E}$clothing).

①　A－B　　②　A－E　　③　B－D　　④　B－E　　⑤　E－D

問2　火の制御と衣服の使用で，人類は寒い北の地域で定住することが可能になった。

It was the control of fire and ($_{A}$humans $_{B}$the use of clothing $_{C}$allowed $_{D}$that $_{E}$to settle) in the cold northern area.

①　C－A　　②　C－D　　③　D－A　　④　D－C　　⑤　E－C

問3　私たちが彼女の計画に賛成できないのは，環境的見地が欠けているからだ。

The reason ($_{A}$is $_{B}$why $_{C}$her plan $_{D}$we cannot agree with $_{E}$that) it lacks an environmental aspect.

①　A－D　　②　C－A　　③　C－B　　④　D－A　　⑤　D－B

問4　技術立国を目指している日本の今後の課題は何だろうか。

What ($_{A}$will $_{B}$Japan $_{C}$face $_{D}$as $_{E}$challenges) it tries to build up its technology?

①　A－C　　②　A－E　　③　B－D　　④　B－E　　⑤　C－D

(☆☆◎◎◎◎◎)

【7】次の各問のA～Fの英文を二人の会話として意味がつながるように並べかえるとき，2番目と4番目にくる最も適切な組合せを選びなさい。ただし，組合せの左側を2番目，右側を4番目とする。

問1　A : Yes. There's one in the Business Center.

B : No, but we have it here in the lobby. You can use any of the tables you see over there.

C : Excuse me. I need to send a fax as soon as possible. Is there a fax machine that I can use?

D : Thanks. And later tonight, I want to use my computer. It's wireless. Do you have wireless service in the rooms?

E : Go across the lobby. Go down the stairs to the first floor, turn left, and it's on your left.

F : Great. Where's that, please?

① A－C　② A－E　③ B－A　④ E－B　⑤ E－D

問2　A : Well, you may want to wait and see. The forecast said we'll have warm days and blue skies by next week.

B : It really has, so I've been thinking about escaping somewhere down south for a few days to thaw out. Maybe even see some of them.

C : Indeed, they're definitely going to be late this year. We've had only a day or two of real spring days. The rest of the time it's been dreary and downright freezing.

D : The weather has been outrageous. It's the middle of April yet it still feels like winter. Isn't it usually the season to view the cherry blossoms now?

E : Even if it did, I can't let that stop me from going. I've heard that too many times before.

F : What do you think about the weather this year?

① A－C　② C－A　③ C－D　④ D－B　⑤ D－C

(☆☆☆◎◎◎◎◎)

【8】次の各問の英文を読み，文脈から考えて文中の(　　)に入る最も適切なものを選びなさい。

問1　Have you ever taken a bullet train in Japan? Bullet trains in Japan are fast but are just slow enough to allow you to enjoy beautiful views of Japan from your window, including a glimpse of Mt. Fuji while traveling from

Tokyo towards Nagoya. Though fast, Japan's bullet trains are not the fastest in the world. Currently, the fastest train is the Shanghai Maglev, traveling at 431 kilometers per hour. However, Japan hopes to unveil a train in 2027 that will move at 603 kilometers per hour, cutting down travel time between Tokyo and Nagoya by nearly 60 minutes. This will have two effects on bullet trains: they will (　　).

① serve less people but will become more enjoyable in seeing Japan's landscape
② turn out to be less convenient and more enjoyable in seeing Japan's landscape
③ be able to hold more people and will become more enjoyable in seeing Japan's landscape
④ become more convenient but less enjoyable in seeing Japan's landscape
⑤ remain unchanged in terms of convenience and enjoyment in seeing Japan's landscape

問2　Technological advancements of the 21st century have allowed people to shop online from the comfort of their homes. For those who enjoy shopping but do not enjoy going out in public, online shopping is a good alternative to shopping in-person, and most online stores are open all the time. Customers can also have items delivered to their homes, saving time and energy. On the other hand, online shopping does have flaws. It does not allow customers to try on or assess their items before purchase, leaving shoppers feeling (　　). It may even lead some people to spend more money on things such as delivery and returns.

① content about their decision to buy items
② discontent with the condition of the items they purchased
③ comfortable in using the items that they bought
④ satisfied with the quality of the items they invested in
⑤ inspired by the convenience of the items they spent money on

問3 In the early stages of film, a movie could have been less than a minute long, in black and white, and with no sound. People gathered to see the films that incorporated new technology. In America in 2018, the top three highest-grossing movies utilized new-age technology to create stunning visual effects and action sequences with powerful movie music scores. It can be assumed that (　　).

① films of the 21st century are often shorter than those from the early stages of film
② movie producers continue to gain attention by using technology
③ the level of technology used in film has decreased over time
④ technology used in film depreciates its appeal
⑤ black and white films are common in today's day and age

問4 With recent enthusiasm over sustainable energy increasing worldwide, countries must consider their impact on the world's ecosystem by utilizing eco-friendly resources such as geothermal, water, wind, and solar energy. In 2007, Japan noted in a report that just 3% of its energy came from renewable resources. With countries such as Iceland and Norway powering nearly 100% of their electrical output with renewable energy, Japan looks to (　　). By 2030, Japan hopes to reach 22% renewable energy, increasing percentages by nearly 20% in comparison to the survey in 2007.

① deplete its natural resources to impact the world's delicate ecosystem
② utilize non-renewable energy as frequently as possible
③ increase renewable energy output in order to leave a smaller carbon footprint
④ rule out renewable energy, so as to stop discussing this topic altogether
⑤ decrease energy output from non-renewable and renewable resources

問5 Team-teaching can be successful if both teachers make time to talk about the lesson plan before going into the classroom. It is important for homeroom teachers and ALTs to talk about lesson plans in order to establish classroom roles. This will help the homeroom teacher and the ALT (　　), and in turn, will help students to feel more comfortable speaking English in their classroom, too. The two teachers should plan activities, make materials, determine the goal of the class, and give feedback to each other after the class finishes in order to establish a positive relationship.

① become more aware when their partner is not following the plan
② feet more nervous and hopeless in the classroom
③ teach classes without planning beforehand
④ plan for a class after the lesson finishes
⑤ feel more comfortable and confident in teaching in English in the classroom

(☆☆☆◎◎◎◎◎)

【9】次の英文を読んで，あとの問に答えなさい。

People tend to believe that happiness exists, but that it must be journeyed for and sought after in order to be obtained. Perhaps happiness feels elusive because it can be difficult to (A)<u>discern</u>, which is why many people try to define their happiness by physical displays of wealth or beauty. These days, social media has made it more apparent than ever that happiness is not strictly tangible.

Online sites and apps allow people to post pictures or updates, and naturally the majority of these posts depict peoples' best, most curated moments. Although this seems like an innocuous way for people to validate or celebrate their own experiences, the trouble may come later when online followers view these posts and inevitably begin to draw comparisons between themselves and the posters. Users of social media frequently report strong feelings of envy and dissatisfaction when viewing other peoples' perfectly filtered pictures and descriptions of achievements. This is not so dissimilar from the Greek fable of King Midas.

Midas was a wealthy and prosperous king who lived in a beautiful palace filled with a bounty of food, friends, and family, and his kingdom was peaceful. For a long time he was pleased, until one day he heard rumors of another king far away who had riches of gold which surpassed anything Midas had ever known. This thought cast a dark shadow upon Midas. "I wish," he implored, "that everything I touched would turn to gold!"

Later that day, Midas reached out for a red rose, and it became a golden blossom in his hand. Midas was ecstatic that his wish had come true, and wherever he went he left a path of shining gold. Eventually he reached for food and drink, and they too became hard lumps of gold. The king was dismayed, and grew both hungry and thirsty. Midas' daughter came to him. "Father, are you all right?" she asked, and took his hand. Just like that, in the place where Midas' daughter stood just a moment before was a lifeless golden statue of her likeness. King Midas was horrified, and he realized the error of his ways.

Although the story of King Midas is ancient in origin, its lessons are still relevant today. The Midas tale shows that tangible wealth is not so much a reflection of happiness as self-esteem is. Users of social media should be wary of deriving a sense of worth based on how they are doing relative to others. Otherwise they, as Midas did, run the risk of taking for granted the true happiness right in front of them, like the warmth of friendly and familial love.

問1 Choose the most appropriate word to rephrase the underlined (A),

① inherit

② submit

③ gain

④ pinpoint

⑤ disguise

問2 According to the passage, why is it problematic when people share their positive experiences online?

① Because the people sharing may become too proud of themselves.

② Because the people sharing may lose a sense of privacy.

③ Because viewers cannot help but compare themselves with the people sharing.

④ Because viewers can share their own positive experiences in reply.

⑤ Because online sites take advantage of people sharing and viewing these experiences.

問3 Which phrase can be used to summarize the moral of the fable of King Midas?

① Being happy is letting go of things that make you sad.

② Failure is the result of people not trying.

③ You must be the change you wish to see in the world.

④ Second-hand gold is as good as new.

⑤ Happiness is not a physical state but a state of mind.

(☆☆☆◎◎◎◎◎)

【10】次の英文を読んで，あとの問に答えなさい。

When talking about manners, people tend to speak nostalgically about how folks were more polite “back in the olden days,” but are manners truly a thing of the past? It is a common belief that manners were better fifty or more years ago. In a recent survey it was found that 74 percent of Americans think manners have steadily (A) over time. Those who participated in the survey generally agreed on what they considered ill-mannered, however there were definite differences in opinion regarding certain behaviors.

One such area of contention in particular was technology. When asked whether or not it is acceptable behavior to use smartphones during mealtimes, roughly half of participants between the ages of 18 and 29 responded that such behavior would be acceptable. In contrast, only 22 percent of participants over the age of 60 agreed. This could indicate that differences of opinion regarding acceptable behavior emerge based on age, and a change in manners over generations. What could be the reason for this change? A number of experts blame electronic devices.

Indeed, smartphones have become a key instrument in how young people interact with each other. The ever-increasing amount of time young people spend on their smartphones pulls them away from (B) interactions with peers and adults, giving them less time to speak kindly with others. Furthermore, communicating in brief snippets with texts could distort the way words are used and intended, leading to a perception of rudeness and lack of tact both on their devices and in person.

Whether they are deteriorating due to technology or simply changing along with the times, the importance of manners cannot be ignored. At their core, good manners are more than a set of rules for how to say and do things correctly. Manners also reflect respect for oneself and for others, and it is crucial for children to learn to connect (C) with strength, determination, and appreciation. Young people are depending on the adults around them, especially parents and teachers, to show them how to be trustworthy and considerate to others so that they can take these skills with them through school, work, relationships, and forward into adulthood.

問1 According to the passage, what do the results of the survey regarding smartphone usage during mealtimes suggest?

① More young people responded to the survey than people over the age of 60.

② The generation gap plays an important role in how manners are perceived.

③ Most young people believe using smartphones during meals is acceptable.

④ Manners are getting worse year after year because of smartphones.

⑤ What is considered acceptable behavior for each generation is invariable.

問2 Choose the most appropriate combination of words to fill in (A), (B), and (C).

① A deteriorated　B personal　C civility
② A collapsed　B public　C incivility
③ A improved　B individual　C rudeness
④ A ameliorated　B private　C discourtesy
⑤ A enhanced　B impersonal　C courtesy

問3　The main point of the third paragraph is to demonstrate that
① children are much more knowledgeable about technology than their parents.
② communication via electronic devices is more efficient than speaking in person.
③ children should spend more time practicing on electronic devices with others.
④ poor manners among young people should be ignored because it is unintended.
⑤ young people can be seen as rude because smartphones have changed the way they communicate.

問4　What is the main topic of this passage?
① Technology is to blame for manners worsening in America.
② Young people are ill-mannered until they become adults.
③ Manners have changed so much that they have become irrelevant.
④ Manners are crucial and should be modeled by adults for young people.
⑤ People are dependent on electronic devices and no longer need manners.

(☆☆☆☆◎◎◎◎◎)

【11】次の英文を読んで，あとの問に答えなさい。

On a recent Saturday, I headed out to run my weekend errands. They consisted of grocery shopping, dropping off dry-cleaning, lunch, and then soccer practice. I hadn't even backed out of the driveway when my 5-year-old started his standard rapid-fire line of questioning. "How many whales are in the ocean? Can ashes from a volcano burn you? What do butterflies eat? Why does the moon change in size? What is your favorite animal? Mine is a rabbit!"

Once at soccer practice, I sat with my friend Marie, a fellow parent of a boy on the soccer team. (A) We chatted as we watched the kids dribble up and down the field, and Marie asked me how my morning was. "The questions just kept coming and coming," I said with exasperation. "It is maddening!"

Marie looked at me. "At least your son is still curious!" she said. She went on to tell me about her own family. Marie is a mother of three, and she explained that her eldest daughters asked many questions when they were younger too, (B) "As time passes, they stop asking, you know," Marie told me. "It could be because they become too busy, or they only want to hang out with friends. I hope it isn't because they've lost interest in the world. Whatever the case, believe me when I say that the second those questions disappear, you'll miss them."

That's when it hit me. Curiosity is a trait I deeply admire in others. In fact, my own desire to learn as a young woman was so pronounced, and it wasn't until the busyness and responsibilities of adulthood got the best of me that I stopped having time to ask questions for myself anymore. (C) I want him to be constantly seeking more knowledge. The questions he asks are draining at times, yes. Even worse than a child who asks 58 questions on a 15-minute car ride though would be a child who asks none at all.

While some curiosity is innate, it is a trait that must be continuously fostered. Inquisitiveness ebbs and flows, depending on our age, stage of life, and the people around us. This is reassuring because parents can play an active role in cultivating a child's ability to ask questions and seek answers, but it is cumbersome because doing so requires a great deal of persistence and patience. (D)

I realize now that when I ignore my son's inquiries, I may be stunting his desire to learn. The best way for parents to nurture children's curiosity is to stay curious themselves. As we get older, we have a tendency to fall back on what we know and stop asking questions. (　Z　), curiosity is like a muscle: it atrophies without use. To keep it strong, we need to adopt the perspective of young children and remain intensely aware of what we don't know.

I am horribly unprepared for all the questions my son will ask me. (　E　) I don't know what stars are made of, or who invented the first train. I'm not even sure I know why the sky is blue. The one thing I do know is that I have a powerful motivation for staying curious: I don't want to disappoint my son.

問1　Choose the most appropriate transition for (　Z　).

① For example
② As a result
③ To begin with
④ However
⑤ Accordingly

問2　Place the following sentence in the correct placement in the passage from (　A　) to (　E　).

"That being said, curiosity is a characteristic I am desperate for my son to have."

問3　According to the passage, which of the following statements is untrue?

① The narrator was irritated by her son firing so many questions while out doing chores.
② Through chatting with her friend, the narrator realized the value of her son asking about many things.
③ The narrator used to ask questions for herself but became too busy with adult responsibilities.
④ Curiosity is inherent, and once this trait is set it cannot be changed by anyone.
⑤ If adults do not stay curious then they cannot help children foster their

own curiosity.

問4　According to the passage, which statement is true?

① It is difficult to make time to answer questions as a parent, so children should save their questions for school time only.

② Adult responsibilities can often help mothers and fathers become more inquisitive because they are so frequent.

③ It is necessary to cultivate and maintain curiosity because even as adults people do not understand everything.

④ When people get older, it becomes easier for them to answer children's questions because they have learned everything.

⑤ Adults should stay curious so as to know more than their children at all times, and therefore remain superior.

(☆☆☆◎◎◎◎◎)

【中学校】

【1】次の文は，「中学校学習指導要領解説　外国語編」(平成29年文部科学省)「第1章　総説」「2　外国語科改訂の趣旨と要点」「(2)　改訂の要点」の一部である。次の①～⑤に当てはまる語句を書きなさい。ただし，同じ番号には同じ語句が入る。

> 中央教育審議会答申を踏まえ，目標及び内容等に関して，次のような改善を図った。
>
> －　中　略　－
>
> 今回の改訂では，小学校中学年に新たに(　①　)を導入し，三つの資質・能力の下で，英語の目標として「聞くこと」，「話すこと[やり取り]」，「話すこと[発表]」の三つの領域を設定し，(　②　)面を中心とした外国語を用いたコミュニケーションを図る素地を育成した上で，高学年において「読むこと」，「書くこと」を加えた教科として(　③　)を導入し，五つの領域の(　④　)を通して，コミュニケーションを図る(　⑤　)となる資質・能力を育成することとしている。中学校段階では，こうし

た小学校での学びを踏まえ，五つの領域の(　④　)を通してコミュニケーションを図る資質・能力を育成することとしている。

(☆☆☆◎◎◎◎)

【2】次の文は，「中学校学習指導要領」(平成29年3月告示)「第2章　各教科」「第9節　外国語」「第2　各言語の目標及び内容等」の一部である。次の①～⑤に当てはまる語句を書きなさい。ただし，同じ番号には同じ語句が入る。

英語

1　目標

英語学習の特質を踏まえ，以下に示す，聞くこと，読むこと，話すこと[やり取り]，話すこと[発表]，書くことの五つの領域別に設定する目標の実現を目指した指導を通して，第1の(1)及び(2)に示す資質・能力を一体的に育成するとともに，その過程を通して，第1の(3)に示す資質・能力を育成する。

－　中　略　－

(3)　話すこと[やり取り]

ア　関心のある事柄について，簡単な語句や文を用いて(　①　)で伝え合うことができるようにする。

イ　日常的な話題について，事実や自分の考え，気持ちなどを(　②　)し，簡単な語句や文を用いて伝えたり，相手からの質問に答えたりすることができるようにする。

ウ　社会的な話題に関して聞いたり読んだりしたことについて，考えたことや感じたこと，その(　③　)などを，簡単な語句や文を用いて述べ合うことができるようにする。

－　中　略　－

(5)　書くこと

ア　関心のある事柄について，簡単な語句や文を用いて(　④　)に書くことができるようにする。

イ　日常的な話題について，事実や自分の考え，気持ちなどを(　②　)し，簡単な語句や文を用いて(　⑤　)のある文章を書くことができるようにする。

ウ　社会的な話題に関して聞いたり読んだりしたことについて，考えたことや感じたこと，その(　③　)などを，簡単な語句や文を用いて書くことができるようにする。

(☆☆☆◎◎◎◎)

【3】次の文は，「中学校学習指導要領」(平成29年3月告示)「第2章　各教科」「第9節　外国語」「第2　各言語の目標及び内容等」「英語」「3　指導計画の作成と内容の取扱い」の一部である。次の①～⑥に当てはまる語句を書きなさい。ただし，同じ番号には同じ語句が入る。

(2)　2の内容に示す事項については，次の事項に配慮するものとする。

－　中　略　－

イ　音声指導に当たっては，日本語との違いに留意しながら，発音練習などを通して2の(1)のアに示す言語材料を継続して指導するとともに，音声指導の補助として，必要に応じて発音表記を用いて指導することもできることに留意すること。

また，発音と(　①　)とを関連付けて指導すること。

－　中　略　－

エ　文法事項の指導に当たっては，次の事項に留意すること。

(ア)　英語の特質を理解させるために，関連のある文法事項はまとめて整理するなど，効果的な指導ができるよう工夫すること。

(イ)　文法はコミュニケーションを(　②　)ものであることを踏まえ，コミュニケーションの目的を達成する上での必要性や有用性を実感させた上でその知識を活用させたり，繰り返し使用することで当該文法事項の規則性や構造などについて(　③　)を促したりするなど，(　④　)と効果的に関連付けて指導すること。

－　中　略　－

オ　辞書の使い方に慣れ，活用できるようにすること。

カ　身近な事柄について，友達に質問をしたり質問に答えたりする力を育成するため，ペア・ワーク，グループ・ワークなどの(　⑤　)について適宜工夫すること。その際，他者とコミュニケーションを行うことに課題がある生徒については，個々の生徒の特性に応じて指導内容や指導方法を工夫すること。

－　中　略　－

ク　各単元や各時間の指導に当たっては，コミュニケーションを行う目的，場面，状況などを明確に設定し，(　④　)を通して育成すべき資質・能力を明確に示すことにより，生徒が学習の(　⑥　)を立てたり，振り返ったりすることができるようにすること。

(☆☆☆◎◎◎◎)

【高等学校】

【1】次の文は，「評価規準の作成，評価方法等の工夫改善のための参考資料(高等学校外国語)」(平成24年7月国立教育政策研究所)の「第2編　外国語科における評価規準の作成，評価方法等の工夫改善」「第2章　コミュニケーション英語Ⅰ」「5　評価に関する事例」の一部である。文中の①～⑤に当てはまる語句をあとの語群から一つずつ選んで記号で答えなさい。ただし，同じ番号には同じ語句が入る。

(1)　外国語科における観点別評価について

－　中　略　－

(イ)　改訂の趣旨を踏まえた指導のより一層の充実

高等学校では，中学校に比べ言語材料や教材の題材・内容も高度になり，それらを生徒に理解させるためには相応の工夫と時間が必要となる。しかし，今回の改訂では，「聞くこと」や「読むこと」など理解の能力に関わる受信型の指導ばかりではなく，学んで得た知識を活用し，「話すこと」や「書くこと」を通じて(　①　)することができる(　②　)の能力の育成を強く求めている。4技能を総合的に育成する指導を通じて，生徒が4技能を(　③　)に活用できるよう，(　④　)を充実させることが必要となる。また，文法指導を(　④　)と一体化して行ったり，授業は英語で行うことを基本としたりすることの趣旨は，受信だけではなく(　①　)にも活用できる知識や技能を生徒が得られるよう，指導をより一層充実するというところにある。これらのことを踏まえ，各学校における観点ごとの評価規準の設定や指導及び評価の実施に当たっては，学期や学年を通じて「外国語理解の能力」と「外国語(　②　)の能力」双方において計画的にバランスよく行うことが必要になる。

また，「言語や文化についての知識・理解」については，単に知識を暗記しているといった評価規準ではなく，知識や理解が(　⑤　)のコミュニケーションを目的とした言語運用に資する形で身に付いているかを問う評価規準の設定が必要である。

《語群》

ア	一体的	イ	運用	ウ	音読活動	エ	現実
オ	語彙指導	カ	送信	キ	実際	ク	統合的
ケ	特別活動	コ	発信	サ	発表	シ	表現
ス	言語活動	セ	網羅的				

(☆☆☆◎◎)

【2】次の文は，「高等学校学習指導要領」(平成21年3月告示)「第2章　各学科に共通する各教科」「第8節　外国語」「第3款　英語に関する各科目に共通する内容等」に示されている「言語の働きの例」を英訳したものの一部である。文中の①～③に当てはまる語を下の語群から一つずつ選んで記号で答えなさい。

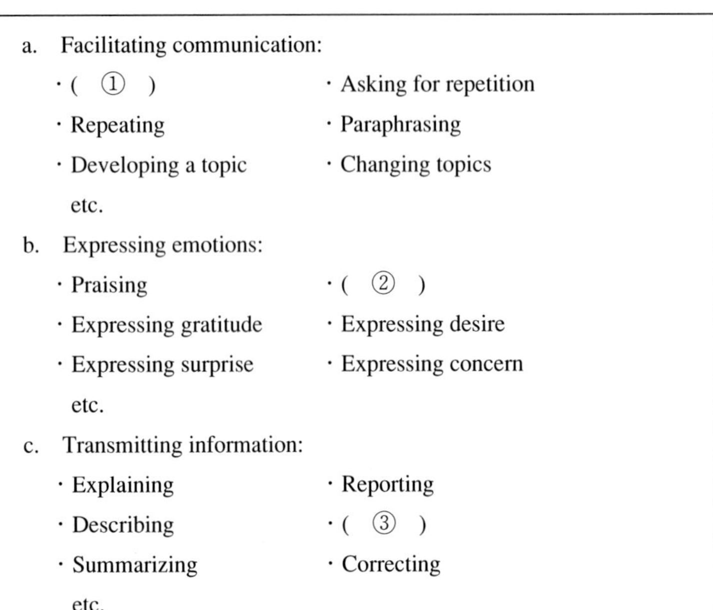
a. Facilitating communication:
- (①) ・Asking for repetition
- Repeating ・Paraphrasing
- Developing a topic ・Changing topics

etc.

b. Expressing emotions:
- Praising ・(②)
- Expressing gratitude ・Expressing desire
- Expressing surprise ・Expressing concern

etc.

c. Transmitting information:
- Explaining ・Reporting
- Describing ・(③)
- Summarizing ・Correcting

etc.

《語群》

ア	Agreeing	イ	Assuming	ウ	Apologizing	エ	Inferring
オ	Nodding	カ	Offering	キ	Permitting	ク	Reasoning
ケ	Requesting						

(☆☆☆◎◎◎◎)

【3】次の文は，「高等学校学習指導要領解説　外国語編・英語編」(平成22年文部科学省)「第1章　総説」「第1節　改訂の趣旨」「3　外国語科改訂の要点」の一部である。これを読んで，あとの各問に答えなさい。

(1) 外国語科改訂の要点

① 目標は，外国語を通じて，言語や文化に対する理解を深め，積極的にコミュニケーションを図ろうとする態度の育成を図り，情報や考えなどを的確に理解したり適切に伝えたりする(①)を養うこととした。

② 英語を履修する場合には，これまでの選択必履修制を改め，(A)「コミュニケーション英語Ⅰ」をすべての生徒に履修させる科目とすることとした。

― 中 略 ―

④ 中学校における学習との円滑な接続を図る科目として「コミュニケーション英語基礎」を新たに設けるとともに，(B)言語の使用場面の例や言語の働きの例についても，中学校との(②)を重視した改善を図った。

⑤ 指導する語数を充実し，例えば，「コミュニケーション英語Ⅰ」「コミュニケーション英語Ⅱ」及び「コミュニケーション英語Ⅲ」をすべて履修した場合，高等学校で(③)語，中高で3,000語を指導することとした。

問1 文中の①～③に当てはまる語句や数字を書きなさい。

問2 下線部(A)について，「高等学校学習指導要領」(平成21年3月告示)「第2章 各学科に共通する各教科」「第8節 外国語」「第2款 各科目」「第2 コミュニケーション英語Ⅰ」「2 内容」では，次のような事項について指導するよう配慮するものとする，と示されている。以下の文中の④～⑦に当てはまる語句を書きなさい。

ア リズムや(④)などの英語の音声的な特徴，話す速度，声の大きさなどに注意しながら聞いたり話したりすること。

イ 内容の要点を示す語句や文，(⑤)を示す語句などに注意しながら読んだり書いたりすること。

ウ (⑥)と(⑦)などを区別して，理解したり伝えたりすること。

問3　下線部(B)について，「高等学校学習指導要領解説　外国語編・英語編」(平成22年文部科学省)「第3章　英語に関する各科目に共通する内容等」では，次のように示されている。文中の⑧～⑩に当てはまる語句をそれぞれ書きなさい。ただし，同じ番号には同じ語句が入る。

> 高等学校においては，中学校での指導を踏まえ，「(　⑧　)での活動」及び「(　⑨　)での活動」が新たに加えられている。中学校では「(　⑧　)の行事」の場面が取り上げられ，日本の(　⑩　)文化など(　⑧　)の行事について説明する活動が扱われているが，高等学校における「(　⑧　)での活動」の場面では，ボランティア活動等，より広範囲にわたる(　⑧　)での社会活動の場面を扱う。「(　⑨　)での活動」とは，国際化が進展する中，英語を使って国内外の(　⑨　)で働く場面を想定したものである。

(☆☆☆◎◎◎◎)

解答・解説

【中高共通】

【1】Question 1　①　　Question 2　④　　Question 3　③

〈解説〉やや長めの対話文と設問文を聞き，問題用紙に印刷された選択肢から適切な解答を選ぶ4択問題である。放送は2回ある。ホテルのフロント係と客との会話で，Question 1は客が電話をかけてきた理由，Question3は客がホテル付近のレストランについて聞いた理由を問うシンプルな問題である。Question 2は，ブラウン夫妻のホテル料金をたずねているので，1泊95〔ドル〕×2〔泊〕×2〔人〕＝380〔ドル〕という計算が必要となる。

【2】≪A≫ Question 1 ③ Question 2 ② Question 3 ④
≪B≫ Question 1 ④ Question 2 ② Question 3 ③

〈解説〉250語程度の英文A及び英文Bと，それぞれ3つの設問文が2回放送される。英文Aは「砂糖の功罪」についてのスピーチ，英文Bは「脳の構造と働き」についてのパッセージである。英文全体を把握すべき問いも含まれているので，あらかじめ選択肢に目を通しておきたい。英文Bには脳の部位に関する専門用語がいくつか提示され，そのうちの1つの機能を答える問題がある。耳慣れない専門用語であっても，部位ごとの機能を聞き分けてメモを取るようにすること。

【3】Question 1 No.2 Question 2 No.1 Question 3 No.4

〈解説〉【1】【2】と違い，選択肢は問題用紙に印刷されていない。250語程度のエッセイと3つの設問及び4つの選択肢を聞き取り，解答しなければならない。あせって聞き逃さないように落ち着いて臨みたい。初回の放送ではエッセイの概要をつかみ，設問を把握した後2回目の放送で再確認するつもりで聞くこと。トピックは，幼児を一人で寝かせる文化と，親と一緒に寝かせる文化を比較した話者の見解である。

【4】No.3，No.5 (順不同)

〈解説〉英文は，ラジオで流れる交通情報と天気予報である。読み上げられる6つの選択肢から，英文の内容に合致するものを2つ選ぶ。放送は2回あるが，情報量が多く展開が早い。話の流れを把握すると同時に，聞き取った情報をできる限りメモをして，設問に臨みたい。日頃からテレビ・ラジオのニュース等に慣れておくことが必要である。

【5】問1 ④ 問2 ③ 問3 ② 問4 ① 問5 ⑤

〈解説〉問1 「ここに駐車はできません。あそこの標識は，このあたりが駐車禁止であると示しています」。towaway zone「駐車禁止区域」。問2 「この用紙に書いた住所が間違っている場合は，赤ペンで線を引いて消し，その下に正しい住所を活字体で書いてください」。cross ～

out「～を線で消す」，print「(文字を)活字体で書く」。　問3「あなたがラッシュアワーに車で帰宅しなかったのは賢明だった。高速道路で5キロ以上の渋滞があった」。sensible「賢明な」。形式主語構文で，it isの後に人の性格や態度を表す語が来た場合，意味上の主語を表す前置詞はforではなくofを用いる。　問4「そのバイクはこれまで20年間，ガレージに保管されきちんと手入れされてきた。だからその年月にもかかわらず真新しい状態だった」。mint condition「真新しい，新品同様の」。　問5「通りを歩いていると，風が吹き，足元の落ち葉がカサカサと鳴った」。rustle「パラパラ・カサカサと音を立てる」。

【6】問1　④　　問2　③　　問3　④　　問4　①

〈解説〉問1　整序するとprovides customers with clothing at reasonable pricesとなる。provide A with B「AにBを供給する」。　問2　整序するとthe use of clothing that allowed humans to settleとなる。強調構文となっている。　問3　整序するとwhy we cannot agree with her plan is thatとなる。whyはreasonを先行詞とする関係副詞である。　問4　整序するとchallenges will Japan face asとなる。「日本はどんな課題に直面するのか」と読み換えて考える。

【7】問1　②　　問2　④

〈解説〉問1　宿泊客とホテルの従業員との会話。どちらの発言かを区別しながら，話の流れをつくると，C→A→F→E→D→Bとなる。
問2　天候についての会話。「桜の開花が遅れているので，南部に行って桜を見たい」という流れを読み取り，並べ替えると，F→D→C→B→A→Eとなる。

【8】問1　④　　問2　②　　問3　②　　問4　③　　問5　⑤

〈解説〉問1　2027年に発表される時速603kmの新型新幹線がもたらす影響を表す内容が解答となるので，④「便利にはなるが，日本の景色が楽しめなくなる」が適切。　問2　ネットショッピングの功罪に関する文章である。空所にはそれについての欠点に当たる文章が入るので，②「購入した品物の状態に不満がある」が適切。　問3「2018年，アメリカで興行収入トップ3の映画が，新時代のテクノロジーを駆使して，力強い映画音楽とともに驚くべき視覚効果とアクションシーンを作り出した」と述べられているので，それに続く内容を考えると，②「映画製作者はテクノロジーの活用によって注目を集め続ける」が適切。　問4　アイスランドやノルウェーなどの国が，再生可能エネルギーで電気出力のほぼ100%をまかなっているという文章に続く日本の対応は，③「二酸化炭素排出量を削減するために，再生可能エネルギーの産出量を増やす」が適切。　問5　ALTと日本人教師が前もって授業プランについて話し合うことが大切だという趣旨の文である。これによりALTと日本人教師がどのようなことをできるようになるのかを考えると，⑤「教室で英語を教えるのに自信を持てる」が適切。

【9】問1　④　　問2　③　　問3　⑤

〈解説〉問1　下線部(A)のdiscernは「見定める，判別する，気づく」の意。直後に，「多くの人が富や美など物理的なものを使って幸福をはっきり表そうとしている」と述べられていることから推測すると，pinpoint「正確に示す，指摘する」が適切。　問2　第2段落の2文目の後半から，③「(投稿されたものを)見る人たちは，自分たちと投稿者とをつい比べてしまう」が適切。cannot help but ～「～せずにはいられない」。問3　最終段落の2文目，4文目から，⑤「幸福とは物理的なものではなく，心の状態だ」が適切。

【10】問1　②　　問2　①　　問3　⑤　　問4　④

〈解説〉問1　第2段落の4文目から，②の「マナーがどのように受け止められるかに関して，世代間のギャップは重要な役割を果たしている」が適切。　問2　直前の文より，空所Aにはネガティブな意味の語が入るので，deterioratedかcollapsedが入ると推測できる。また，空所Bの直後にあるinteractionから，personal interaction「個人的な交流」が適切と推測できる。さらに空所Cの文章の前半部分で，「マナーは自己と他者への敬意を映し出す」と述べていることから，Cにcivility「礼儀正しさ」を入れると，「子供たちが，強さ，決断力，感謝の気持ちを，礼儀正しさと結びつけて考えるようになることが重要だ」という意味になり，文意が通る。　問3　第3段落の要旨は，「若者がスマートフォンを使用する時間が増えたせいで，友達や大人との個人的なやり取りが減り，さらに文字を使って断片的なやり取りしかしないことで言葉が曲解され，無礼や気配りに欠けると受け止められてしまう」。よって⑤「スマートフォンがコミュニケーションの仕方を変えたために，若者は無礼だと思われることがある」が適切。　問4　①「アメリカでのマナーの悪化は科学技術のせいである」は，最終段落の内容から判断して趣旨とは言えない。②「若者は大人になるまでマナーが悪い」，③「マナーはあまりにも変わってしまったので無意味だ」，⑤「人々は電子機器に依存し，もはやマナーを必要としない」という記述は本文にない。④「マナーは重要で，若者のために大人が手本を見せるべきだ」は最終段落の最終文に合致する。

【11】問1　④　　問2　C　　問3　④　　問4　③

〈解説〉問1　設問は「空所Zに最も適切な転換語を入れなさい」という意味。空所Zの直前で，「歳をとるにつれて，私たちは自分たちの知識に頼り，質問をするのを止める」という内容が書かれており，直後では「好奇心は筋肉のようなもので，使わなければ衰える」とある。よって，逆接を表すHowever「しかしながら」が適切とわかる。

問2　設問は「以下の英文を空所AからEの中の適切な場所に入れなさい」という意味。挿入文の意味は「とはいえ，好奇心は私が息子に絶対持って欲しい特質だ」。空所Cの直後にある「私は彼に常に知識欲を持って欲しい」が，挿入文の言い換えと考えられる。　問3　本文の内容と合致しない記述を選ぶ問題。①は第1段落の3文目，②は第3段落最終文から第4段落2文目まで，③は第4段落の3文目，⑤は第6段落の2文目に合致する。本文では，「人はやがて好奇心を失ってしまう」

と述べているので，④「好奇心は生来のもので，この特性はだれにも変えることができない」とは合致しない。　問4　本文の内容と合致する記述を選ぶ問題。最終段落の2文目～4文目から，③「人は，大人になってもすべてを理解しているわけではないので，好奇心を育て，維持することが必要だ」が適切。

【中学校】

【1】①　外国語活動　②　音声　③　外国語　④　言語活動　⑤　基礎

〈解説〉平成30(2018)年度から一部先行実施されていた新中学校学習指導要領(平成29年3月告示)は，令和3(2021)年度から全面実施となる。改訂の趣旨や要点を十分に把握した上で，新学習指導要領の目標や細かい内容までも読み込んでおきたい。さらに小学校と中学校の学習指導要領を比較し，知識の整理をしておくほか，「中学校学習指導要領比較対照表【外国語】」も熟読しておきたい。

【2】①　即興　②　整理　③　理由　④　正確　⑤　まとまり

〈解説〉学習指導要領解説外国語編(平成29年7月)を参照しながら，「第1　目標」と「第2　各言語の目標及び内容等」にしっかり目を通しておくこと。目的や活動内容などを理解しておくとともに，キーワード(「即興」,「やり取り」,「言語活動」など)にも注目しよう。特に「話すこと[やり取り]」は，今回の改訂で新たに領域として設定されたものであるから，重点的に目を通しておきたい。また「即興」や「即興性」も新しい用語であるので，詳細な説明をおさえておくこと。

【3】①　綴り(つづり)　②　支える　③　気付き　④　言語活動　⑤　学習形態　⑥　見通し

〈解説〉①　「発音と綴りとを関連付けて指導すること」については，小学校の外国語科で「音声と文字とを関連付けて指導すること」とされていることを考慮する必要がある。　②③④　文法をその伝える内容や目的，場面，状況といったことと分離せずに，それらと密接に関連させた形で，効果的な導入，指導，練習方法を工夫することが求められることを示すものである。　⑤　指導に当たっては，活動の目的に応じて，全体学習，個人学習，ペア・ワーク，グループ・ワークなど様々な学習形態を活用していくことが重要である。　⑥　生徒がコミュニケーションを行う目的や場面，状況などを意識して学習に臨むことができるよう，どのような言語活動を行うのかを明確に示す必要がある。これにより，生徒自らが学習の見通しを立て，主体的に学習に取り組み，言語活動の質の高まりによる自分の考えの変容について，自ら学習のまとめを行ったり，振り返りを行ったりすることが促される。

【高等学校】

【1】①　コ　　②　シ　　③　ク　　④　ス　　⑤　キ

〈解説〉「評価規準の作成，評価方法等の工夫改善のための参考資料(高等学校外国語)」(平成24年7月国立教育政策研究所)からの出題。過去にも同資料から出題されているので一読の必要があるだろう。ただし，本資料は現行の高等学校学習指導要領(平成21年3月告示)に即しているので，新学習指導要領(平成30年3月告示)の内容と混同しないように注意したい。本資料では，「観点別評価は，学習指導要領における目標の達成状況を内容のまとまりごとに分析的に評価し，指導に役立てるための，目標に準拠した評価であり，観点別評価を行うことは，学習指導要領改訂の趣旨を踏まえた指導をより一層充実させる上で重要な意味をもつ」と示されている。

【2】①　オ　　②　ウ　　③　ク

〈解説〉各科目について目標や内容を空欄記述式で解答できるようにしておくことは必須。本問は現行の高等学校学習指導要領(平成21年3月告示)の英訳版からの出題である。キーワードになる語句は日本語のみならず，英語も全て暗記しておきたい。なお，新学習指導要領の英訳版は，令和2(2020)年1月現在まだ公表されていない。したがって，さしあたり平成21年の英訳版を活用し，新学習指導要領と重なるキーワードの英訳をおさえておくとよいだろう。

【3】問1　①　コミュニケーション能力　②　系統性　③　1800
問2　④　イントネーション　⑤　つながり　⑥　事実
⑦　意見　問3　⑧　地域　⑨　職場　⑩　伝統

〈解説〉学習指導要領及び同解説の内容を読み込んでおこう。本問は現行の高等学習指導要領解説からの出題であるが，今後は，新高等学校学習指導要領(平成30年3月告示)及び同解説外国語編・英語編(平成30年7月)からの出題にも備えておきたい。

2019年度　実施問題

【中高共通】

【１】次に読まれる英文を聞き，1～3の設問に対する答として最も適切なものを，四つの選択肢の中から一つ選びなさい。
(英文及び設問は2回読まれる。)

Receptionist : May I help you?
Ken : Yes. I'm looking for an English teacher.
Receptionist : Well, what's your name, and what are your goals for studying English?
Ken : My name is Ken, and I have to work in L.A. from September, but I can't speak English well.
I have to improve.
Receptionist : Our English school has many courses and teachers. We can help.
Do you have any particular needs?
Ken : I'm not sure. What courses do you offer?
Receptionist : Well, you don't have a lot of time, so I recommend our intensive course. This course offers many opportunities to use English every lesson.
Ken : I'm interested.
Receptionist : O.K. We offer both full day and half day classes. Which would you prefer?
Ken : I'd prefer full day classes.
Receptionist : Then you should take our Intensive B course.
Ken : Intensive B? What's the difference?
Receptionist : Intensive B is held every Saturday, so you don't have to worry about your work schedule.

Ken　　　　　: That's good. Weekends are better for me. How long is the course?

Receptionist　: Three months.

Ken　　　　　: What about the cost?

Receptionist　: Each month is 7,000 yen.

Ken　　　　　: That's great. I'll sign up.

Question 1 : What is Ken's reason for studying English?

① He can speak English well.

② He needs to because he is going to work in L.A.

③ He has no chance to speak English in his daily life.

④ He is interested in traveling all over the world.

Question 2 : Why did Ken sign up for the Intensive B course?

① The course runs for three consecutive weeks.

② The course has opportunities to read English books.

③ He is interested in half day classes after work.

④ He wants full day classes during the weekend.

Question 3 : How much does the course cost for three months?

① 7,000 yen.

② 14,000 yen.

③ 21,000 yen.

④ 28,000 yen.

(☆☆◎◎◎◎)

【2】次に読まれる英文≪A≫及び英文≪B≫について，それぞれの1～3の設問に対する答として最も適切なものを，四つの選択肢の中から一つ選びなさい。

(英文及び設問は2回読まれる。)

≪A≫

Hello. I'm John. Let me tell you about what I do in my free time.

Have you ever been to a coffee shop? I love going to coffee shops.

Whenever I go to a café, I always have a cup of coffee. I especially like drinking strong coffee. Some people say drinking too much coffee is harmful to your body because it has so much caffeine. Also, some researchers indicate that ingesting too much caffeine can cause a variety of problems, from restlessness to muscle spasms.

I always take these studies with a grain of salt, though. Actually, my main reason for going to cafés isn't to drink coffee. Rather, I like to read books and magazines. I don't buy them for myself, so I read the ones at coffee shops. Reading them is enjoyable and relaxing. As a plus, I've made friends with a number of café owners and regular customers, too. It's interesting to be surrounded by other people, instead of being home alone.

Coffee drinkers have gathered together as far back as the 1600's. Today, drinking coffee isn't the only thing to do at cafés. If you want a chance to relax and meet new people, go to a coffee shop!

Question 1: According to the passage, why do some people say drinking too much coffee can be harmful to the body?

① Because it has so much caffeine.

② Because it has so much salt.

③ Because it leads to success.

④ Because it is not well-researched.

Question 2: According to the passage, what is John's main reason for going to coffee shops?

① He enjoys drinking strong coffee.

② He enjoys reading books and magazines.

③ He was invited by the owner of the coffee shop.

④ He prefers being home alone.

Question 3: According to the passage, which statement is true?

① Some researchers say drinking strong coffee can be good for your health.

② Drinking coffee is the only thing to do at coffee shops.

③ John feels sad because he can't buy books or magazines.

④ John made friends with a number of people who own coffee shops.

≪B≫

My name is Bryan, a bank clerk in Chicago. These days I often think about ethics in business. It is getting more and more important in today's society. Companies take on social responsibilities and have a lot of influence, and behaving in an ethical way is necessary to win public confidence. They should make good decisions to improve society.

The meaning of "ethics" varies depending on business. For a bank, it often means not investing in companies or doing business with people who abuse human rights or harm the environment. In order to follow this path, some companies have to turn down a lot of money-making opportunities. Our bank is a successful example of this practice. We advertised that we wouldn't invest peoples' money in unethical businesses and we've seen our number of accounts grow.

If you are employed by a food trading company, especially dealing with exotic imports such as fruits and nuts, ethical practice for you means not taking advantage of the local workers. They should be paid a fair wage, and given a voice in the kind of crops grown and in fixing the prices. You should not use these people as cheap labor but invest in their communities and in their lives.

Question 1 : According to the passage, which statement is true about ethics in business?

① The meaning of "ethics" is the same in all businesses.

② It's a matter relevant to companies' social liabilities.

③ Today more companies are reluctant to apply it.

④ It is less significant in banks than food trading.

Question 2 : According to the passage, what happened to Bryan's bank?

① It got involved with unethical businesses and fell into a financial crisis.

② It succeeded in promoting environmental preservation business.

③ It was forced to work with people who violated human rights.

④ It attracted more customers after the announcement of its ethics policy.

Question 3 : According to the passage, which statement is true about the food trading business?

① It should be the company's right to determine the selling price of the product.

② Local workers want to make good use of their money to stimulate the labor market.

③ Companies should be respectful to local workers and should not exploit them.

④ The wage of local workers should match the quantity of crops they produce.

(☆☆◎◎◎◎)

【3】次に読まれる英文を聞き，1～3の設問に対する答として最も適切なものを，その後に読まれる四つの選択肢の中から一つ選びなさい。
(英文，設問及び選択肢は2回読まれる。)

If you are a teacher, you must have encountered some "critical incidents". A critical incident is an unexpected event that occurs in class, and it helps to trigger insights about some aspects of teaching.

Take my own experience as an example. John was an excellent student in my writing course. His essays were clearly better than those of the other students, so I always marked them with an "A" and said good things about them. In class, I spent a lot of time helping other students struggling with writing their essays, and often had to rewrite them. At the end of the semester, John said to me, "If you had marked my essays lower, I would have worked harder. I wanted to improve my writing." I was upset to think he felt he hadn't been pushed enough in class, and that he hadn't learned very much. I learned that I shouldn't judge students only by comparing them with others. Instead, I should judge them on their own terms. Otherwise I won't help them grow.

This incident was "critical" for me because it prompted me to stop and reflect on the meaning of the event and consider its long-term implications. Analyzing incidents of this kind can serve as an important part of a teacher's professional development. Those incidents appear insignificant at first glance, but they soon become "critical" when you reflect on them and consider how and why they occurred.

Question 1: According to the passage, what is a "critical incident" ?

No. 1　It is an experience shared by a teacher and an excellent student.

No. 2　It is a teacher's failure in class about how to deal with students.

No. 3　It is a trigger for a student's practice to think more critically.

No. 4　It is an occurrence which inspires a teacher to improve their teaching.

Question 2: According to the passage, why was John's remark upsetting?

No. 1　The teacher realized John had not been satisfied or helped.

No. 2　The teacher never highly evaluated his essays compared with other students'.

No. 3　The teacher knew John had always had difficulties in completing essays in class.

No. 4　The teacher had spent a lot of time rewriting John's essays.

Question 3: According to the passage, which statement is true?

No. 1　A good teacher can anticipate when and how a critical incident occurs in class.

No. 2　The teacher's experience was "critical" because it proved John's capabilities.

No. 3　The other students in class asked John to rewrite their essays because they were struggling.

No. 4　The positive impact of a critical incident is not immediately apparent before reflection.

(☆☆☆◎◎◎◎)

【4】次に読まれる英文を聞き，英文の内容に合致するものを，その後に読まれる六つの選択肢の中から二つ選びなさい。
(英文及び選択肢は2回読まれる。)

I have two daughters, Jenifer and Evelyn. Jenifer is ten years old and Evelyn is five, and they are always getting along well. Last week I overheard Jenifer saying to her sister, "You've been watching cartoons on the computer too long. It's my turn to play a computer game." I expected Evelyn would burst into tears, but she looked Jenifer right in the eye and said, "Who says you get to decide? I haven't been watching very long and your game goes on forever! I should get the same time!" That was a great surprise for me, and I felt I was witnessing a major turning point in their relationship. Evelyn was standing up to her big sister and actually bargaining with her. After a few minutes of give-and-take, they decided together that Evelyn could watch 15 minutes more of cartoons and then Jenifer could play her game. Both seemed happy with the compromise.

Young children's everyday lives are filled with situations like sharing toys, getting along with siblings, and settling arguments with peers. There is always potential for conflict. Successful negotiation can be defined as the art of finding and implementing solutions that make everyone involved feel satisfied. If you help your children learn how to negotiate when they are young, it will pay off in many ways. They'll be better able to handle conflicts without resorting to violence, and they'll become more empathetic to others. They'll also feel secure about their ability to make their way through challenging social situations.

No. 1　Jenifer was trying to teach her sister how to negotiate and work things out.

No. 2　The turning point in the sisters' relationship was caused by their father's interference.

No. 3　Jenifer and Evelyn reached an agreement about their time allotment for using the computer.

No. 4　Negotiation skills are not helpful for parents in preventing conflicts with their children.

No. 5　You can prepare children for a confrontational situation by teaching them how to negotiate.

No. 6　Negotiation skills help children sympathize with people who solve problems by means of violence.

(☆☆☆☆◎◎◎◎)

以上で英語リスニングテストを終わります。

【5】英文の意味が通るように，(　　)内に入る最も適切なものを選びなさい。

問1　The (　　) of the dinosaurs still mystifies many scientists.

①　malpractice　②　compromise　③　sacrifice
④　franchise　⑤　demise

問2　The theory of relativity seemed (　　) when first introduced.

①　indivisible　②　indelible　③　implausible
④　inconsolable　⑤　insatiable

問3　With a sharp knife, cut the end of the stems (　　) so that the flowers have new, clear access to water.

①　flexibly　②　cowardly　③　religiously　④　diagonally
⑤　responsively

問4　The introduction of new technology proved to be (　　) for everyone involved.

①　attentive　②　lucrative　③　conservative　④　distinctive
⑤　accumulative

問5　Greater London is divided, for (　　) purposes, into 32 boroughs plus the City. This is to help manage the city's affairs more easily.

① momentary　② administrative　③ dietary　④ critical
⑤ compulsive

(☆☆☆◎◎◎◎)

【6】次の各問の日本文の意味を表す英文を作るために，(　　)内のA～Eの語句を正しく並べかえたとき，2番目と4番目にくる最も適切な組合せを選びなさい。

ただし，組合せの左側を2番目，右側を4番目とする。なお，文頭にくる語も小文字で表している。

問1　新しいメガネは，以前買ったものの3倍の値段だった。

My new glasses ($_{A}$the last pair $_{B}$as $_{C}$cost me $_{D}$three times $_{E}$as much) that I bought.

① A－E　② D－A　③ D－B　④ E－D　⑤ E－B

問2　あるとき列車に乗ったら，一人の青年が私の隣に座るとすぐに小説を読み始めた。

Once, when I took a ride in a train, a young passenger ($_{A}$than $_{B}$had $_{C}$sat down $_{D}$no sooner $_{E}$beside me) he began to read a novel.

① B－A　② B－E　③ D－C　④ D－E　⑤ E－B

問3　彼女はあれだけ才能がありながら，いつも謙虚に振る舞う。だからみんなに好かれるのも当たり前だ。

With all her talent she always behaves with modesty, ($_{A}$that $_{B}$no $_{C}$so $_{D}$it is $_{E}$wonder) that she should be loved by everyone.

① A－B　② A－E　③ B－A　④ B－C　⑤ C－B

問4　考え込むときはいつものことだったが，彼は腕を組んで部屋の中を歩き回った。

($_{A}$when $_{B}$usual $_{C}$was $_{D}$with him $_{E}$as) absorbed in thought, he walked about the room with folded arms.

① B－C　② B－D　③ C－D　④ E－B　⑤ E－D

(☆☆◎◎◎◎)

【7】次の各問のA～Fの英文を二人の会話として意味がつながるように並べかえたとき，2番目と4番目にくる最も適切な組合せを選びなさい。ただし，組合せの左側を2番目，右側を4番目とする。

問1 A: That sounds tough. Is that about the big project for the new product?

B: I'm sure they'll like it. Then I'd better leave you alone. Good luck to you.

C: Would you like a cup of tea?

D: Yes. It has to be eye-catching and persuasive enough to grab their attention, especially that of the executives.

E: Thanks. I'll do my best.

F: No, thanks. I'm in a rush today. I've got to prepare the presentation for tomorrow's meeting.

① D－E　② D－F　③ E－D　④ F－D　⑤ F－E

問2 A: They say the Chinese developed it using a very pure form of clay, and it became known in Europe in the late 17th century.

B: Yes, I have. Cups and saucers mainly.

C: Oh, you know a lot about history. Is that why you've been collecting them?

D: I gather you've been collecting antique porcelain, haven't you?

E: Tell me a bit about porcelain. Who invented it first?

F: No, actually I have a dream to open a pretty tea-room. I'd like to serve tea in my antique cups.

① A－E　② A－F　③ B－A　④ B－E　⑤ D－C

(☆☆◎◎◎◎)

【8】次の各問の英文を読み，文脈から考えて文中の(　　)に入る最も適切なものを選びなさい。

問1 Have you ever had a lucid dream? During a lucid dream, the dreamer is aware that what they're experiencing is a dream and is often able to change its course. For example, if they know that they're dreaming, they can say to themselves, "This is a dream, so I can fly," and then suddenly they're flying through the air like a bird. Research has shown that (　　) can increase your likelihood of having these kinds of dreams. Scientists believe that this is because it helps us recognize patterns that often occur in our dreams, which then allows us to realize that we're dreaming.

① dreaming about flying in the sky
② sleeping for a long time every day
③ keeping a journal of your dreams
④ taking medicine occasionally before sleeping
⑤ refraining from looking at your smart phone

問2 What kind of diet do you have? Traditional belief says that a healthy diet is high in carbohydrate rich foods like grains, bread, and rice; moderate in protein rich foods like meat, chicken, and fish; and low in high fat foods such as butter and cheese. Recently, though, some research has suggested that a (　　) diet is more similar to what our ancestors ate. Since our ancestors ate mostly meat and animal fat, these people believe that our bodies evolved to eat this kind of food. As nutritional science improves, hopefully we will learn more about our bodies and how they work.

① more bread, less rice
② high sugar and salt
③ heavy on fish, light on meat
④ low carbohydrate, high fat
⑤ no vegetable oil, only animal fat

問3 In Japan, it's not unusual for people to have very long commute times compared to people in other countries. Although there is plenty of research concerning the negative impacts of long commute times, there can be some benefits, particularly for those who ride the bus or train. This time can be spent focusing on what we need to accomplish for the day, studying, reading, or even just relaxing. In today's hectic society, it's important to (　　), including the time we spend commuting to work, in order for us to get the most out of our free time.

① focus on our work
② use our free time efficiently
③ make our commute times shorter
④ focus on the positive aspects of things
⑤ be environmentally conscious by taking the train or bus

問4 The 26th U.S. President, Theodore Roosevelt, was famous for loving Japanese culture, particularly samurai culture and martial arts. He was actually the first American ever to earn a brown belt in judo, and often encouraged his colleagues and famous American athletes of the time to learn the sport. Although he is well-known for being a very physical person, he was actually sickly and weak as a child and preferred books to sports. Due to this experience, he grew up to be an individual (　　).

① who was strong and intelligent
② who was strong, yet sickly
③ who was weak and mean
④ with a debilitating illness
⑤ with a distaste for sports

問5 We often talk about the importance of clarifying the daily goal of each lesson when we teach our students. It helps them to better understand the day's activities and the reason for doing each task. However, it's also important to (　　). By reminding students each class of their long-term objective, and connecting it to the day's activities, we can improve students' understanding, motivation, and focus.

① make students do large projects
② use the goal that is written in the textbook
③ let students decide their own goals for studying English
④ tell the situation of the activity students do in the lesson
⑤ confirm the goals of the whole unit in addition to the short-term goals

(☆☆☆◎◎◎◎)

【９】次の英文を読んで，あとの問に答えなさい。

What makes learning enjoyable? Students often say that their teacher is the most important element. A good teacher is able to make all the difference. Then what makes a good teacher?

Some people believe that being good at teaching is a natural talent, but anyone can learn to teach. One must complete a training course in order to become a professional teacher. Being well informed in a specific field of study is essential before beginning. The course will provide the necessary skills to effectively pass knowledge onto students. Trainee teachers learn classroom management, how to design and plan a syllabus, and most importantly, a variety of methods to help students comprehend new ideas and concepts.

The huge majority of teachers do their job because they love it. This doesn't mean that they do not receive good pay. However, their equivalents in other professions enjoy considerably better terms of employment. Where teachers are fortunate is in having a high level of job satisfaction, which derives from the fact that they are equipping others with the skills to fulfill their ambitions. To see the light of understanding flash in a student's eyes can make a whole lesson worthwhile for any teacher.

As individuals, teachers are of course not perfect. They also have some tough days. A suitable comparison for teaching is acting. Even if teachers have a personal problem, when they are in the classroom the show must go on. The class is watching and depending on teachers so they must do their best. Perhaps the most frustrating thing of all is when a student shows no interest in studying and becomes disorderly. Motivating students is a very important factor of teaching, and it is also the most difficult. No two students have the same reason for studying, and motivating each one is a ceaseless task. One way teachers can demonstrate how fun and fulfilling studying can be is by learning alongside their students. Education is an amazing opportunity that should not be wasted. Everyone is learning all the time, and learners should "seize the day."

問1　本文の内容に合うように，次の問の答として最も適切なものを選びなさい。

According to the passage, what is the hardest part of teaching?

① Being paid less than equivalents in other professions.
② Having to practice acting skills in front of a lot of people.
③ Not being able to leave a class when unwell or having a problem.
④ Passing the training course and learning a variety of skills.
⑤ Finding ways to inspire and encourage every single student to study.

問2　次の問の答として最も適切なものを選びなさい。

According to the passage, which of the following statements is true?

① A teacher's quality is of little consequence to students' enjoyment while earning.
② All students share the same incentives for studying.
③ Only those with an innate talent are able to become good teachers.
④ Teachers get a sense of happiness and achievement when they help students.
⑤ Once teachers complete their training, their studying is completely finished.

問3　本文の内容に合うように，次の問の答として最も適切なものを選びなさい。

What is the author's advice for all learners?

① To respect all teachers for their completion of the highly difficult training course and ability to motivate.
② To go into acting rather than teaching if they want to receive a higher salary.
③ To make the most of learning whenever and wherever they can do so.
④ To become disorderly as a way of testing trainee teacher's classroom management skills.
⑤ To watch their teachers carefully when they have personal problems to

find out how to deal with tough days.

(☆☆☆◎◎◎◎)

【10】次の英文を読んで，あとの問に答えなさい。

Cursive script has been disappearing in the United States. It has declined because of the invasion of technology, beginning with the typewriter and then the computer. As a result, when asked to write a message, essay, or application form, many Americans opt for printing, the form of writing they learned at the start of elementary school, rather than the smoother, interconnected script they were taught later. Some specialists in graphology believe that handwriting is a reflection of character, and that the shift from cursive letters to printed letters suggests a transition from community to selfishness. Unlike interconnected cursive letters, separate printed ones consist of perpendicular strokes that, as one graphologist said, "stand on their own and reflect the single self."

The return to printing also perhaps indicates a lack of time in the nation's classrooms. Schools may still teach cursive script, but they rarely make time to practice it the old-fashioned way with copybooks and extended repetition. This is not only true for American schools but for Japanese schools as well. For many years Japanese teachers were required to teach cursive script alongside print in their English lessons. Then in 2002, the standardized curriculum for English language teaching made cursive optional rather than mandatory. Most Japanese teachers quickly dropped cursive from their classes in order to focus on other aspects of the English language. The modern curriculum, whether in Japan or America, is too crowded, and demands on teachers too pressing.

Now that many American adults print like grade schoolers, handwriting speed has become very slow. Ironically this decline in handwriting speed has not led to gains in legibility. The U.S. Post Office gives us one of the best examples of this nation-wide handwriting trend. In spite of significant improvements in its automated reading systems, postal workers must still individually and personally process many handwritten addresses because they are impossible for machines to read. There are some larger post offices that send illegible addresses to decoders. Despite these efforts, a huge amount of mail is undelivered every year because their addresses are illegible.

However, it may be too early to give up on handwriting. Now that standardized tests for college entrance exams require essays, readable cursive script may make a comeback, as nobody wants to risk a college rejection by wasting time printing an entire essay exam.

(注) cursive: the handwriting style of joining letters together

問1 本文の内容に合うように，次の問の答として最も適切なものを選びなさい。

According to the passage, which of the following is the main cause of the decrease in cursive handwriting?

① The slowness and general inefficiency people experience when they write messages and other official forms in cursive.

② The inability of schools worldwide to teach students handwriting effectively.

③ The U.S. Post Office urging Americans to stop handwriting addresses due to the growing amount of undelivered letters.

④ The shift in society to print handwriting as a way to express self-confidence.

⑤ The need for handwriting has decreased along with the increase in technological innovations.

問2 本文の内容に合うように，次の問の答として最も適切なものを選びなさい。

According to the passage, which statement best explains what a graphologist is?

① Someone who studies handwriting as a means to infer the writer's personality or values.

② Someone who teaches how to write cursive script beautifully and more smoothly.
③ Someone who studies the effect of technology on handwriting.
④ Someone who composes graphs to express change over time.
⑤ Someone who studies the psychology of selfishness in community settings.

問3　本文の内容に合うように，次の英語に続く最も適切なものを選びなさい。

The main point of the third paragraph is to demonstrate that

① address-reading technology is not helpful.
② the U.S. Post Office needs more decoders.
③ handwriting legibility in America is declining.
④ handwriting speed has slowed significantly.
⑤ postal workers prefer processing handwritten addresses.

問4　本文の内容に合うように，次の問の答として最も適切なものを選びなさい。

What is the main topic of this passage?

① The failure of parents to teach their children how to print legibly.
② The gradual decline of cursive handwriting being practiced over the years.
③ The superiority of Japanese teachers to American teachers in administering cursive script lessons in their English classes.
④ The curriculum in modern schools is too difficult for teachers because they must teach both print and cursive handwriting.
⑤ The faulty automated machinery in the U.S. Post Office has led to an increase in job opportunities.

(☆☆☆◎◎◎◎)

【11】次の英文を読んで，あとの問に答えなさい。

I was driving alone from Hershey to Raleigh last night. It was middle of the night and I was almost late for a meeting, and if anyone asked me, I'd be very embarrassed to admit how fast I was driving. (A)

While driving along an open highway, eventually I came upon a traffic light. I was totally by myself on the road, but as I drew close to the light, it turned red, so I stepped on the brakes and came to a stop. I looked all around me. There was nobody. No cars. Absolutely nothing. I couldn't see even a suggestion of head lights. I was the only human being for at least a mile in any direction. But there I sat, waiting for the light change. (B)

Why didn't I run the light? There was clearly no policeman anywhere in the vicinity, so there obviously would have been no danger in running it. (C)

At the end of the night, after I'd met some acquaintances in Raleigh and had climbed into bed, I again started to wonder why I'd stopped for that light. I think I stopped because it's part of a pact we've all made with each other. Of course it is a law, but it is also a promise, one we trust each other to hold in great respect: we must stop for red lights. For most of us, including myself, it isn't the law which stops us from doing something wrong so much as the fear of going against social conventions and receiving disapproval from our peers. (D)

Isn't it amazing that we ever trust one another to do the right thing? It's what we do. Trust is instinctual. (E)

In fact, our society entirely depends on reciprocal trust, not distrust. If we suddenly stopped trusting each other most of the time, this whole thing for us would be ruined. In one country, the government had a hard time getting any money because many people simply didn't pay their taxes. In another country, the government pretended to enforce the law, but in the end they simply had to trust that people would pay what they owed. If a revolt were to take place, many governments have had to admit that they would be unable to do anything at all.

The bottom line is we do what we say we'll do. We turn up when we say we'll turn up. I was so proud of myself for not going through that red light.

And inasmuch as nobody would have known about my good behavior on the road from Hershey to Raleigh, I had to tell somebody.

問1　本文の内容に合うように，次の問の答として最も適切なものを選びなさい。

What did the author do while he was driving from Hershey to Raleigh?

① He behaved himself according to the conventions we all share.

② He saw other cars going through the traffic lights.

③ He was asked a question but refused to answer it.

④ He thought it was too dangerous to go through the light.

⑤ He talked with his friends on his cell phone because he was very lonely.

問2　本文の内容に合うように，次の問の答として最も適切なものを選びなさい。

Which statement would the author most likely agree with?

① Don't worry about breaking the law until you get caught.

② Traffic laws are the most important laws in our society.

③ Governments cannot trust people to follow their rules.

④ Running a red light is a breach of trust like breaking a promise.

⑤ More often than not, people will end up letting each other down.

問3　次の問の答として最も適切なものを選びなさい。

According to the passage, which of the following statements is true?

① On the way to Raleigh from Hershey, the author was caught by the police.

② The author told some of his acquaintances that he had ignored a traffic light.

③ People are apt to stop themselves from doing something to avoid social ridicule.

④ It is difficult for people to trust each other because society would fall apart.

⑤ The author regretted not running the light because it was late at night.

問4　次の一文を本文中の(　A　)～(　E　)のいずれかに挿入する場合，最も適切な箇所を記号で答えなさい。

We have to make a deliberate decision to mistrust someone or to be suspicious, or questioning.

(☆☆☆◎◎◎◎)

【中学校】

【1】次の文は，「中学校学習指導要領解説　外国語編」(平成29年文部科学省)「第1章　総説」「2　外国語科改訂の趣旨と要点」「(1)　改訂の趣旨」の一部である。次の①～④に当てはまる語句を書きなさい。

・中学校においては，小学校における外国語活動の成果として，英語で積極的にコミュニケーションを図ろうとする態度が育成され，「聞くこと」及び「話すこと」の活動を行うことに慣れているといった変容が生徒に見られること等も踏まえ，授業における教師の英語使用や生徒の英語による言語活動の割合などが改善されてきている。

・一方，授業では依然として，文法・語彙等の(　①　)がどれだけ身に付いたかという点に重点が置かれ，外国語によるコミュニケーション能力の育成を意識した取組，特に「話すこと」及び「書くこと」などの言語活動が適切に行われていないことや「(　②　)」・「(　③　)」を意識した言語活動が十分ではないこと，読んだことについて意見を述べ合うなど，複数の領域を(　④　)した言語活動が十分に行われていないことなどの課題がある。

(☆☆◎◎◎◎)

【2】「中学校学習指導要領」(平成29年3月告示)「第2章　各教科」「第9節　外国語」「第1　目標」について，次の①～⑥に当てはまる語句を書きなさい。

第1　目標

外国語によるコミュニケーションにおける見方・考え方を働かせ，外国語による聞くこと，読むこと，話すこと，書くことの(　①　)を通して，簡単な情報や考えなどを理解したり表現したり伝え合ったりするコミュニケーションを図る資質・能力を次のとおり育成することを目指す。

(1)　外国語の音声や語彙，(　②　)，文法，言語の働きなどを理解するとともに，これらの知識を，聞くこと，読むこと，話すこと，書くことによる実際のコミュニケーションにおいて活用できる技能を身に付けるようにする。

(2)　コミュニケーションを行う目的や場面，(　③　)などに応じて，日常的な話題や(　④　)な話題について，外国語で簡単な情報や考えなどを理解したり，これらを活用して表現したり伝え合ったりすることができる力を養う。

(3)　外国語の背景にある文化に対する理解を深め，聞き手，読み手，話し手，書き手に(　⑤　)しながら，(　⑥　)に外国語を用いてコミュニケーションを図ろうとする態度を養う。

(☆☆☆◎◎◎◎)

【3】「中学校学習指導要領解説　外国語編」(平成29年文部科学省)「第2章　外国語科の目標及び内容」「第2節　英語」「2　内容」「(3)言語活動及び言語の働きに関する事項」「②　言語の働きに関する事項」「イ　言語の働きの例」「(イ)気持ちを伝える」には，言語の働きの例として，下のア～オが挙げられている。

【表現例】の①～⑥は，それぞれア～オのどの働きの表現の例であるか。記号で答えなさい。

ア　礼を言う イ　苦情を言う ウ　褒める エ　謝る オ　歓迎する

【表現例】

A: I'd like you to join the party.
B: Sorry I can't. ①But thanks anyway.

A: ②I like your shoes.
B: Thank you.

A: My name is Yasuko, from Japan. Great to finally meet you.
B: Hello. I'm Bob. ③I've been looking forward to your visit.

A: ④This computer is not working.
B: Oh, really? I'll check it out soon.

A: It's time to say good-bye. We'll miss you.
B: I had a great time here. ⑤I really appreciate it.

A: ⑥I apologize for my mistake.
B: Don't worry about it.

(☆☆◎◎◎)

【高等学校】

【1】次の文は，「高等学校学習指導要領」(平成21年3月告示)「第2章　各学科に共通する各教科」「第8節　外国語」「第2款　各科目」「第2　コミュニケーション英語Ⅰ」の一部である。

> 2　内容
> (1)　生徒が情報や考えなどを理解したり伝えたりすることを実践するように具体的な言語の使用場面を設定して，次のような言語活動を英語で行う。
> ア　事物に関する紹介や(　①　)などを聞いて，情報や考えなどを理解したり，(　②　)や要点をとらえたりする。
> イ　説明や物語などを読んで，情報や考えなどを理解したり，(　②　)や要点をとらえたりする。また，聞き手に伝わるように(　③　)する。
> ウ　聞いたり読んだりしたこと，学んだことや経験したことに基づき，情報や考えなどについて，話し合ったり意見の(　④　)をしたりする。
> エ　聞いたり読んだりしたこと，学んだことや経験したことに基づき，情報や考えなどについて，(　⑤　)に書く。
> (2)　(1)に示す言語活動を効果的に行うために，次のような事項について指導するよう配慮するものとする。
> ア　(　⑥　)やイントネーションなどの英語の音声的な特徴，話す(　⑦　)，声の大きさなどに注意しながら聞いたり話したりすること。
> イ　内容の要点を示す語句や文，<u>つながりを示す語句</u>などに注意しながら読んだり書いたりすること。
> ウ　(　⑧　)と意見などを区別して，理解したり伝えたりすること。

問1　文中の①～⑧に当てはまる語句を書きなさい。ただし，同じ番号には同じ語句が入るものとする。

問2　下線部の「つながりを示す語句」について，「高等学校学習指導要領解説　外国語・英語編」(平成22年文部科学省)には，次のア～キの例が挙げられている。①～⑦は，それぞれア～キのどれにあてはまるか。記号で答えなさい。

ア	順序を表す語句(first, second, lastly など)
イ	出典を表す語句(according to など)
ウ	付加情報を表す語句(furthermore, in addition など)
エ	要約を表す語句(to sum up, to conclude など)
オ	同列を表す語句(in other words, that is to say など)
カ	結果を表す語句(therefore, as a result など)
キ	対比を表す語句(however, on the other hand など)

① in a nutshell　② on the contrary　③ at the outset
④ namely　⑤ accordingly　⑥ to boot
⑦ to quote

(☆☆☆◎◎◎◎)

【2】次の英文は，文部科学省のリーフレット*Overview of the Ministry of Education, Culture, Sports, Science and Technology (September, 2016)* "*Introduction of the Bureaus: Elementary and Secondary Education Bureau*" の一部である。

文中の①～⑥に当てはまる語をあとの《語群》から選んで記号で答えなさい。ただし，同じ番号には同じ記号が入るものとする。

Cultivating a "Competency (Ikiru chikara)"

MEXT established the National Curriculum Standards as a broad standard for each school to organize school curriculums to ensure a fixed standard of education throughout the country.

The current National Curriculum Standards revised in 2008 and 2009 aim to nurture in children "competency." This revision enhances educational contents and increases the number of classes in order that children acquire (　①　) knowledge and skills, (　②　) the ability to think, make decisions and (　③　) themselves to solve problems by using acquired knowledge and skills, cultivate motivations to learn, and (　②　) good study habits.

(中略)

The National Curriculum Standards have been under deliberation by the Central Council for Education since November 2014. The council is discussing revisions to the National Curriculum Standards suitable for a new era with the aim of realizing a "curriculum open to (　④　)." In addition to identifying competencies that will be required in the future, the council works on implementing (　⑤　), interactive, and deep learning (improving classes from the perspective of active learning), reassessing subjects, and enhancing curriculum management as well as learning (　⑥　).

《語群》

ア	objective	イ	oppress	ウ	sophisticated
エ	assessment	オ	structural	カ	express
キ	proactive	ク	interpretation	ケ	predominate
コ	society	サ	global	シ	accuracy
ス	foster	セ	counsel	ソ	fundamental

(☆☆☆◎◎◎)

解答・解説

【中高共通】

【1】Question1　②　　Question2　④　　Question3　③

〈解説〉167 wordsからなる英文(対話文)と3つの設問を聞いて，選択肢で答える形式。選択肢は問題用紙に印刷されており，設問も特に難しくない。Question3は，3カ月間の授業料を尋ねているので月に7000[円]×3[カ月]＝21,000[円]という計算をする程度で，他は会話文からそのまま解答できる素直な質問となっている。

【2】≪A≫ Question1 ① Question2 ② Question3 ④
≪B≫ Question1 ② Question2 ④ Question3 ③

〈解説〉Aは189 words，Bは206 wordsからなる英文(スピーチ)と，それぞれ3つの設問を聞いて，選択肢で答える形式。選択肢は問題用紙に印刷されているが，やや長めである。キーワードとその周辺の情報で答えを導くことのできる【1】と異なり，スピーチ全体やパラグラフ全体を把握すべき問いが含まれている。事前に選択肢に目を通しておきたい。

【3】Question1 No. 4 Question2 No. 1 Question3 No. 4

〈解説〉239 wordsの長さからなる英文(エッセイ)と3つの設問を聞き，それぞれ4つずつ読み上げられる選択肢で答える形式。【1】，【2】と異なり，問題用紙には選択肢が印刷されておらず，読まれる英文量も多いことから，差がつく問題になると思われる。1度目は全体の把握を中心に，設問を把握した後の2度目は，答えを再確認するつもりで聞くこと。

【4】No. 3，No. 5

〈解説〉253 wordsの長さからなる英文(エッセイ)を聞いて，内容に合致するものを，読み上げられる6つの選択肢の中から2つ選ぶ形式。細部にとらわれずに話の流れを把握する聞き方をすることが求められている。

【5】問1 ⑤ 問2 ③ 問3 ④ 問4 ② 問5 ②

〈解説〉問1 「恐竜の絶滅はいまだに多くの科学者に謎を与えている」。

demise「消滅」。　問2 「相対性理論は最初に発表された時，信じがたく思えた」。implausible「もっともらしくない」。　問3 「鋭いナイフで，花が新鮮できれいな水を吸水するよう斜めに茎の端を切りなさい」。diagonally「対角線に」。　問4 「新しい技術の導入は関係者全員にとって利益があることがわかった」。lucrative「儲かる」。
問5 「グレーター・ロンドンは，行政上の理由で，32区と1市に分割されている。これで容易に市政を行うことができる」。administrative「行政に関する」。

【6】問1　③　　問2　④　　問3　①　　問4　③
〈解説〉問1　整序すると，cost me three times as much as the last pairとなる。
問2　整序すると，had no sooner sat down beside me thanとなる。no sooner … than ～「…するとすぐに～」。　問3　整序すると，so that it is no wonderとなる。so that「その結果」。it is no wonder that ～「～でも少しも不思議ではない」。　問4　整序すると，As was usual with him whenとなる。as is usual with ～「～にはよくあることだが」。when (he was) absorbed in thought「(彼が)考え込んだときは」。

【7】問1　④　　問2　③
〈解説〉問1　プレゼンの準備に忙しい人と同僚の会話だと想像できる。どちらのせりふかを区別しながら，話の流れをつくる。C→F→A→D→B→Eとなる。　問2　アンティークの磁器製品収集家とそれについて質問している人の会話。D→B→E→A→C→Fとなる。

【8】問1　③　　問2　④　　問3　②　　問4　①　　問5　⑤
〈解説〉問1　直後の理由を表す文「それは夢でしばしば起こるパターンを私たちが認識するのに役立つ」から，それが指す内容を考える。③「夢の記録をつけること」が正解。　問2「しかし近年では…」と伝統的に信じられてきた健康的な食事とは逆の内容が続くことから，④「低炭水化物で高脂肪の」が適切。　問3　長時間の通勤が，ためにな

ることもあるという流れから，②「自由時間を効果的に使う」ことが大切である。　問4　セオドア・ルーズベルト大統領は柔道の茶帯をとった最初のアメリカ人であるが，子どもの頃は病気がちで弱く，スポーツより本を好んでいた。この経験で彼は成長し，①「強くて聡明な」人になった。　問5　個々のレッスンの目標を明確にすることと同様に重要なことが解答にあたる。⑤「短期目標に加えて，ユニット全体の目標を確認する」が正解。

【9】問1　⑤　　問2　④　　問3　③

〈解説〉問1　質問は「教えることの最も難しいところはどこか」。第4段落の7，8文目より，⑤「勉強するよう，どの生徒も奮起させ励ます方法を見つけること」。　問2　第3段落の4文目を参照。equip ～ with …「～に…を身に付けさせる」。④「教師は生徒を援助する時，幸福感や達成感を得る」が正解。　問3　質問は「学習者に対する筆者のアドバイスは何か」。第4段落の最後の文が筆者のメッセージとなっている。seize the day「一日一日を大切にする，今を楽しむ」。③「学べる時はいつでもどこでも，学習を最大限に活用すること」が適切。make the most of ～「～を最大限に活用する，存分に楽しむ」。

【10】問1　⑤　　問2　①　　問3　③　　問4　②

〈解説〉問1　質問は「筆記体の減少の主原因はどれか」。第1段落の2文目より，⑤「筆記体の必要性が技術革新の拡大に伴い減ってきている」。問2　質問は「筆跡学者とは何か上手く説明しているものはどれか」。第1段落の4文目から，①「書き手の性格や価値観を推測する手段として筆跡を研究している人」が正しい。　問3　第3段落の要旨は，「多くのアメリカ人が活字体で字を書き，書く速度は遅くなったが，それにより文字が判読しやすくなったわけではない」。よって③「アメリカにおける手書きの読みやすさは低下している」。　問4　①「子どもに判読できるよう活字体の書き方を教えるのに親が失敗したこと」や，③「日本の教師がアメリカの教師より筆記体のレッスンが優れていること」，⑤「合衆国郵政省の欠陥のある自動機械が雇用機会を増やした」などは記述がない。④「最近の学校のカリキュラムは教師にとって困難になっている」ことは書かれているが，理由は「活字体と筆記体を両方教えなければならないから」ではない。②「長年にわたる筆記体のゆるやかな減少」が正しい。

【11】問1　①　　問2　④　　問3　③　　問4　E

〈解説〉問1　質問は「ハーシーからローリーまで筆者が車を運転している間，何をしたか」。車も人もいなかったが，赤信号で止まったとする第2段落の内容から，①「私たちが共有するしきたりに従って行動した」。　問2　質問は「筆者が最も賛同するのはどれか」。第4段落の最後の文を参照。「自分も含め私たちの多くにとって，間違ったことをさせないのは法律ではなく，社会のしきたりに反することや仲間から非難を受けることへの恐れである」から，④「赤信号を無視することは，約束を破ること同様，信頼をこわすことである」。　問3　筆者は信号無視はしていないので，①②⑤は不適切。第6段落の1文目「実際私たちの社会は不信ではなく，相互信頼にもっぱら頼っている」から，④は誤り。③「人々は社会的嘲笑を避けるために行動を止める傾向にある」が正解。　問4　挿入文は「私たちは誰かを信用しなかったり，疑ったり，不審に思うには，よく考えて判断することが必要だ」。信用について話題が及ぶのは第5段落以降である。よってEが適切。

【中学校】

【1】①　知識　　②　やり取り　　③　即興性　　④　統合

〈解説〉改訂の趣旨や要点を十分に把握したうえで，新学習指導要領の目標や細かい内容までも読み込んでおきたい。特に「やり取り」は今回の改訂で新たに領域として設定されたものであるから，重点的に目を通しておくこと。また「即興性」も新しい語彙となるので，詳細な説明をおさえておくこと。

【2】① 言語活動 ② 表現 ③ 状況 ④ 社会的 ⑤ 配慮 ⑥ 主体的

〈解説〉目標は現行の学習指導要領よりかなり詳細に記されている。根幹を成すものとしてしっかり読み込んで全文完璧に頭に入れておきたい。

【3】① ア ② ウ ③ オ ④ イ ⑤ ア ⑥ エ

〈解説〉出題元を確認しておくこと。小学校の児童が，どのような表現を学んできているか把握し，繰り返し使用させることで定着を図ることや，新しい表現を使用させ内容の広がりや深まりを持たせるよう工夫することが大切である。

【高等学校】

【1】問1 ① 対話 ② 概要 ③ 音読 ④ 交換 ⑤ 簡潔 ⑥ リズム ⑦ 速度 ⑧ 事実 問2 ① エ ② キ ③ ア ④ オ ⑤ カ ⑥ ウ ⑦ イ

〈解説〉問1 一般的な出題方法，出題内容である。各科目について目標や内容を空欄記述式で解答できるようにしておくことは必須。なお，本問は現行の高等学校学習指導要領(平成21年3月告示)からの出題であるが，今後は，平成30年3月告示の新学習指導要領及び同解説外国語編・英語編(平成30年7月)からの出題に備えておきたい。 問2 文やパラグラフを論理的につなげる表現として，生徒に提示してライティング指導に役立てたい。 ① in a nutshell「簡単に言えば」。
② on the contrary「逆に」。 ③ at the outset「最初は」。
④ namely「すなわち」。 ⑤ accordingly「したがって」。
⑥ to boot「その上」。 ⑦ to quote「引用すると」。

【2】① ソ ② ス ③ カ ④ コ ⑤ キ ⑥ エ

〈解説〉文科省からの資料にはできるだけ目を通しておくことが望ましい。しかし初見であっても，昨今の英語教育の成果や課題等を認識しておけば解答するのに困ることはない。　① fundamental knowledge「基礎的・基本的な知識」。　② foster the ability to think「思考力を育成する」, foster good study habits「望ましい学習習慣を確立する」。
③ (the ability to) express themselves「自己表現する(能力)」。
④ curriculum open to society「社会に開かれた教育課程」。
⑤ proactive, interactive, and deep learning「主体的・対話的で深い学び」。　⑥ learning assessment「学習評価」。

2018年度　実施問題

福　岡　県

【中高共通】

【1】次に読まれる英文を聞き，1～3の設問に対する答として最も適当なものを，四つの選択肢の中から一つ選びなさい。

(英文及び設問は2回読まれる。)

Lucy : Hi, Jeff.

Jeff : Hi, Lucy. Did I tell you about the new apartment I'm renting?

Lucy : No. You finally found one, right?

Jeff : Yes. It's about one mile from the campus. It has a big living room plus two bedrooms.

Lucy : That sounds nice. Is there a washer in the unit?

Jeff : No, there isn't. I have to get one.

Lucy : Oh, I see. How's the rent?

Jeff : it's 1,000 dollars a month.

Lucy : Oh, it's kind of high.

Jeff : It's not too bad because Mike is sharing it with me. However, I was worried at first because we had to put down <u>three months' rent as a security deposit as well as the first month's rent.</u>

Lucy : That's kind of expensive.

Jeff : Yeah, but the good thing is that all the utilities are included.

Lucy : That's hard to believe. You really lucked out.
How are you and your roommate getting along?

Jeff : Well, we're doing well except for meals. None of us are chefs. We're already sick of cereal and sandwiches. I miss homemade cooking.

Question 1 : What did Jeff find?

① A new apartment near the campus.

② A large apartment with one bedroom.

③ A small unit with a washer and dryer.

④ A new roommate who is rich.

Question 2 : How much did Jeff and Mike have to pay at first?

① 1,000 dollars.

② 2,000 dollars.

③ 3,000 dollars.

④ 4,000 dollars.

Question 3 : Why does Jeff miss homemade cooking?

① Because he is good at cooking.

② Because he likes cereal and sandwiches.

③ Because no one in his apartment cooks well.

④ Because he doesn't have to pay the utilities.

(☆☆☆◎◎◎◎)

【2】次に読まれる英文≪A≫及び英文≪B≫について，それぞれの1～3の設問に対する答として最も適切なものを，四つの選択肢の中から一つ選びなさい。(英文及び設問は2回読まれる。)

≪A≫

Let's talk about the history of spices.

About 5,000 years ago, they were first used in China mainly to restore people to health. The information of their medical properties and their prominent flavors spread rapidly. An enormous market for spices grew around the Mediterranean coastal areas.

In Rome, spices were used in place of money. Peppercorns were a preferred form of payment. This was convenient because they were small and they weren't as heavy as coins. The trading value was high because there was such a high demand for pepper. People in Rome could purchase several sheep for a pound of pepper. Therefore only the richest Romans could afford to season their food with pepper, and it symbolized high status. Most people couldn't afford to use their pepper for cooking. In fact, over the centuries, people in Europe mainly used spices to preserve foods and to cover up the taste of foods that were rotten or diseased. Spices were so important for those reasons that they indirectly led to the exploration of the world. Most European explorers set out to find new ways to get these precious goods.

Question 1 : According to the passage, how were spices mostly used in China?

① To pay for sheep.

② To flavor food.

③ To season according to taste.

④ To get over illness.

Question 2 : According to the passage, what was the main purpose of using pepper on foods?

① To distinguish among social classes.

② To prevent from rotting and gloss over the taste of foods.

③ To magnify the smell of the foods and enjoy the flavor.

④ To enlarge the nutritional value of the foods.

Question 3 : According to the passage, which statement is true?

① People in China exhausted most of their spices.

② Supplies of coins were too limited.

③ In Rome, pepper was a status symbol used as a food seasoning.

④ People in Rome tried to create new routes for medical treatments.

≪B≫

I'm Steve, a businessman in New York.

On that morning I wasn't sure what to expect, though I had consulted with coaches and friends and had been given lots of advice on how to run the race.

Years before, I had run track in high school, but not at my university. Then I got busy with work and forgot about running. However, when my wife pointed out that I was putting on weight, I got back into running.

At first it was hard to go even one mile, but with effort, I was soon entering 5 kilometer races and breaking the 25 minute barrier. Still, I never thought about trying a marathon. That is, not until I realized that I was going to turn 40 years old. I thought I should do something memorable.

So there I was, getting ready to run through the city of New York along with so many ordinary people. Super runners would take off much earlier so they wouldn't get caught in us. They were in pursuit of world class times and placings or large amounts of money. But we were just running after our own goals. I wanted to see if I could run the race in under four hours.

Question 1 : According to the passage, why did Steve get back into running?

① His friend gave him advice on running.

② He wanted to do a fun thing besides working.

③ His wife made a comment about his weight.

④ He found it hard to run even one mile.

Question 2 : According to the passage, when did Steve decide to run a marathon race?

① When he realized his 40s were getting closer and felt like doing something.

② When he entered a 5 kilometer race and ran under 25 minutes.

③ When he felt he should improve his mental health before turning 40.

④ When he wanted to run in the race with top class runners as a memory.

Question 3 : According to the passage, which statement is true?

① Steve was uneasy because he'd had no opportunity to talk with his coaches before the race.

② Steve's running experience had been as a high school student and rather extensive during his university days.

③ Steve had no interest in his time in the race, as well as his ranking or large amounts of money.

④ Steve knew why the starting time for super runners was different from that of ordinary runners.

(☆☆☆☆◎◎◎◎)

【3】次に読まれる英文を聞き，1～3の設問に対する答として最も適切なものを，その後に読まれる四つの選択肢の中から一つ選びなさい。
(英文，設問及び選択肢は2回読まれる。)

There are a lot of volcanoes on Earth. A volcano is a vent which transfers molten rock, known as magma, from deep within the Earth to the Earth's surface. The molten rock that erupts from the volcano, called lava, builds up a hill or mountain around the vent.

Volcanoes can be different in appearance. Shield volcanoes have a broad, flattened, dome-like shape. They are formed when the mostly fluid magma erupts gently. The lava flows from shield volcanoes are usually only one to ten meters thick, but they may extend for great distances away from the vent. The volcanoes of Hawaii and Iceland are typical shield volcanoes. Composite volcanoes, which are also known as stratovolcanoes, form tall, steep, cone-shaped mountains. These are created by a cycle of quiet eruptions of fluid lava, followed by explosive eruptions of less fluid lava. They erupt less frequently than shield volcanoes.

A volcano may exhibit different styles of eruption at different times, and eruptions may change from one type to another as the eruption progresses. The least violent type of eruption is termed "Hawaiian" and is characterized by extensive fluid lava flows from central vents. It is occasionally accompanied by lava fountains. Vulcanian eruptions are characterized by short, thick flows around vents. Very sticky or solid fragments of lava are violently ejected from these vents. The most violent eruptions include the exclusive ejection of a large volume of volcanic ash, followed by the collapse of the central part of the volcano.

Question 1 : According to the passage, how are shield volcanoes formed?

No.1　Fluid lava makes a steep hill surrounding the vent.

No.2 The very runny magma erupts gently from the vent.

No.3 The sticky or solid lava erupts quietly again and again.

No.4 The lava extends broadly after a series of violent eruptions.

Question 2 : According to the passage, what is a characteristic of a "Hawaiian" eruption?

No.1 It often makes progress when the volcano has a flattened, dome-like shape.

No.2 It is the most violent eruption, and the central part of the vent usually collapses.

No.3 It is one of the characteristics of tall, steep, cone-shaped mountains.

No.4 It is not as violent as a Vulcanian eruption, and the fluid lava extends broadly.

Question 3 : According to the passage, which statement is true?

No.1 The appearance of volcanoes is closely related to their age and location.

No.2 Most of the volcanoes in Iceland are tall, cone-shaped mountains called stratovolcanoes.

No.3 In the formation process of composite volcanoes, explosive eruptions sometimes occur after quiet ones.

No.4 Violent ejection of a large volume of ash is always observed when the volcanoes in Hawaii erupt.

(☆☆☆☆☆◎◎◎◎)

【4】次に読まれる英文を聞き，英文の内容に合致するものを，その後に読まれる六つの選択肢の中から二つ選びなさい。

(英文及び選択肢は2回読まれる。)

In Japan, American musicals attract many people. You might have enjoyed one. Some famous musicals were made into movies and became very popular.

The American musical is one of the unique literary art forms. A lot of people in Japan think of musicals as mainly singing and dancing, so some might question that claim. Italy and Germany have their operas, Great Britain has its musical comedies, and Japan has Noh and Kabuki. All of them include singing and dancing in their performances. The distinction lies in the integration of song and dance into the advancement of the story and how they increase dramatic effect. In opera, for example, the story is fully revealed through song. Dialogue is minimal and dance is merely decorative. In the British musical comedy, song and dance are entertainment between acts. They may enhance the dramatic effect, but essentially interrupt the story. The role of song and dance in Japanese traditional theater is much the same. In the American musical, song is used both to develop character and plot and advance the storyline. The musical *Show Boat* in the 1920s is often cited as the first example of this element. The 1940s musical *Oklahoma!* does the same with dance. In the American musical, story is always the strongest element, so plots are often adapted from other genres. *West Side Story* is clearly a modern version of *Romeo and Juliet*. Song and dance in these works don't stop the action, but carry it forward, and that is the unique contribution of the American musical.

No.1 The difference between a musical and an opera is the uniqueness of the performance.

No.2 In Italian opera, dance has a major role in carrying the story forward.

No.3 In Japanese Noh, song increases the dramatic effect, but dance is only an entertainment between acts.

No.4 The musical *Oklahoma!* is mentioned as an example of dance carrying the story forward.

No.5 *West Side Story* has a very powerful storyline, so dance is merely decorative.

No.6 In the American musical, song and dance are integrated without interrupting the story.

以上で英語リスニングテストはすべて終わりました。

(☆☆☆☆☆◎◎◎◎)

【5】英文の意味が通るように，(　　)内に入る最も適切なものを選びなさい。

問1　Our library is not large enough to (　　) all the students at the same time.

① compromise　② accommodate　③ customize
④ integrate　⑤ account

問2　Beth overcame many (　　) circumstances on her way to becoming a teacher.

① conventional　② constructive　③ reverse
④ adverse　⑤ relevant

問3　Curiosity will (　　) fear even more than bravery will.

① conquer　② win　③ notch
④ prevail　⑤ represent

問4　The (　　) motion of our planet as it turns on its axis creates the change of seasons.

① perpendicular　② periodical　③ persistent
④ perceptible　⑤ perfidious

問5　It was necessary for all the participants of the new plan to (　　) with each other, so they had a party before the first meeting.

① mingle　② contribute　③ evaluate
④ deliver　⑤ estrange

(☆☆☆◎◎◎◎◎)

【6】次の各問の日本文の意味を表す英文を作るために，(　　)内のA～Eの語句を正しく並べかえるとき，2番目と4番目にくる最も適切な組合せを選びなさい。

ただし，組合せの左側を2番目，右側を4番目とする。なお，文頭にくる語も小文字で表している。

問1　体を動かすと，筋肉が作られ脂肪が減ることで新陳代謝が上昇する。

Physical activity ($_A$muscle $_B$creating $_C$boosts $_D$by $_E$metabolism) and reducing fat.

①　A－C　　②　B－C　　③　B－D　　④　E－A
⑤　E－B

問2　雪が降るやら冷たい風が吹くやらで，今年の収穫は遅くなりそうだ。

($_A$the snow $_B$with $_C$and $_D$the cold winds $_E$what), crops are likely to be late this year.

①　A－D　　②　A－B　　③　B－C　　④　B－A
⑤　C－E

問3　その話をすべて聞いて，私は初めてその作家の偉大さがわかった。

Not until I ($_A$realize $_B$I $_C$did $_D$the whole story $_E$heard) how great the writer was.

①　A－E　　②　B－E　　③　D－A　　④　D－B
⑤　D－C

問4　よく比較される熱帯の森林のように，サンゴ礁は多くの生物の宝庫である。

Like the tropical forests ($_A$to $_B$often be $_C$can $_D$compared $_E$they), reefs are repositories of vast biological wealth.

①　A－C　　②　D－C　　③　D－E　　④　C－B
⑤　C－D

(☆☆☆◎◎◎◎)

【7】次の各問のA～Eの英文を二人の会話として意味がつながるように並べかえるとき，2番目と4番目にくる最も適切な組合せを選びなさい。ただし，組合せの左側を2番目，右側を4番目とする。

問1　A : Good thinking. I think visiting a country is the best way to learn its language.

B : Yes, I'm going to London. I'm going to pick up some current English there.

C : Your English has improved a lot. Which class do you plan to register for during the next term?

D : That's good. Well, do you have any plans for the holiday?

E : Well, I can get by in everyday conversation, but I really need to brush up my technical language. I'll apply for the business class.

①　B－D　②　B－E　③　D－A　④　E－B

⑤　E－D

問2　A : The reason I prefer Japanese dishes is that they are prepared to retain as much of the natural color and taste of ingredients as possible.

B : You are a perfect Japanologist. Let's go to a sushi bar this evening.

C : Yes. Though plain white rice did not seem tasty at first, now I'm afraid I can't live without rice and miso soup. I also like tofu, tempura, and, especially, sashimi.

D : I'm happy to hear that. A distinct feature of Japanese cuisine has long been the consumption of raw seafood supplied by surrounding Japan.

E : You use your chopsticks perfectly. Have you gotten used to Japanese food?

①　A－C　②　A－D　③　C－A　④　C－B

⑤　D－C

(☆☆☆◎◎◎◎)

【8】次の各問の英文を読み，文脈から考えて文中の(　　)に入る最も適切なものを選びなさい。

問1　Most adults need between seven and nine hours of sleep each night.

When you go to bed, do you set your alarm for the same time every morning? This might not be the best for our bodies. When sleeping, our bodies go through what is called a "sleep cycle." Each cycle takes about ninety minutes. If we wake ourselves up in the middle of a cycle using an alarm, we might feel (　　). Instead, we should arrange our bedtime and alarm so that we wake up in-between cycles, which will make us feel refreshed and ready for the day.

① we don't want to sleep more
② we slept enough to be energized
③ refreshed and ready for getting up
④ energized or well rested
⑤ drowsy or unrested

問2 In Japan, there is a certain type of doll called a *daruma*. This is one of the traditions of Buddhism. When you decide on a goal or a project, you paint in the right eye of the *daruma*. As time passes, you can look at the doll and be reminded of your goal. In this way, we can stay motivated and conscious of our path and actions. Once the goal is achieved or the project is finished, you paint in the left eye. This particular Japanese tradition represents (　　).

① the ideals of continued effort and persistence
② the celebration of the culture of painting
③ the custom that people paint on their special days
④ the nature of people losing their motivation to achieve their goals
⑤ the merit of telling our goals or projects to others

問3 When learning English, it can be difficult for students to remember the mountain of new words and grammar structures in front of them. Studies have shown most people will only remember roughly forty percent of newly learned material after one day has passed. As teachers, (　　). Repeated exposure to new vocabulary or grammatical structures is necessary for students to effectively memorize information.

① we need to teach students as many words and phrases as quickly as possible

② we need to ask students to memorize vocabulary on their own so we can focus on grammatical phrases

③ we need to let students see and use vocabulary and phrases from previous lessons again and again over a long period of time

④ we must not forget to make students memorize model sentences from the textbook

⑤ we need to let students remember new words and grammar structures on the day they have just learned them

問4 The words we use when defining a goal for a lesson or unit are extremely important. What do you want to achieve? What should the students be able to do by the time they're finished with the lesson? It's important to clearly define this goal using carefully selected words. A goal needs to be (　　). By doing this, we can more easily evaluate the students' performance and make changes to future lessons.

① rough so students can easily understand what will happen in the lesson

② specific, measurable, and designed so that all students in the class can realistically achieve it

③ written on the blackboard at the beginning of every lesson with a lot of explanation

④ vague enough so that all students feel like they can achieve it in the lesson

⑤ written in English so students prepare themselves mentally for studying English

問5 Recently, students in Japan have started studying English in elementary school. The connection between English education in elementary school and junior high school is important. One thing junior high school teachers can do is (　　). If junior high school English teachers do so, students can realize that they're already familiar with the topic and can gain confidence in their ability to learn.

① use new materials students haven't seen before when introducing connected points in the classroom

② use materials from elementary school only when teaching difficult grammar points for students to understand

③ use materials from elementary school when introducing new points in the classroom

④ reteach all expressions students learned in elementary school

⑤ scold students for not remembering what they have learned in elementary school

(☆☆☆☆◎◎◎◎)

【9】次の英文を読んで，あとの問に答えなさい。

There is a difference in emphasis between studying to acquire knowledge and studying to acquire the ability to use knowledge and to do things. Traditionally, high schools in Japan have greatly focused upon the former, but nowadays, under the buzz words "active learning," they are redesigning classes and curriculums in which students can learn proactively, interactively, and more thoroughly. This does not minimize the place of knowledge itself — which is in fact subordinate to the ability to use knowledge, but an indispensable subordinate. Intelligent thoughts and actions are always based on (A) knowledge.

One of the most valuable abilities you can develop is the ability to study. And in this case, to study is not something you do the night before the exam. Rather, you have to learn how to study so you can independently (B) and think it through to a successful solution. Mastering a method of doing something is also an accomplishment that can only be achieved through genuine study. Learning to study effectively is far more important than merely acquiring a particular body of information. In most fields, information may quickly become out of date, whereas analyzing a problem, gathering the necessary information, and interpreting that information are skills that will not tarnish quite so quickly. Knowing how to study means knowing how to think, observe, organize, and analyze information.

Learning to study means that you are (　C　).

問1　(　A　)に入る最も適切なものを選びなさい。

①　vague　②　little　③　superficial　④　sound
⑤　a little

問2　(　B　)に入る最も適切なものを選びなさい。

①　pass the exam　②　approach a novel problem
③　choose the choice　④　tackle the test
⑤　avoid any trouble

問3　(　C　)に入る最も適切なものを選びなさい。

①　having a hard time　②　preparing for the exam
③　learning to think and to live　④　doing research on the exam
⑤　being promoted to a professor

(☆☆☆☆◎◎◎◎)

【10】次の英文を読んで，あとの問に答えなさい。

Our planet is revolving around the sun. The revolution and the rotation of the earth and its satellite have a tremendous effect on the surface of the earth; the revolution together with the inclination of the axis makes seasons in many parts of our planet, and the rotation makes day and night. They also affect the atmosphere of the earth. One of the greatest effects of the atmosphere is its vast "automatic air-conditioning system." Our planet is heated strongly at lower latitudes, feebly at higher latitudes, and moisture is generated mostly in the great oceans. The atmosphere distributes this heat and moisture and as a result, large areas of the land's surface will become habitable environments. However, this automatic air-conditioning system of our planet is (　A　). In fact, it doesn't work in polar regions, in desert areas, and on mountain summits where you would never feel comfortable. Still, as a whole, the atmosphere does work as automatic air-conditioning system because it succeeds in making most of the earth's lands habitable.

There are two main functions of the air-conditioning system: one is the regulation of air temperature and the other is that of humidity. Together with these functions, the atmosphere's ability to provide precipitation on a regular basis contributes to the creation of weather and climate patterns. Weather is the changes at a certain period of time in temperature, humidity, pressure, cloudiness, and rainfall, while climate is the change of weather conditions over a period of years. When you focus on climate, the ア<u>variability</u> of temperature and rainfall with the seasons is very important.

Solar energy is quite strong and influential in creating and affecting the kinetic energy of the atmosphere. If it were not for the atmosphere, the sun would directly heat the surface of the earth, and all the energy that reaches it from the sun would be immediately radiated back into space from its heated surface. Like the moon, the temperature during the day and at night would become significantly different. An atmosphere effectively keeps these temperature extremes stable. Our atmosphere plays an important role as an efficient system, which allows the energy of sunlight in freely but at the same time (　B　) its escape.

問1　(　A　)に入る最も適切なものを選びなさい。

① absolutely perfect
② far from perfect
③ cannot be helped
④ can be appreciated
⑤ by no means inefficient

問2　下線部アの意味として最も適切なものを選びなさい。

① a category of things distinguished from some common quality
② something a little different from others of the same type
③ something unlikely to alter
④ the state of being susceptible to attack

⑤　the quality of being subject to change

問3　(　B　)に入る最も適切なものを選びなさい。

①　hinders　②　finds　③　reinforces　④　admires

⑤　activates

問4　本文の内容に合致しないものを一つ選びなさい。

①　The atmosphere can make hot places less hot and vice versa.

②　The atmosphere provides us with habitable regions.

③　Weather and climate exist because of the performance of the atmosphere.

④　Climate is defined as long-term weather patterns.

⑤　Because of the atmosphere, it gets hot during the day, and cold at night.

(☆☆☆◎◎◎◎)

【11】次の英文を読んで，あとの問に答えなさい。

What is a "good friend?" It seems that although many will cry with you, few can sincerely (　ア　) with you. If you were tremendously sad, many of your friends would probably feel sympathy for you or shed tears with you. But the deeper your sorrow is, the less your mind would be eased, for the greater sorrow they show, the more miserable you would feel. You would say to yourself, "I am unhappy, as many of my friends feel sorry for me." Therefore, イ<u>in my opinion</u>, sympathy is not a good reaction of a good friend. A good friend should be one who can enjoy your success without envy; one who can say, "That was wonderful! You can do it again, ever better if you want!" — and mean it. Nothing taxes a friendship more than the prosperity of one and not the other. Even the closest of friendships often cannot withstand such strain and collapse. Small wonder many minor friendships go down the drain for the same reason.

(A) What makes a friendship last? It seems that most good friends usually have similar tastes. (B) There also usually seems to exist a parallelism of personality traits — especially in the fundamental values of life such as honesty, sincerity, loyalty, and dependability. More often than not, birds of a feather do fly together. I don't think it matters at all whether one prefers soccer or science to another's baseball or literature. (C) With not many people on this earth will you find this much in common. When you find one, hang on to him, for a good friend found is a rare treasure. (D)

Initiating or maintaining a good friendship involves reaching out, time, thoughtfulness and care, a phone call at least once a month, a lunch every two months or so. Do not allow too much time to pass by without contact. (E) Good friendships need tending. Just as a farmer's fence gets checked and repaired regularly to prevent his cattle from wandering away, so too must the bonds of friendship be checked and any snags repaired to avert a good friend — through (ウ) — from wandering off.

問1 (ア)に入る最も適切なものを番号で答えなさい。

① get angry　② lament　③ adore　④ rejoice

⑤ relieve

問2 下線部イについて，筆者が考えるgood friendはどのような言動をとるか。最も適切なものを番号で答えなさい。

① stand by you when you are weary and feeling small

② cheer you up when you have enough confidence

③ show you his or her feelings straightforwardly without secrets

④ be pleased with your victory as if it were his or her victory

⑤ make the most of the privilege of your friendship to succeed

問3 次の一文を本文中の(A)～(E)のいずれかに挿入する場合，最も適切な箇所を記号で答えなさい。

They generally like and dislike many of the same things.

問4 (ウ)に入る最も適切なものを番号で答えなさい。

① neglect　② negotiation　③ correction　④ affection

⑤ collaboration

(☆☆☆◎◎◎◎)

【中学校】

【1】「評価規準の作成，評価方法等の工夫改善のための参考資料(中学校外国語)」(平成23年11月国立教育政策研究所)において，「第2編　評価規準に盛り込むべき事項等」「第2　内容のまとまりごとの評価規準に盛り込むべき事項及び評価規準の設定例」が示されている。

次の①～⑥の評価規準は，どの観点において設定されているものか，下のア～エからそれぞれ一つずつ選び，記号で答えなさい。

① 間違うことを恐れず積極的に自分の考えなどを話している。

② 話されている内容から話し手の意向を理解することができる。

③ 適切な声量や明瞭さで音読することができる。

④ 基本的なイントネーションの違いを理解している。

⑤ 場面や状況にふさわしい表現を用いて話すことができる。

⑥ 文字や符号を使い分ける知識を身に付けている。

ア　コミュニケーションへの関心・意欲・態度

イ　外国語表現の能力

ウ　外国語理解の能力

エ　言語や文化についての知識・理解

(☆☆☆☆◎◎◎◎)

【2】「中学校学習指導要領」(平成20年告示)「第2章　各教科」「第9節　外国語」「第2　各言語の目標及び内容等」「英語」「2　内容」について，次の各問に答えなさい。

問1　次の文は，「(2)　言語活動の取扱い」の一部である。次の①及び②に当てはまる語句を書きなさい。

> イ　生徒の学習段階を考慮して各学年の指導に当たっては，次のような点に配慮するものとする。
>
> (ア)　第1学年における言語活動
>
> 小学校における外国語活動を通じて(　①　)面を中心としたコミュニケーションに対する積極的な態度などの一定の

素地が育成されることを踏まえ，身近な言語の使用場面や言語の働きに配慮した言語活動を行わせること。その際，自分の気持ちや身の回りの出来事などの中から(　②　)表現を用いてコミュニケーションを図れるような話題を取り上げること。

問2　次の文は，「(4)　言語材料の取扱い」の一部である。次の③～⑥に当てはまる語句を書きなさい。

ア　発音と(　③　)とを関連付けて指導すること。
イ　文法については，コミュニケーションを(　④　)ものであることを踏まえ，言語活動と効果的に関連付けて指導すること。
ウ　文法事項の取扱いについては，用語や用法の区別などの指導が中心とならないよう配慮し，実際に(　⑤　)できるように指導すること。また，語順や修飾関係などにおける日本語との違いに留意して指導すること。
エ　英語の特質を理解させるために，関連のある文法事項は(　⑥　)をもって整理するなど，効果的な指導ができるよう工夫すること。

(☆☆☆☆◎◎◎◎)

【3】「中学校学習指導要領解説　外国語編」(平成20年文部科学省)「第2章　外国語科の目標及び内容」「第2節　英語」「2　内容」「(1)　言語活動」について，次の各問に答えなさい。

問1　次の文は，「ア　聞くこと」の指導事項の一つである。下線部の例として，学習指導要領解説には，Do you have a pen? という問い掛けに対して，YesやNoを使って答えることの他に，どのようなことが示されているか説明しなさい。

(ウ)　質問や依頼などを聞いて<u>適切に応じること</u>。

問2　次の文は，「ウ　読むこと」の指導事項の一つである「(オ)　話の内容や書き手の意見などに対して感想を述べたり賛否やその理由を示したりなどすることができるよう，書かれた内容や考え方などをとらえること。」の解説の一部である。次の①～④に当てはまる語句を書きなさい。ただし，同じ番号には同じ語句が入るものとする。

> 外国語を用いたコミュニケーション能力を身に付けられるよう，4技能を(　①　)的に育成していくためには，「読むこと」の活動であっても，単に(　②　)等を得ることにとどまるのではなく，「読むこと」を通して得た(　②　)等について，自らの体験や考えなどに照らして「話すこと」や「書くこと」と結び付けることが大切である。「読むこと」について，そうした活動につながる活動とするためには，単に内容を理解するだけでなく，読み手として(　③　)的に考えたり，判断したりしながら理解していくことが必要となる。
>
> 「感想を述べたり賛否やその理由を示したりなどする」とは，学習段階に応じて，既習の表現を用いて，読み手としての感想や意見，賛否及びその理由を表現させることであり，話の内容や書き手の意見などを適切に理解することが前提となる。このように，(　④　)をもって読んだり，読んだ後に感想等を表現し合ったりする活動を計画的・系統的に行わせることが大切である。

(☆☆☆☆◎◎◎◎)

【高等学校】

【1】次の文は，「高等学校学習指導要領解説　外国語編・英語編」(平成22年文部科学省)「第1部　外国語編」「第3章　英語に関する各科目に

共通する内容等」の一部である。これを読んで，以下の問に答えなさい。

> 言語活動を行うに当たっては，例えば，次に示すような言語の使用場面や言語の働きの中から，各科目の目標を達成するのにふさわしいものを適宜取り上げ，(　①　)的に組み合わせて活用する。
>
> (中略)
>
> また，言語の働きについては，
>
> a　コミュニケーションを円滑にする
>
> b　気持ちを伝える
>
> c　情報を伝える
>
> d　考えや意図を伝える
>
> e　相手の行動を(　②　)
>
> の五つを設定し，それぞれに具体例を示している。

問1　文中の①及び②に当てはまる語句を書きなさい。

問2　学習指導要領解説には，「a　コミュニケーションを円滑にする」について，例が六つあげられている。そのうちの三つを書きなさい。

(☆☆☆☆☆◎◎◎◎)

【2】次の各問に答えなさい。

問1　次の文は，「高等学校学習指導要領解説　外国語編・英語編」(平成22年文部科学省)「第1部　外国語編」「第3章　英語に関する各科目に共通する内容等」の一部である，文中の①～⑤に当てはまる語句を書きなさい。ただし，同じ番号には同じ語句が入るものとする。

> 英語に関する各科目については，その(　①　)にかんがみ，生徒が英語に触れる機会を充実するとともに，授業を実際のコミュニケーションの場面とするため，授業は英語で行うことを基本とする。その際，生徒の(　②　)の程度に応じた英語を用いるよう十分配慮するものとする。

(中略)

「生徒の(　②　)の程度に応じた英語」で授業を行うためには，(　③　)の選択，発話の速さなどについて，十分配慮することが必要である。特に，生徒の英語によるコミュニケーション能力に懸念がある場合は，教師は，生徒の理解の状況を把握するように努めながら，簡単な英語を用いてゆっくり話すこと等に十分配慮することとなる。

(中略)

なお，音声で行うコミュニケーションと文字を用いて行うコミュニケーションでは，指導の重点も変わりうる。音声で行うコミュニケーションにおいては，限られた時間の中で，意味の伝達を行うことが重要であり，生徒が，(　④　)を大切にして発話したり会話したりするよう指導する必要がある。このため，教師は，生徒がコミュニケーションを積極的に行おうとする態度を損なわないよう配慮しつつ，意味が伝わらないおそれがあるものは正しく言い換えるといった指導を行うことが考えられる。一方，文字で行うコミュニケーションでは，正確さや(　⑤　)が一層重要となる。

問2　次の文は，「高等学校学習指導要領」(平成21年3月告示)「第2章　各学科に共通する各教科」「第8節　外国語」「第2款　各科目」に示されている外国語の各科目の目標を英訳したものである。文中のA～Eに当てはまる語をあとの語群から選び，記号で答えなさい。

English Communication Ⅰ

To develop students' basic abilities such as (　A　) understanding and (　B　) conveying information, ideas, etc., while fostering a positive attitude toward communication through the English language.

English Expression Ⅰ

To develop students' abilities to evaluate facts, opinions, etc.

from multiple (C) and communicate through (D) and a range of expression, while fostering a positive attitude toward communication through the English language.

English Conversation

To develop students' abilities to hold conversations on (E) topics, while fostering a positive attitude toward communication through the English language.

《語群》

ア	comprehensively	イ	international	ウ	everyday
エ	accurately	オ	objectively	カ	social
キ	methods	ク	observation	ケ	appropriately
コ	perspectives	サ	activities	シ	reasoning

(☆☆☆☆☆◎◎◎◎)

【3】「グローバル化に対応した英語教育改革実施計画」(平成25年12月文部科学省)について，以下の問に答えなさい。

問1 「1. グローバル化に対応した新たな英語教育の在り方」には，高等学校ではどのような能力を養うと示されているか。次の文の空欄に当てはまる語句をそれぞれ書きなさい。

( )について( )を理解できる，英語話者とある程度流暢に( )ができる能力を養う

問2 「2. 新たな英語教育の在り方実現のための体制整備」には，「小・中・高の各段階を通じて英語教育を充実し，生徒の英語力を向上」とある。高校卒業段階でどの程度以上の英語力をつけさせると示されているか。英検及びTOEFL iBTそれぞれについて書きなさい。

(☆☆☆☆☆◎◎◎◎)

福 岡 市

【中学校】

【1】Please complete the following English sentences by choosing the most appropriate word or phrase to replace the blanks.

問1　He had spent all his money (　　) the time his mother's birthday came.

①　till　　②　by　　③　during　　④　until　　⑤　since

問2　At the end of the workday on Thursday, we (　　) overtime four days in a row.

①　will have been working　　②　would have been working

③　have been working　　④　are working

⑤　will be working

問3　We were taught that Revolutionary War (　　) in 1783.

①　was ending　　②　had ended　　③　ends

④　has ended　　⑤　ended

問4　I thought that she would not attend the conference, as she (　　) the previous day.

①　is sick　　②　had been sick　　③　was sick

④　would be sick　　⑤　would have been sick

問5　Even though (　　), I still don't trust him.

①　he came to make up with me　　②　he'll come to talk to me

③　he has dinner with me　　④　he went library to study with me

⑤　he came to make friends with me

(☆☆☆◎◎◎◎)

【2】次の各問の日本文の意味を表す英文を作るために，(　　)内のA～Eの語句を正しく並べかえるとき，2番目と4番目にくる最も適切な組合せを選びなさい。ただし，組合せの左側を2番目，右側を4番目とする。

問1　明日の百より今日の五十

A bird in the hand is ($_{A}$<u>bush</u> $_{B}$<u>the</u> $_{C}$<u>two</u> $_{D}$<u>worth</u> $_{E}$<u>in</u>).

① C－E　② E－D　③ C－B　④ A－B　⑤ D－C

問2　3つの三角形は底辺を共有し，その底辺の長さは旗の全長の3分の1に当たる。

Three triangles share a common base, ($_A$of $_B$is $_C$the $_D$which $_E$length) one-third of the full length of the flag.

① E－A　② B－E　③ B－C　④ D－E　⑤ E－D

問3　わが社は銀行からの融資を取りつけることでどうにかやっていくことができた。

Our company managed to ($_A$water $_B$above $_C$its $_D$keep $_E$head) by securing a bank loan.

① A－C　② E－C　③ C－B　④ B－C　⑤ B－D

問4　その劇は最初から最後まで夢中になってみていた。

The play had ($_A$my seat $_B$the edge $_C$of $_D$me $_E$on) from start to finish.

① C－B　② E－C　③ E－D　④ B－C　⑤ B－A

(☆☆☆☆◎◎◎◎)

【3】次の各問のA～Eの英文を二人の会話として意味がつながるように並べかえるとき，2番目と4番目にくる最も適切な組合せを選びなさい。ただし，組合せの左側を2番目，右側を4番目とする。

問1　A：Yes, of course.

B：Excuse me. Is this Mr. Taylor's office?

C：I am sorry, but he's in another meeting at the moment, Mr. Hawkins. Could you wait a few minutes?

D：Yes, I'm Chris Hawkins. I have an appointment to see Mr. Taylor.

E：Yes, it is. Can I help you?

① B－A　② E－B　③ E－C　④ B－C　⑤ B－D

問2　A：Let me check that I got that right.

B：I want to get to the ball park. Do you know how to get there?

C：OK. Thanks for your help.

D：Of course. Just hop on that train and go five stops. It's right there.

E ：You're right, but go just five stops instead of four.

① A－C　② D－E　③ A－E　④ D－A　⑤ D－B

(☆☆☆◎◎◎◎)

【4】次の各問の英文を読み，文脈から考えて文中の(　　)に入る最も適切なものを選びなさい。

Integrated curriculum can be defined in a variety of ways. For our purposes, we focus on linking language with other curricular areas, on linking the various language skills, on linking the academic with the social and emotional aspects of students' lives, on linking different ways of learning, and on linking classroom activities to the wider world. Sometimes these links are small connections within a single lesson, and at other times, the links involve larger concepts that unify a course of study. Many opportunities to make connections between various parts of the curriculum present themselves, and (1).

Many of the ideas advocated in this book are supported by the findings of recent research on how the brain works. Integrated Curriculum is one example. Brain research tells us that our minds are constantly looking for connections (Jensen, 2008). Integrated Curriculum guides students to find and create the many connections that exist to be explored.

A key to link between Curricular Integration in education generally, and the CLT paradigm shift in second language education, lies in the concept of going from whole to part rather than from part to whole. For instance, under the traditional education model, students study a given historical period, e.g., the 19th century, in an atomistic way. In history class, they study key events, people and movements, In science class, in another year or semester, they discuss notable scientific discoveries from the 19th century. In first or second language class, in yet another year or semester, they read literature from the period. Thus, (2).

－Essentials for Successful English Language Teaching. Thomas S. C.

Farrell & George M. Jacobs

*CLT Communicative Language Teaching　コミュニカティヴ教授法

問1　(　1　)

① it is really teachers' faults if the learners blow or lose these opportunities

② it is the responsibility of teachers and administrators to recognize and reinforce these opportunities

③ it is impossible for every teacher or administrator to restrict and give these opportunities

④ it is the learners' autonomy in the classroom to be able to take these opportunities

⑤ it is the very integration of curriculum that teachers and administrators should have these opportunities

問2　(　2　)

① teachers create great opportunities for students to learn context-free facts

② students have wonderful opportunities to learn the every detail in each subject area

③ students have fun to make some scientific hypotheses in science class may be more important for them

④ students miss valuable opportunities for understanding context

⑤ teachers give a good bottom-up opportunities to learn subject matters

We have already argued that skillful language usage is an indispensable inextricable part of what it means to be a successful writer. Most readers would no doubt agree with this assertion, but it is not the same as claiming that explicit language instruction is valuable and appropriate within the context of a writing course. Indeed, experts have argued and provided evidence that, at least sometimes, it is not (Hartwell, 1985); Krashen, 1982, 1984). Over the past several decades, L1 researchers have consistently challenged the practice of teaching grammar and punctuation rules in composition courses. The basic argument is that (1). What is needed, rather, are opportunities to put them into practice: "Language cannot be learned in isolation but only by manipulating it in meaningful contexts" (Frodesen & Holten, 2003, p. 143).

L2 scholars and teachers have also questioned the efficacy of grammar instruction, noting that "the return on grammar instruction is often disappointing. Teachers find that even when a grammatical feature has been covered and practiced, students may not use it accurately in their own writing" (Frodesen & Holten, 2003, p. 142). Nonetheless, it has also been noted that L2 writers do not have the same "felt sense" of correctness nor intuitive grasp of the grammatical rules of English, so formal instruction may be more important for them (Ferris, 1999b; Frodesen & Holten, 2003; Reid, 1998a).

It should be evident from the above discussion that overgeneralized and haphazard language instruction will not help student writers. Unfortunately, for the reasons discussed in the first part of this chapter, much grammar teaching provided by writing teachers is ineffective. In a recent longitudinal study of L2 university freshmen in a developmental writing course for multilingual students, the participants described having received extensive grammar instruction in their secondary English courses but also said (2) and often weren't sure how to apply it to their own writing (Ferris et al., 2013).

—Teaching L2 Composition (Third Edition). Dana R. Ferris & John S. Hedgcock

問3 (1)

① student writers already have an intuitive sense of rules of their language

② students have to learn the grammatical rules of their language in their everyday life

③ the rules of their own language are very difficult to learn for even L1 speakers

④ students don't have to learn the rules of their language because of its difficulty

⑤ the rules and principles of their language are universally innate

問4 (2)

① it is very important for them to use language in their school life

② grammar is indispensable to write a composition in L2

③ they don't understand it or didn't remember much of it

④ university writing courses are effective for L2 English learners

⑤ they use their own grammatical knowledge to write in L2

(☆☆☆☆◎◎◎◎◎)

【5】Read this passage and answer the questions below.

Since prehistoric times, humans have made use of plants, roots, animals and minerals as medicine. Old books and excavated articles have shown that our ancestors had a surprisingly wide range of pharmacological knowledge.

Natural medicines have played a central role in medicine since ancient times, but (A). On the Greek island Lemnos in the Aegean Sea, (B). It is surprising that (C) by carving the place they were manufactured as early as 2500 years ago.

Modern pharmacology began to develop in the latter half of the eighteenth century. (D)Breakthrough remedies and antibiotics were discovered, and many diseases which had distressed people were eradicated. People may have forgotten that the word medicine used to mean "magic spell." Now it seems to mean nothing but medication.

In this way, medicine is filled with our ancestors' wisdom and devotion. However, many medicines have side effects. Therefore, in order to gain the maximum efficacy and avoid the side effects of a particular medicine, when and how to take it are very important considerations.

When to take a medicine is directed in the prescription and is based on meals; for example before or after meals. That is because we can remember when to take medicine more easily when it is based on meals. So when exactly does "before meals" refer to? It means 30 minutes before a meal. Similarly, "after meals" means 30 minutes after a meal.

People often misunderstand what the word "*shokkan*" means. "*shokkan*" means not during a meal but rather between meals. One is supposed to take their medicine between two hours after a meal and two hours before their next meal. If you take medicine during a meal, its efficacy weakens because what you have eaten influences the amount and speed of absorption of the medicine.

By the way, when you take medicine, what do you drink with it? Do you ever take it with juice, tea or coffee? Naturally it is best to take medicine with water. Be sure to never take it with alcohol. If you drink alcohol before or after taking medicine, (　E　) because the effect of the medicine becomes too strong. Doctors recommend you avoid even such things as fish and vegetables pickled in sake lees as well as sweets containing alcohol.

—Living Well, Eating Well. John Norman, Hiroshi Ishibashi, Sumiko Akiyoshi & Fujiko Motoyama

問1　Choose the most appropriate combination of sentences (a), (b) and (c) to fill in the blanks (　A　), (　B　) and (　C　).

(a)　medicinal tablets were made of clay with a trademark carved on them in about 500 B.C

(b)　some people knew that soil contains elements that are good for one's health

(c)　some people knew how to enhance the commercial value of medicines

	A	B	C
①	(a)	(b)	(c)
②	(b)	(c)	(a)
③	(b)	(a)	(c)
④	(c)	(a)	(b)
⑤	(c)	(b)	(a)

問2 Choose the most accurate statement for the underlined part (D).

① conservative ② epoch-making ③ far-reaching

④ independent ⑤ far-flung

問3 Fill in the blank (E) with the most appropriate phrase.

① doctors can be very happy

② you can sleep very well

③ the medicine can work well

④ it can be dangerous

⑤ you can be healthier

問4 Choose the most accurate statement according to the passage.

① Few ancestors knew that plants, roots and animals were so useful for eating that they had them every day.

② Many people always remember that medicine has a magical spelling because serious diseases were wiped out.

③ Medicine is full of our ancestors' efforts and knowledge and has been developed by their sacrificial acts.

④ In order to avoid the side effects of medicine, we need to carefully handle the prescription before taking it.

⑤ You can take medicine with special foods such as fish and vegetables pickled in sake lees because it's healthy.

(☆☆☆☆◎◎◎◎)

【6】Read this passage and answer the questions below.

In *CBLT, teachers often say that their main concern is with making sure students learn the academic content. They recognize the importance of language learning but they often think that, given enough time and comprehensible input, students will gradually develop their knowledge of and ability to use the new language. As we have seen, they may also assume that the ability to use language for social interaction is evidence that students have reached age-appropriate L2 (A)proficiency. Evidence from research in a variety of language learning settings, including a great variety of CBLT contexts, shows that students benefit from instructional guidance that focuses their attention on language itself.

One of the questions that is often asked about instruction that focuses on language is whether it should be provided in separate lessons or integrated into content-based lessons (Spada & Lightbown, 2008). We will (　B　) that the answer to that question is that both kinds of instruction are important for CBLT students, with the added observation that when language-focused instruction is separated from content classes, it should include focus on language features — vocabulary, grammar, style — that students will need while doing their academic work. Furthermore, during content-based lessons, the language features that were in focus in the language-focused instruction should be highlighted, and feedback on students' use of these features should be offered.

When learners produce spoken or written language in a CBLT context, a teacher or peer may respond by continuing the conversation or reacting to the ideas that have been expressed. (　C　), in the sense that the learner may see these responses as confirmation that what they said was understood. Alternatively, the interlocutor or reader might ask for clarification or show in some other way that the meaning was unclear or inappropriate. A peer would probably ask for clarification. A teacher might request clarification or tell the learner more explicitly that something is incorrect. Either of these responses would be a kind of corrective feedback to the learner, indicating that something in the speech or written text did not quite accomplish its intended goals.

Teachers often express a reluctance to interrupt students to give feedback on a language error during a classroom activity where the focus is on academic content. They feel more comfortable offering feedback that focuses on what students are trying to communicate. In the CBLT context, this has been interpreted to mean, for example, that feedback on language form should be offered during a separate language-focused class, not during mathematics or science lessons. If they do provide feedback during content-focused lessons, they tend to provide implicit feedback, often in the form of a recast (a kind of 'echo' that retains the learner's meaning but in a correct form) rather than by offering a more explicit response to the *form* as opposed to the *content* of what students are saying.

－Focus on Content-Based Language Teaching. Patsy M. Lightbown

*CBLT Content-Based Language Teaching　内容重視言語学習

問1　Choose the most appropriate definition for the underlined part (A).

① willingness to communicate in every situation

② acquisition which occurs around puberty

③ input which can be turned into intake

④ competence or skills in doing or using something

⑤ interlanguage produced during the course of learning

問2　Fill in the blank (　B　) with the most appropriate word.

① suggest　② see　③ indicate　④ interpret

⑤ imagine

問3　Fill in the blank (　C　) with the most appropriate phrase.

① This could be seen as implicit feedback

② This could be seen as explicit feedback

③ This could be seen as peer feedback

④ This could be seen as positive feedback

⑤ This could be seen as negative feedback

問4　What is the suggestion given by the writer, which could be helpful for the teachers? Choose the most appropriate statement below.

① It relies heavily on teachers whether language itself should be taught in separate lessons or content-based lessons.

② Students can learn vocabulary and grammar while they learn the academic content during mathematics or science lessons.

③ Even in academic content-based lessons, teacher are willing to give feedback when the students make errors.

④ Peer feedback is not always correct so that only teachers should let the students notice their own errors autonomously.

⑤ When you give feedback to the linguistic form, you should use the form of a recast, in which teachers repeat the erroneous part in a correct form.

(☆☆☆☆☆◎◎◎◎◎)

【7】Read this passage and answer the questions below.

Whether we like it or not, the world we live in has changed a great deal in the last hundred years, and it is likely to change even more in the next hundred. Some people would like to stop these changes and (　A　) what they see as a purer and simpler age. But as history shows, the past was not that wonderful. It was not so bad for a privileged minority, though even they had to do without modern medicine, and childbirth was highly risky for women. But for the vast majority of the population, life was nasty and short.

Anyway, even if one wanted to, one couldn't put the clock back to an earlier age. Knowledge and techniques can't just be forgotten. (　B　) Even if all government money for research were cut off, the force of competition would still bring about advances in technology. Moreover, one cannot stop inquiring minds from thinking about basic science, whether or not they were paid for it.

If we accept that we cannot prevent science and technology from changing our world, we can at least try to ensure that the changes they make are in the right directions. In a democratic society, this means that the public needs to have a basic understanding of science, so that it can make informed decisions and not leave them in the hands of experts. (C), the public has a rather ambivalent attitude toward science. It has come to expect the steady increase in the standard of living that new developments in science and technology have brought to continue, but it also distrusts science because it doesn't understand it. This distrust is evident in the cartoon figure of the mad scientist working in his laboratory to produce a Frankenstein. But the public also has a great interest in science, as is shown by the large audiences for science fiction.

What can be done to harness this interest and give the public the scientific background it needs to make informed decisions on subjects like acid rain, the greenhouse effect, nuclear weapons, and genetic engineering? Clearly, the basis must lie in what is taught in schools. But in schools science is often presented in a day and uniteresting manner. Children must learn it by rote to pass examinations, and they don't see relevance to the world around them. Moreover, science is often taught in terms of equations. Although equations are a concise and accurate way of describing mathematical ideas, they frighten most people.

Scientists and engineers tend to express their ideas in the form of equations because they need to know the precise value of quantities. But for the rest of us, a qualitative grasp of scientific concepts is sufficient, and this can be conveyed by words and diagrams, without the use of equations.

—NEWS WEEK

問1 Fill in the blank (A) with the most appropriate word.

① look back to ② give rise to ③ set up to

④ go back to ⑤ live up to

問2 Fill in the blank (B) with the most appropriate sentence below.

① Everyone can prevent further advances in the future.

② Nor can one prevent further advances in the future.

③ Nor anyone can prevent further advances in the future.

④ No one cannot prevent further advances in the future.

⑤　Nor one can prevent further advances in the future.

問3　Fill in the blank (　C　) with the most appropriate words.

①　For the meantime　　②　In the meanwhile　　③　At the moment

④　For the moment　　⑤　To the moment

問4　What is the suggestion given by the writer? Choose the most appropriate statement below.

①　We have to pay much attention to the changes happened over the past hundred years.

②　We have a difficult way of seeing advances in science and technology at the same time.

③　We need to make quick decisions to solve the problems such as acid rain, the greenhouse effect, nuclear weapons, and genetic engineering.

④　We need to learn and understand scientific evidence in order to have a better future lives.

⑤　We have to learn as many equations by heart as possible to pass the entrance examinations.

(☆☆☆☆◎◎◎◎◎)

【8】次の文は，「評価規準の作成，評価方法等の工夫改善のための参考資料(中学校　外国語)」(平成23年11月国立教育政策研究所教育課程研究センター)において，「第2編　評価規準に盛り込むべき事項等」「第2　内容のまとまりごとの評価規準に盛り込むべき事項及び評価規準の設定例」が示されている。

次のA～Eの評価規準は，どの観点において設定されるものか，あとのア～エからそれぞれ一つずつ選び，正しい組合せをあとの［　　］の①～⑤から一つ選びなさい。

A　基本的な強勢やイントネーションなどの違いを理解している。

B　伝言や手紙などを読んで，その内容にあわせて適切に応じることができる。

C　うまく書けないところがあっても知っている語句や表現を用いて

書き続けている。

D　話を続けるために必要なつなぎ言葉や相づちをうつ表現などを知っている。

E　正しい強勢，イントネーション，区切りなどを用いて音読することができる。

ア　コミュニケーションへの関心・意欲・態度
イ　外国語表現の能力
ウ　外国語理解の能力
エ　言語や文化についての知識・理解

	A	B	C	D	E
①	イ	ウ	ア	エ	ア
②	ウ	ア	エ	ア	イ
③	イ	ア	ウ	イ	エ
④	エ	ウ	ア	エ	イ
⑤	エ	イ	ウ	ア	ア

(☆☆☆☆◎◎◎◎)

【9】問1　次の文は，中学校学習指導要領(平成20年3月告示　平成27年3月一部改正)「第2章　各教科」「第9節　外国語」「第2　各言語の目標及び内容等」の「英語　2　内容」の「(1)言語活動」の一部を抜粋したものである。文中の(　A　)～(　E　)に当てはまる語句の正しい組合せを，あとの[　　]の①～⑤から一つ選びなさい。ただし，同じ記号には同じ語句が入る。

英語を理解し，英語で表現できる実践的な運用能力を養うため，次の言語活動を3学年間を通して行わせる。
エ　書くこと
主として次の事項について指導する。
(ア)　文字や符号を(　A　)し，語と語の区切りなどに注意して正しく書くこと。

(イ)　語と語の(　B　)などに注意して正しく文を書くこと。
(ウ)　聞いたり読んだりしたことについてメモをとったり，感想，(　C　)やその理由を書いたりなどすること。
(エ)　身近な場面における出来事や体験したことなどについて，自分の考えや(　D　)などを書くこと。
(オ)　自分の考えや(　D　)などが読み手に正しく(　E　)ように，文と文の(　B　)などに注意して文章を書くこと。

	A	B	C	D	E
①	識別	つながり	賛否	計　画	理解してもらう
②	認識	連　　結	賛否	気持ち	理解される
③	識別	連　　結	意見	気持ち	伝　わ　る
④	認識	つながり	意見	計　画	伝　わ　る
⑤	識別	つながり	賛否	気持ち	伝　わ　る

問2　次の文は，中学校学習指導要領解説外国語編(平成20年　文部科学省)「第2章　外国語の目標及び内容等」の「第2節　英語」「2 内容」「(3)言語材料」の一部を抜粋したものである。文中の(　A　)～(　E　)に当てはまる語句の正しい組合せを，あとの［　］の①～⑤から一つ選びなさい。ただし，同じ記号には同じ語句が入る。

言語材料は，英語の目標の達成を図るためのものでなければならない。コミュニケーション能力を養うため，言語材料を一層(　A　)かつ適切に用いて，更に活発で多様な言語活動を行うようにする必要がある。言語材料は，「音声」，「文字及び符号」，「語，連語及び(　B　)」及び「文法事項」の四つから構成されている。そのうち今回は以下に示す事項について改善を行った。

(ア)　言語材料の改善事項

「語，連語及び(　B　)」については，指導する語の総数を(　C　)語程度とした。これは，より豊かな表現を可能にし，コミュニケーションを(　D　)にもより充実できるようにするためには語数の増加が必要と考えたことによるものである。また，語数の増加は，増加した語彙を活用しうる言語活動の充実と切り離して考えることはできないものであり，授業時数が各学年とも(　E　)時間から140時間に増加したことで，生徒に過度の負担を負わせることなく，言語活動の一層の充実を図ることが可能となった。

	A	B	C	D	E
①	柔軟的	熟語表現	1200	表現的	100
②	弾力的	慣用表現	1200	内容的	105
③	柔軟的	熟語表現	1300	表現的	105
④	柔軟的	慣用表現	1200	内容的	105
⑤	弾力的	慣用表現	1300	表現的	100

問3　次の文は，中学校学習指導要領解説外国語編(平成20年　文部科学省)「第2章　外国語の目標及び内容等」の「第2節　英語」「3 指導計画の作成と内容の取扱い」「(1)指導計画の作成上の配慮事項」の一部を抜粋したものである。文中の(　A　)～(　E　)に当てはまる語句の正しい組合せを，あとの□の①～⑤から一つ選びなさい。

(1)　指導計画の作成に当たっては，次の事項に配慮するものとする。

キ　生徒の実態や教材の内容などに応じて，コンピュータや情報通信ネットワーク，教育機器などを有効活用したり，ネイティブ・スピーカーなどの協力を得たりなどすること。

また，ペアワーク，グループワークなどの(　A　)を適宜工夫すること。

指導に当たり，(　B　)を効果的に使うことによって教材が具体化され，生徒にとって身近なものとしてとらえられるようになる。また，生徒の興味・関心を高め，自ら学習しようとする態度を育成することができると考えられる。こういった(　C　)をより一層高めることができるものとして，また，生徒が自分の学習の進度に合わせて活用できるものとして，コンピュータの様々なソフトウェアを活用することなども考えられる。

コンピュータや情報通信ネットワークを使うことによって，教材に関する資料や情報を入手したり，電子メールによって情報を英語で(　D　)したりすることもできる。このような活動を通して，生徒一人一人が(　E　)に世界とかかわっていこうとする態度を育成することもでき，教育機器は英語教育にとって大切な役目を果たすものと考えられる。

	A	B	C	D	E
①	学習形態	視聴覚機器	教育効果	発信	主体的
②	学習隊形	視聴覚教材	学習効果	発信	協働的
③	学習形態	視聴覚機器	教育効果	共有	協働的
④	学習隊形	視聴覚教材	教育効果	共有	協働的
⑤	学習形態	視聴覚教材	学習効果	発信	主体的

(☆☆☆☆◎◎◎◎)

【10】次の文は，「グローバル化に対応した英語教育改革実施計画」(平成25年12月文部科学省)の「1．グローバル化に対応した新たな英語教育の在り方」及び「2．新たな英語教育の在り方に実現のための体制整備」の一部について示したものである。以下の設問に答えなさい。

問1　以下は中学校における英語教育の在り方についてである。文中の(　ア　)～(　オ　)に当てはまる語句の正しい組合せを，あとの□の①～⑤から一つ選びなさい。ただし，同じ記号には同じ語句が入る。

○中学校
・身近な話題についての理解や簡単な(ア), 表現ができる能力を養う
・授業を英語で行うことを基本とする
(課題)
小学校における英語教育の(イ)に伴い, 中・高等学校における英語教育の目標・(ウ)も(イ)するため, 中学校において授業を基本的に英語で行うことや, 高等学校において発表, 討論, 交渉等の高度な言語活動を行うことが可能となるよう, 教員の(エ)・英語力を向上させることが急務(全英語科教員について, 必要な英語力(英検(オ), TOEFL iBT 80点程度等以上)を確保)。

	ア	イ	ウ	エ	オ
①	意見交換	高度化	教材	統率力	準1級
②	情報交換	特殊化	内容	統率力	準1級
③	情報交換	高度化	内容	指導力	準1級
④	情報交換	高度化	教材	指導力	1級
⑤	意見交換	特殊化	内容	指導力	1級

問2 以下は小学校における英語教育の在り方についてである。文中の(ア)～(オ)に当てはまる語句の正しい組合せを, あとの［　］の①～⑤から一つ選びなさい。ただし, 同じ記号には同じ語句が入る。

○小学校中学年：活動型
・コミュニケーション能力の素地を養う
・(ア)を中心に指導
○小学校高学年：教科型
(「(イ)授業」も活用)
・初歩的な英語の運用能力を養う
・英語指導力を備えた(ア)に加えて(ウ)の積極的活用

(課題)
小学校高学年における英語教育の教科化に伴う指導内容の高度化・指導時間増に対応する必要がある中，現状では不足する(　エ　)英語指導力を備えた(　ウ　)としても指導が可能な人材の確保が急務。
また，小学校中学年からの英語教育(活動型)の開始に伴い，中学年の(　ア　)も外国語活動の指導を行う必要が生じるため，研修をはじめとした(　オ　)の大幅な強化が不可欠。

	ア	イ	ウ	エ	オ
①	ALT等	インクルーシブ	専科教員	流暢な	指導体制
②	学級担任	モジュール	専科教員	高度な	協力体制
③	ALT等	モジュール	地域住民	流暢な	協力体制
④	学級担任	モジュール	専科教員	高度な	指導体制
⑤	学級担任	インクルーシブ	地域住民	流暢な	指導体制

(☆☆☆☆☆◎◎◎◎)

【高等学校】

【1】 Please complete the following English sentences by choosing the most appropriate word or replace the blanks.

問1 After years of working, I have some savings and want to go for my dream, but I don't know if (　　) in the university after 40.

① I am so young as to study　② I am young enough to study
③ I am too old to study　④ I am old enough to study
⑤ I am too young to study

問2 "It didn't matter so much what you did (　　) the lecture," Dr. Smith explains.

① for　② between　③ up to　④ during　⑤ while

問3 Bill said that he didn't like the party, and he (　　) to go home.

① wants　② wanted　③ has wanted
④ has been wanting　⑤ had wanted

問4 The problem is that it hasn't worked, and it's time we stopped

(　　) around the problem.

① dance　② dancing　③ being danced　④ to dance
⑤ to be danced

問5　HUMPER Inc. snacks are made (　　) a special blend of real cheese seasoning to give each bite the perfect pop.

① of　② with　③ into　④ out of　⑤ between

(☆☆☆◎◎◎◎)

【2】次の各問の日本文の意味を表す英文を作るために，(　　)内のA～Eの語句を正しく並べかえるとき，2番目と4番目にくる最も適切な組合せを選びなさい。ただし，組合せの左側を2番目，右側を4番目とする。

問1　このクラスには音楽の天才だと思われる子どもが一人いる。

There is a child in this class (${}_{A}$is ${}_{B}$a musical genius ${}_{C}$believe ${}_{D}$I ${}_{E}$who).

① C－D　② B－E　③ C－A　④ D－A　⑤ E－B

問2　この写真を見ると，おじのことを思わずにはいられない。

I(${}_{A}$see ${}_{B}$thinking ${}_{C}$without ${}_{D}$this picture ${}_{E}$never) of my uncle.

① A－C　② A－E　③ B－E　④ B－D　⑤ D－C

問3　あなたたちは「類は友を呼ぶ」ということわざを聞いたことがあるだろう。新しい研究論文によって，このことわざに関するもうひとつの例が見つかった。

You're probably heard the adage "(${}_{A}$together ${}_{B}$birds ${}_{C}$flock ${}_{D}$of ${}_{E}$a feather)." A new research paper has found another example of this maxim.

① B－A　② E－C　③ D－B　④ D－C　⑤ E－A

問4　そんなに利益は出ないだろうが，好機は逃さないに越したことはないと経営者たちは考えている。

Managers believe that there will not be much profit, and that it is beat to "(${}_{A}$hay ${}_{B}$make ${}_{C}$the sun ${}_{D}$while ${}_{E}$shines)".

① A－C　② A－D　③ B－C　④ D－E　⑤ E－B

(☆☆☆◎◎◎◎)

【3】次の各問のA～Eの英文を二人の会話として意味がつながるように並べかえるとき，2番目と4番目にくる最も適切な組合せを選びなさい。ただし，組合せの左側を2番目，右側を4番目とする。

問1　A: You don't know anyone who's looking for a roommate, do you?

B: Okay. Why don't you put an ad in the newspaper? Or, better yet, you could sign up at the housing office. They post notices on a big bulletin board, and there are always people looking for roommates.

C: Yeah. I could do that, but I just keep hoping I'll find out that one of my friends is looking for a roommate. I'd rather live with someone I know.

D: I do. Or rather, I did. But she's getting married in the fall, so I have to find somebody else.

E: Not really. But I thought you had a roommate.

① A－B　② A－E　③ D－C　④ E－B　⑤ E－C

問2　A: …I, …uh…I don't know. Is there much difference …in the price, I mean?

B: Excuse me. Do you work here?

C: Oh, well, um, I'm looking for a book for … for English 100.

D: Okay. Textbooks are in the back of the store. Did you want a new book or a used book?

E: Yes, I do. How can I help you?

① A－D　② A－C　③ C－B　④ E－B　⑤ E－D

(☆☆☆◎◎◎◎)

【4】次の各問の英文を読み，文脈から考えて文中の(　　)に入る最も適切なものを選びなさい。

問1　Every three years, half a million 15-year-olds in 69 countries take a two-hour test designed to gauge their ability to think. Unlike other exams, the PISA, as it is known, does not assess what teenagers have memorized. Instead, it asks them to solve problems they haven't seen before, to identify patterns that are not obvious and to make compelling written arguments. It tests the skills, in other words, (　　).

① the ability to calculate quickly

② the ability to memorize a lot of English idioms

③ the ability to imitate others completely

④ that machines have not yet mastered

⑤ that machines have already mastered

問2 *Active learning* is generally defined as any instructional method that engages students in the learning process. In short, active learning requires students to do meaningful learning activities and think about what they are doing. While this definition could include (　　), in practice active learning refers to activities that are introduced into the classroom. The core elements of active learning are student activity and engagement in the learning process. Active learning is often contrasted to the traditional lecture where students passively receive information from the instructor.

① work in small groups toward a common goal

② traditional activities such as homework

③ self-assessment of team functioning

④ problem-solving tasks that are introduced at the beginning of the instruction

⑤ interactions rather than learning as a solitary activity

問3 It is important for (　　) whose goals for L2 use do not include identification with native speakers of the language nor membership in its native speech communities. Indeed, adopting this goal may be considered "imperialistic" in many social and political settings, and in any case, is certainly unrealistic for most beginning learners beyond the stage of puberty. To be valid, criteria for assessing relative L2 achievement must take into account the needs, goals, and circumstances of second language learners.

① language learners to accept the fact that "native-like" production is neither intended nor desired by many teachers

② language learners to know the fact that "native-like" production is both intended and desired by many teachers

③ language teachers to accept the fact that "native-like" production is neither intended nor desired by many learners

④ language teachers to know the fact that "native-like" production is both intended and desired by many learners

⑤ language teachers to accept the fact that "nonnative-like" production is neither intended nor desired by many learners

問4 Today, receiving a wedding invitation for a Catholic bride and a Hindu groom for an intercultural or an interfaith wedding is not unusual, and stirs anticipation for a splendid affair! Couples from different faiths and cultures have the opportunity to bring tradition from both backgrounds to the wedding festivities.

( ). Did you know that in the Greek Orthodox, Hindu, and Jewish belief systems it is customary to break an item at the ceremony's end? Greek tradition is to drink from a wine glass and toss it! Jewish vows include the groom stepping on a glass, while Hindus crush a pot. Jewish tradition calls for marriage vows to be held under a chuppa while in Hindu culture, vows are held under a mandap — the symbolism represents the couple's first home.

① Create and encourage open communication with a single side of the family early in the engagement

② When you take a closer peek into wedding customs and belief systems, you'll discover surprising similarities

③ Few religious officiants are more than willing to conduct the ceremony jointly and provide creative ideas to honor both traditions

④ You need not discuss the planning process and select certain traditions from each culture

⑤ If you are planning the ceremony in a park, garden or on a lake or beach, special licensing will be needed

(☆☆☆☆◎◎◎◎)

【5】 Read this passage and answer the questions below.

On a routine visit to a doctor's surgery, you might expect to have your blood pressure and BMI measured, and be asked a few questions about diet, exercise and alcohol intake. One thing the doctor probably won't ask is "how do you sleep?"

If we're serious about preventive health, that is a serious oversight. Poor sleep is a major risk factor for obesity, diabetes, mood disorders and immune malfunction. Put simply, poor sleep can shorten your life. How to fix the problem?

Although there are habits and tricks to sleeping we can all adopt, everyone's needs are different. Why this should be so is not well understood.

Perhaps the biggest gap is a lack of research into women's sleep. Women typically report poorer quality and more disrupted sleep, and their risk of insomnia is 40 percent higher than men's. This gender difference is strongly associated with a greater risk of depression and a host of other illnesses. However, women and female animals are underrepresented in studies of sleep and its disorders, and the reason for sex differences in sleep behavior is unknown.

Then there are teenagers. Their hormonal turmoil has serious effects on their ability to switch off, but current wisdom leaves a lot to be desired. Parents might think they need to lay down the law on sleep, but research indicates that positive discussion between parents and teenagers is the best option.

At the other end of the age spectrum, older adults have a problem with sleeping pills. Paradoxically, (A). The conclusion for seniors? Sleep medication use does not appear to promote sleep health.

With the profusion of sleep monitoring tech now at our disposal, doctors have the chance to intervene in an individualised way. And, unlike being urged to eat five a day or drink less than 21 a week, being advised (　B　) is something we can all welcome.

問1　Fill in the blank (　A　) with the most appropriate sentence.

① taking them often makes illnesses better

② taking them often makes illnesses worse

③ taking them often makes sleep problems worse

④ taking them often makes sleep problems better

⑤ taking them often has nothing to do with sleep problems

問2　According to the passage, which statement is NOT true?

① Some teenagers have difficulty in resting because of hormonal problems.

② Doctors can intervene thanks to recent technology.

③ Poor sleep may cause physical disorders.

④ Parents should make rules about sleep for their children.

⑤ Women have more tendency for sleeplessness than men.

問3　According to the passage, which statement is true about sleep?

① Frequent long, distressing and vivid dreams often cause problems like insomnia.

② Sleep is linked to your health and longevity.

③ Nightmares can make it difficult to sleep and interfere with daytime functioning.

④ Poor sleep among the elderly may in part account for problems with memory.

⑤ A midafternoon nap of about 20 minutes can improve alertness and productivity.

問4　Fill in the blank (　B　) with the most appropriate phrase.

① how to spend a day in order to make sleep problems better

② how often sleeping pills we should take a day

③ how to get the right number of hours' sleep a night

④ why older adults have a problem with sleeping pills.

⑤ why women report poorer quality and more disrupted sleep

(☆☆☆☆◎◎◎◎◎)

【6】Read this passage and answer the questions below.

Teaching based on a linguistic content, whether this is specified in structural terms as a list of grammatical features or in notional/functional terms as in the weak version of communicative language teaching (CLT), has traditionally employed a methodological procedure consisting of present-practice-produce (PPP). That is, a language item is first presented to the learners by means of examples with or without explanation. This item is then practiced in a controlled manner using what we have called 'exercises'. Finally opportunities for using the item in free language production are provided. It is in this 'production' stage that tasks have been employed. Implicit in PPP is the idea that it is possible to lead learners from controlled to automatic use of new language features by means of text-manipulation exercises that structure language for the learner followed by text-creation tasks where learners structure language for themselves.

The view of language learning that underlies this approach to language teaching has been criticized on a number of grounds. PPP views language as a series of 'products' that can be acquired sequentially as 'accumulated entities'. However, second language acquisition (SLA) research has shown that learners do not acquire a language in this way. Rather they construct a series of systems, known as interlanguages, which are (A) grammaticized and restructured as learners incorporate new features. Furthermore, research on developmental sequences has shown that learners pass through a series of transitional stages in acquiring a specific grammatical feature such as negatives, often taking months or even years before they arrive at the target form of the rule. In other words, L2 acquisition is a 'process' that is incompatible with teaching seen as the presentation and practice of a series of 'products'.

There are practical problems with PPP as well. Clearly, the production stage calls for 'grammar tasks', i.e. tasks that will elicit the feature that is the target of the lesson. However, it is not easy to design tasks that require learners to use a targeted structure, as learners can always fall back on their strategic competence to circumvent it. (　B　).
However, this would encourage the learners to focus primarily on form with the result that the task then ceases to be a task as it has been defined in this chapter, and becomes instead an exercise.

However, despite these criticisms and problems and despite the doubts as to whether PPP can deliver what it promises, i.e. the ability to use the structures taught in real communication, it has proved highly durable. This is because it affords teachers procedures for maintaining control of the classroom, thus reinforcing their power over students and also because the procedures themselves are eminently trainable.

問1　Choose the most accurate statement about present-practice-produce (PPP).

① PPP aims to investigate which kind of input works best for language acquisition.

② PPP aims to develop the ability of learners to use language in real communication.

③ PPP aims to ensure the acquisition of certain grammatical features.

④ PPP aims to develop learner's automatic procedural knowledge.

⑤ PPP aims to compare learners' own norms with the target norms exemplified in the feedback.

問2　Fill in the blank (　A　) with the most appropriate word.

① gradually　② occasionally　③ frequently

④ absolutely　⑤ obviously

問3　Fill in the blank (　B　) with the most appropriate sentence.

① One way out of this problem is to choose the linguistic and nonlinguistic resources needed, and there must be a clearly defined outcome

② One way out of this problem is to overcome learners' linguistic deficiencies in order to say what they want to say

③ One way out of this problem is to make it clear to the learners that they must use the targeted structure when they perform the task

④ One way out of this problem is to integrate their extensive knowledge and executing communication

⑤ One way out of this problem is to comprehend input without having to pay close attention to linguistic form

問4 With which of the following statements would the author of the passage most likely agree?

① Teachers are required to design better tasks so that their students can develop their competence.

② PPP has a lot of problems, so it should be avoided in the English language classroom.

③ Students have acquired a targeted structure if they can produce it.

④ PPP has some criticisms and problems, but it is durable and manageable for teachers.

⑤ A lot of teaching methods have been researched to find out the effective method.

【7】Read this passage and answer the questions below.

Coffee is a crop for which there is a seemingly endless demand. Since the time of colonialism, when the plant was (A) its native Africa and Asia to Central and South America, it has been grown more and more intensively, meaning more coffee is produced on the same amount of land, year after year. To achieve these high levels of production, coffee is typically grown on vast plantations, where the land is cleared of forest, weeds and insects are vigorously controlled, and the full energy of the sun is used for growth.

(B). Most notably, native forest is permanently destroyed in the creation of the plantation. In tropical and semi-tropical areas, this typically represents forest areas containing high floral, faunal, and insect diversity. It is hard to know exactly how much tropical forest and attendant biodiversity has been lost to coffee plantations over the past two hundred years, but the massive declines in forest cover in countries like Mexico in recent decades are closely associated with commodity production, especially coffee. Moreover, by managing this conventional "(C) grown" coffee with intensive chemical inputs, non-target insect and plant species are typically killed and soils tend to degrade, losing nutrients and structure over time. This dependence on monocultural coffee plantation also results in social and economic vulnerability. When prices for coffee collapsed in the late 1990s, many producers around the world became immediately destitute, with no resources at hand for recovery.

(D)

The problem with such a system is straightforward, however. Shade grown coffee, by definition, has lower yields than conventional plantations production. And during periods of low prices, as in the coffee price collapse of recent years, this leaves farmers even more economically vulnerable and indeed encourages them to clear forests for more intensive cultivation of different crops. To be sustained, shade grown coffee must, therefore, be supported somehow, either by consumers who are willing to pay a premium for more green or sustainable production, by governments interested in maintaining forest cover, or through cooperatives that can lower production and transportation costs for farmers. This makes shade grown coffee one of the more promising examples of reconciliation ecology, but raises questions about our willingness to collectively support sustainable enterprise.

問1　Fill in the blank (A) with the most appropriate phrase.

① covered with　② regarded as　③ brought from

④ made in　　⑤ known by

問2 Fill in the blank (B) with the most appropriate sentence.

① A typical meal in the United States may last only a few short minutes

② This makes coffee one of the more promising examples of reconciliation ecology

③ In the 1970s, farm activist warned of the McDonaldization of America

④ The environmental costs of conventional coffee production are extremely high

⑤ Trees are therefore excellent indicators of human economic growth and expansion

問3 Fill in the blank (C) with the most appropriate word or phrase.

① sun　② shade　③ water　④ black light　⑤ wind

問4 [D] に挿入する段落として，以下のA～Eの英文を並びかえるとき，2番目と4番目にくる最も適切な組合せを選びなさい。ただし，組合せの左側を2番目，右側を4番目とする。

A: Instead, coffee bushes were seeded throughout existing forest with other crops, resulting in lower levels of production, but much higher diversity of crops, as well as wild flora or fauna.

B: Originally, coffee was not grown in vast open areas.

C: Such "shade grown" coffee could thrive amidst native vegetation, removing the either／or choice of forest versus coffee, or more generally: environment versus society.

D: For all these reasons, there is growing interest in returning coffee production to its more traditional ecological and social roots.

E: Shade grown coffee systems can vary enormously, from plantations that resemble intensive production but where coffee is simply intercropped with various trees, to systems so resembling native forest that it is difficult for visitors to tell by looking that farming is going on at all.

① A－E　② B－A　③ B－C　④ D－A　⑤ E－C

(☆☆☆☆◎◎◎◎)

【8】次の各問に答えなさい。

問1　次の文は,「評価規準の作成，評価方法等の工夫改善のための参考資料(高等学校　外国語)」(平成24年7月国立教育政策研究所教育課程研究センター)「第1編　総説」「Ⅱ．目標に準拠した学習評価により観点別学習状況の評価を行うことは高等学校の生徒にどのようなメリットがあると考えられるか。」に示されている4つのメリットである。文中の(　A　)～(　C　)に当てはまる語句の正しい組合せを，下の［　　］の①～⑤から一つ選びなさい。

1　全ての生徒に(　A　)を身に付けさせる

2　生徒の(　B　)を向上させる

3　大学等が多様な(　C　)を有する生徒を求めることに応え，生徒の様々な進路希望の実現となる

4　高等学校卒業生についての高等学校側からの質の保証となる

	A	B	C
①	確かな学力	学習意欲	資質能力
②	確かな学力	学習能力	思考力
③	知識や技能	学習意欲	資質能力
④	確かな学力	興味・関心	思考力
⑤	知識や技能	興味・関心	資質能力

問2　次の文は,「高等学校学習指導要領解説　外国語編・英語編」(平成22年文部科学省)「第1部　外国語編」「第1章　総説」「第2節　外国語科の目標」の一部である。文中の(　A　)～(　C　)に当てはまる語句の正しい組合せを，あとの［　　］の①～⑤から一つ選びなさい。

外国語科の目標は，コミュニケーション能力を養うことであり，次の三つの柱から成り立っている。

①　外国語を通じて，言語や文化に対する理解を深めること。

②　外国語を通じて，積極的にコミュニケーションを図ろうとする態度を育成すること。

③　外国語を通じて，情報や考えなどを的確に理解したり適切に伝えたりする能力を養うこと。

―中　略―

③の「情報や考えなどを的確に理解したり適切に伝えたりする」ことができることとは，外国語の音声や文字を使って実際にコミュニケーションを図る能力であり，情報や考えなどを受け手として理解するとともに，送り手として伝える(　A　)コミュニケーション能力を意味する。「的確に理解」するとは，場面や状況，背景，相手の(　B　)などを踏まえて，話し手や書き手の伝えたいことを把握することを意味している。また，「適切に伝え」るとは，場面や状況，背景，相手の(　C　)などを踏まえて，自分が伝えたいことを伝えることを意味している。

	A	B	C
①	双方向の	表情	反応
②	実践的な	表情	心情
③	双方向の	ジェスチャー	反応
④	実践的な	ジェスチャー	心情
⑤	柔軟な	ジェスチャー	反応

問3　次の文は，「高等学校学習指導要領解説　外国語編・英語編」(平成22年文部科学省)「第1部　外国語編」「第2章　外国語科の各科目」「第5節　英語表現Ⅰ」「1　目標」の一部である。文中の(　　)に当てはまるものを，下の□の①～⑤から一つ選びなさい。

「英語表現Ⅰ」の目標は，次の二つの要素から成り立っている。

① 英語を通じて，積極的にコミュニケーションを図ろうとする態度を育成すること。

② 英語を通じて，事実や意見などを多様な観点から考察し，(　　)能力を養うこと。

①	身近な話題について会話する
②	論理の展開や表現の方法を工夫しながら伝える
③	聞くこと，話すこと，読むこと，書くことなどの基礎的な
④	情報や考えなどを的確に理解したり適切に伝えたりする
⑤	情報や考えなどを的確に理解したり適切に伝えたりする基礎的な

(☆☆☆☆◎◎◎◎)

解答・解説

福　岡　県

【中高共通】

【1】Question1　①　　Question 2　④　　Question3　③

〈解説〉Question1　Jeffが1回目と2回目の発言で，新しいアパートで大学から約1マイルと言っている。　Question 2　Jeffの4回目の発言で，家賃が1カ月1,000ドル，5回目の発言でいわゆる敷金が3カ月分と言っているので，合計で4,000ドルである。　Question3　Jeffが最後の発言の中でNone of us are chefs.「2人とも料理ができない」と言っている。シリアルとサンドイッチばかりの食事になり，飽き飽きしているのである。

【2】≪A≫　Question1　④　　Question 2　②　　Question3　③

≪B≫　Question1　③　　Question 2　①　　Question3　④

〈解説〉《A》　Question1　スクリプト第2段落第1文の後半，they were以下に注目する。ここでは，「健康の回復」と述べている。　Question 2　第3段落第8文のpeople以下で，「食料の保存と腐敗の防止」について述べている。　Question3　①は誤り。論旨にはない。②は誤り。第3段落第3文ではコインについては重量しか述べられていない。③は正しい。第3段落第6文にこの意味の記述がある。④は誤り。論旨にはない。

《B》　Question1　スクリプト第3段落第3文のwhenからweightまでに「自分が太ってきたことを妻が指摘した」と述べている。

Question2　第4段落第3文及び第4文から，40代になって初めて何かをしようと思ったことがわかる。　Question3　①はno以下が誤り。第2段落though以下に「コーチに相談した」と述べている。②はextensive以下が誤り。第3段落第1文のbut以下に「大学時代は走らなかった」と述べている。③はno以下が誤り。第5段落第5文に「4時間未満で走ることができるかやってみたかった」と述べている。④は正しい。第5段落第2文及び第3文に「世界記録や順位や賞金を狙う一流選手たちは，一般ランナーたちに巻き込まれないように先にスタートする」と述べている。

【3】Question1　No.2　　Question2　No.4　　Question3　No.3

〈解説〉Question1　スクリプト第2段落第3文に「液体のマグマが徐々に噴出して形成される」とある。　Question2　第3段落第2文では“Hawaiian” eruptionの特徴はleast violent type of eruption「最も穏やかな噴火である」と述べられている。　Question3　No.1は誤り。論旨にはない。No.2はtall以下が誤り。第2段落第2文及び第5文で，アイスランドの火山はゆるやかなドーム型のshield volcanoesだと述べている。No.3は正しい。第2段落第7文にこの意味の記述がある。No.4は誤り。論旨にはない。

【4】No.4，No.6

〈解説〉No.1はbetween以下が誤り。第2段落第4文から，オペラ，ミュージカル，能や歌舞伎のいずれにも歌と踊りが含まれていることがわかる。同第5文で，違いは，ストーリーの進行に伴う歌と踊りの統合と，劇的効果の盛り上げ方であると述べている。No.2はdance以下が誤り。論旨にはない。No.3はsong以下が誤り。第2段落第9文と第10文で，歌も踊りも劇的効果を盛り上げると述べている。No.4は正しい。第2段落第13文と第16文にこの意味の記述がある。No.5はso以下が誤り。論旨にはない。No.6は正しい。第2段落第11文と第14文にこの意味の記述がある。

【5】問1　②　　問2　④　　問3　①　　問4　③　　問5　①

〈解説〉問1「私たちの図書館は全学生を同時に収容するほど大きくはない」の意味で，enoughの位置に注意。　問2「ベスは教員になる途中で多くの不利な環境を克服した」の意味で，on one’s wayは「途中で」

の意味である。　問3「好奇心は勇敢さよりもずっと恐怖を克服する」の意味。　問4「地軸を中心にして地球が自転し続けることで季節の変化が生じる」の意味で，asからaxisまでは挿入と考えればよい。
問5　so以下の「パーティーを開いた」という記述に注目する。mingleは「(会合などで色々な人と)交わる，一緒にする」の意味。「新しい計画の参加者全員が互いに交わることが必要だった」となる。なお，each otherは「相互」という名詞句であり，withが付いて副詞句になる点に注意。

【6】問1　⑤　　問2　③　　問3　④　　問4　⑤
〈解説〉問1　語順はC→E→D→B→Aで，boosts metabolism by creating muscleとなる。「体を動かすことが新陳代謝を上昇させる」と考えればよい。　問2　語順はE→B→A→C→Dで，what with the snow and the cold windsとなる。what with A and Bで「AやらBやら」の意味。
問3　語順はE→D→C→B→Aで，heard the whole story did I realizeとなる。「～して始めて…」の強調構文であり，強調のためにdid Iという語順転倒が起きている。文章全体は，I didn't realize how great the writer was until I heard the whole story.と同じ意味である。　問4　語順はE→C→B→D→Aで，they can often be compared to となる。forestsの後にthatまたはwhichが省略されていると考えればよい。

【7】問1　④　　問2　③
〈解説〉問1　各発言の冒頭を考えると，まずCが最初にくることがわかる。次にEの最初と最後の部分を見ると，Cから続くことがわかる。このEの最後の部分を受けてDが続く。Dの後半の問いに対する答えがBであり，さらにBに対する発言がAである。全体の順番はC→E→D→B→Aとなる。　問2　各発言の冒頭を考えると，まずEが最初にくることがわかる。Eの最後の部分を受けてCが続く。Cの内容を聞いて相手がDの発言で受ける。これを受けてもう一人が自分の論をAで展開する。最後はBである。全体の順番はE→C→D→A→Bとなる。

【8】問1　⑤　　問2　①　　問3　③　　問4　②　　問5　③

〈解説〉問1　第5文では「それぞれのサイクルは約90分」と述べている。したがって，第6文のinからalarmのように，サイクルの途中で目を覚ますと変調をきたす訳である。したがって，⑤の「眠くて疲れがぬけない」が適切である。　問2　第7文のThisからtraditionまでの内容を考えればよい。これは第3文から第6文までに記述されている。各選択肢のofまたはthat以下に注目する。この観点からすると①「たゆまぬ努力と忍耐を重視すること」が適切であるとわかる。　問3　第3文の空欄の前の部分と，第4文の冒頭のRepeatedからstudentsまででは，教師が繰り返しの重要性について述べている。　問4　第4文のcarefully以下と第6文のwe can以下から，②が適切である。ここでは，特に第4文のcarefully selected wordsが②のspecific, measurable, and designedにつながることに注意すること。　問5　空欄の直前は「中学校の教師ができることの一つは」の意味である。続く第4文は「中学校の英語の教師がもしそのことを実践すれば，生徒たちはそのトピックがすでになじみがあるものとわかり，学ぶ自信を得られる」。したがって，③が正解であるとわかる。

【9】問1　④　　問2　②　　問3　③

〈解説〉問1　soundは「健全な」の意味である。　問2　ability to study「学ぶ力」についての記述である。空欄Bの直後のand think以下から考える。novelは「新規の，新たな」の意味である。　問3　第2段落第7文のhow to以下の内容を考えればよい。

【10】問1　②　　問2　⑤　　問3　①　　問4　⑤

〈解説〉問1　地球の温度調節システムについての記述である。空欄Aの直後の第1段落第8文に，砂漠や山頂など快適な温度とは言えない場所の例が提示されている。　問2　variabilityとは「変化性」の意味である。第2段落第3文のwhile climate以下にこのvariabilityの具体的な内容を示している。　問3　第3段落第2文のthe sun would以下では，大気がなかった場合の具体例を提示している。　問4　①は正しい。第1段落第4文に同じ内容の記述がある。②は正しい。第1段落第6文の内容と一致する。③は正しい。第2段落第2文に同じ内容の記述がある。
④は正しい。第2段落第3文のwhile以下の内容と一致する。⑤は誤り。第3段落第4文では「大気には昼夜で極端な温度差が出ないよう安定させる効果がある」という意味のことを述べているが，選択肢⑤では逆である。

【11】問1　④　　問2　④　　問3　(B)　　問4　①
〈解説〉問1　第1段落第2文のalthoughからyouの「ともに泣いてくれる友人は多いけれども」に注目。逆のことを述べるのであるから，④のrejoice「喜ぶ」が適切である。「心からともに喜ぶ友人はめったにいない」となる。　問2　第1段落第7文と第8文に「うらやむことなく，あなたの成功を喜んでくれる友人」が真の友人であると述べている。この内容に最も近いのは④の「自分のことのようにあなたの勝利を喜んでくれる友人」である。　問3　まずは挿入すべき文の意味を考えねばならないが，like以下を考えると，Theyは人だと考えてよい。したがって，「彼らは一般的に，同じ事柄について好き嫌いが同じである」と考えればよい。よって，第2段落第2文と同第4文のbirds以下を考慮すると，(B)の位置に挿入するのが適切である。　問4　第3段落第4文で，塀の修理を例にして友情について述べている。so too以下は具体的な内容で，to avert a good friendは「良い友人を遠ざける」の意味である。

【中学校】

【1】①　ア　②　ウ　③　イ　④　エ　⑤　イ　⑥　エ
〈解説〉評価規準は，学習指導案の作成とも関係するので，基本的な内容はおさえておく必要がある。①は「間違うことを恐れずに積極的に」から，意欲を示している。②は「理解することができる」から外国語理解の能力とわかる。③の「適切な音量や明瞭さ」は表現に関わる事

柄である。④の「基本的なイントネーションの違い」は言語の知識を示している。⑤の「場面や状況にふさわしい表現」から，表現の能力とわかる。⑥の「文字や符号を使い分ける知識」は言語の知識である。

【2】問1 ① 音声 ② 簡単な 問2 ③ 綴り(つづり)
④ 支える ⑤ 活用 ⑥ まとまり

〈解説〉問1 小学校での外国語活動を踏まえた，中学校第1学年の言語活動についての記述である。小学校で音声面を中心とした活動を行ってきた素地を生かすことが重要である。また，その際には「簡単な」表現でコミュニケーションを図れるように配慮することが必要である。
問2 アは，小学校での「話す」「聞く」活動に加えて，中学校では「書く」「読む」学習を行うことに関する記述である。イは，「コミュニケーションを支えるものは文法である」ことを示した記述である。ウは，文法の指導は知識中心ではなく，実際に活用できる指導を実践することを示したものである。エは，文法事項は独立的に扱うのではなく，体系的に指導するように示した記述である。

【3】問1 (相手の意向をくんで，Sure，here it is.などと言いながら，) ペンを差し出すこと。 問2 ① 総合 ② 知識 ③ 主体
④ 目的

〈解説〉問1 「中学校学習指導要領解説 外国語編」(平成20 年7月)では，「第2章 外国語科の目標及び内容 第2節 英語 2 内容 (1) 言語活動 ア 聞くこと」の項目「(ウ) 質問や依頼などを聞いて適切に応じること。」の解説として，解答例の他に「Will you open the window? のような問い掛けに対して，実際に窓を開けるという動作に移したりする」という記述が掲載されている。 問2 同解説の同言語活動「ウ 読むこと」の項目「(オ) 話の内容や書き手の意見などに対して感想を述べたり賛否やその理由を示したりなどすることができるよう，書かれた内容や考え方などをとらえること。」の解説文からの出題である。問題文の直前には，「この指導事項は，今回の改訂で新たに加

えたものである。読んだ後に感想や意見，賛否，また，その理由を示すことを念頭に置いて，話の内容や書き手の意見などを批判的にとらえることができるようになることを示している」という記述がある。この中の「批判的に」という部分は，アクティブ・ラーニングの目標の一つにも通じる内容である。

【高等学校】

【1】問1　①　有機　　②　促す　　問2　・相づちを打つ　・聞き直す　・繰り返す　・言い換える　・話題を発展させる　・話題を変えるのうち3つ

〈解説〉問1　各科目にはそれぞれの目標があるが，言語の使用場面や働きを踏まえて，それらを適切に組み合わせて活用することを示している。このことを「有機的に」と記述しているのである。　問2「高等学校学習指導要領解説　外国語編・英語編」の「第1部　外国語編　第3章　英語に関する各科目に共通する内容等」における「[言語の働きの例] の取扱い　a　コミュニケーションを円滑にする」の項からの出題である。この項目の解説部分には，次のような趣旨が記述されている。「コミュニケーションを円滑にする言語の働きは，中学校においても扱われているが，高等学校においては，さらに，『言い換える』，『話題を発展させる』，『話題を変える』が例として挙げられている。高等学校においては，適切な表現を選択し，意見の交換などをより円滑に進める工夫を行えるよう指導する」。

【2】問1　①　特質　　②　理解　　③　語句　　④　流れ　　⑤　適切さ　　問2　A　エ　　B　ケ　　C　コ　　D　シ　　E　ウ

〈解説〉問1「高等学校学習指導要領解説　外国語編・英語編」の「第3章　英語に関する各科目に共通する内容等　4」の項の内容は次の通りである。「英語に関する各科目については，その特質にかんがみ，生徒が英語に触れる機会を充実するとともに，授業を実際のコミュニケーションの場面とするため，授業は英語で行うことを基本とする。

その際，生徒の理解の程度に応じた英語を用いるよう十分配慮するものとする」。この項の解説中には，①～③に関連して次のような記述がある。「英語に関する各科目の「特質」は，言語に関する技能そのものの習得を目的としていることである」及び「教師の説明や指示を理解できていない生徒がいて，日本語を交えた指導を行う場合であっても，授業を英語で行うことを基本とするという本規定の趣旨を踏まえ，生徒が英語の使用に慣れるような指導の充実を図ることが重要である」。また，④と⑤に関連して，「このため，生徒が書いた英語に誤りや曖昧さがあった場合は，それを正確で適切なものとするよう，文法や語彙を運用する能力を高めながら，きめ細かな指導を行うことが考えられる」という記述がある。　問2　高等学校学習指導要領の外国語の英訳版(Section 8 Foreign Languages)からの出題である。第1段落の“English Communication Ⅰ”は日本語版学習指導要領における「第2　コミュニケーション英語Ⅰ」の目標に相当する。空欄Aと空欄Bを含むasからetc.までの部分は，「情報や考えなどを的確に理解したり，適切に伝えたりする」の意味である。第2段落の“English Expression Ⅰ”は同日本語版「第5　英語表現Ⅰ」の目標に相当する。空欄Cと空欄Dを含むevaluateからexpressionまでの部分は「事実や意見などを多様な観点から考察し，論理の展開や表現の方法を工夫しながら伝える」の意味である。第3段落の“English Conversation”は「第7　英語会話」の目標に相当する。空欄Eを含むholdからtopicsまでの部分は「身近な話題について会話する」の意味である。学習指導要領の日本語版を理解していれば解ける問題であるが，「第2章　第8節　外国語」(Section 8 Foreign Languages)及び「第3章　第13節　英語」英訳版(Section 13 English)については相互参照しつつ理解を深めておきたい。

【3】問1　幅広い話題，抽象的な内容，やりとり　　問2　英検…2級～準1級　　TOEFL iBT…57点程度

〈解説〉問1「グローバル化に対応した英語教育改革実施計画」(平成25年12月)は，初等中等教育段階からのグローバル化に対応した教育環境

作りを進めるため，小・中・高等学校を通じた英語教育改革を計画的に進めることを目的に，文部科学省によって公表されたものである。同計画書は全7ページで構成されており，設問は第1ページの「1．グローバル化に対応した新たな英語教育の在り方」における「高等学校」の第1項からの出題である。　問2　同計画書では，英語力の向上を目指すにあたり「高校卒業段階で英検2級～準1級，TOEFL iBT57点程度以上等」を目標とすることが具体的に記されている。これには「外部検定試験を活用して生徒の英語力を検証するとともに，大学入試においても4技能を測定可能な英検，TOEFL等の資格・検定試験等の活用の普及・拡大」というねらいがある。

福　岡　市

【中学校】

【1】問1　②　　問2　①　　問3　⑤　　問4　②　　問5　①

〈解説〉問1　「～までには」の意味。　問2　「木曜日の時点では連続4日の勤務だ」の意味。　問3　「歴史的過去」と呼ばれる用法。事実として過去形を用いる用法で，時制の一致は適用されない。

問4　過去完了の用法。過去のある時点よりもさらに過去を表す用法。

問5　後半の意味は，「彼を信じない」の意味なので，①以外は不適切。

【2】問1　③　　問2　⑤　　問3　③　　問4　②

〈解説〉問1　カッコ内はworth two in the bushとなるので語順はD→C→E→B→Aである。　問2　カッコ内はthe length of which isとなるので，語順はC→E→A→D→Bである。　問3　カッコ内はkeep its head above waterとなるので，語順はD→C→E→B→Aである。「水面上に頭を保つ」とは，溺れないことなので，「借金をしない」という意味である。

問4　日本文の意味は，「私はその劇を最初から最後まで夢中になってみていた」と考えればよい。英文は無生物主語で，haveの使役用法である。「その劇は私を座席にくぎ付けにした」と考えればよい。カッコ内はme on the edge of my seatとなるので，語順はD→E→B→C→Aである。

【3】問1　③　　問2　②

〈解説〉問1　Bの「Taylorさんのオフィスはこちらですか」以外，最初に来る文章はない。Bの後半を受けるのが，E「何かご用ですか」である。ここをAと間違えないこと。このEを受けてD「Taylorさんとお約束があって伺いました」が続き，それに対してC「ただいま会議中ですのでお待ちください」，A「わかりました」となる。順番はB→E→D→C→Aである。　問2　会話の内容から，まずはB「野球場への行き方をご存じですか」が最初に来て，最後がC「教えてくださってありがとう」である。Bの後半を受けて，Dの道案内が続く。Aは「正しく聞いたかどうか確認したい」という意味なので，Dの後はAとなる。次のEで聞き違いを訂正され，最後にお礼のCが来て，B→D→A→E→Cとなる。

【4】問1　②　　問2　④　　問3　①　　問4　③

〈解説〉問1　空欄1を含む第1段落第4文のManyからcurriculumまでの具体的な内容が，第1段落第2文のlinking languageから文末までである。多様なカリキュラムを関連づけることについて述べている。

問2　第3段落第2文以降で伝統的な教授法，つまり最初に部分的なことを学んでから全体を学ぶことについて記述している。選択肢の①～③及び⑤は前述の教授法を肯定的に捉える内容となっているので，本文とは一致しない。伝統的な教授法では，④「生徒たちは，文脈を理解する貴重な機会を失った」が適切である。　問3　第1段落第4文のL1 researchers以下文末までは，続く第5文冒頭の“The basic argument”に反論する立場である。つまり，「学習者は母語に対して既に直観的な感覚がある」からといって文法や句読法を教えるのではなく，第6文のように，「むしろ意味のある文脈で使いこなす練習をするべきだ」

と述べているのである。　問4　第3段落第2文のmuch以降と同第3文のoften以降で，「学習者は大量に文法事項を教わるが，英語を書くにあたってそれらをどのように生かせばいいのかわからない」と述べていることから判断する。

【5】問1　③　　問2　②　　問3　④　　問4　④
〈解説〉問1　A　第2段落第1文は「自然薬が古来から中心的な役割を果たしてきた」。これに続くのは，(b)「土の中にも健康に有効な成分があることが知られていた」が適切である。　B　第1文の内容を受けるので，第1文に入る(b)のsoil containsに注目すると，これに対応するのは(a)のmade of clayの部分である。したがって空欄Bには(a)が入る。C　(c)のhow to以下を第2段落第3文のby carving the placeが修飾している。2500年前の人が，薬に生産地を刻印することで薬の商業価値を高めていたことに驚いているのである。　問2　下線部(D)からdiscoveredまでは，直前の文章である第3段落第1文「18世紀後半には薬理学の発展が始まった」について，具体的な例を示しており，antibioticsは「抗生物質」の意味である。したがって下線部(D)には②のepoch-making「画期的な」が入るのが適切である。　問3　第7段落第3文に「アルコールで薬を飲むな」と記述している。　問4　①はFew ancestorsが誤り。第1段落の内容と逆の意味になっている。②はMany people always rememberが誤り。第3段落の第3文と第4文で逆のことを述べている。③はby以下が誤り。これは論旨にはない。④は正しい。第4段落第3文のavoid以下で同様のことを述べている。⑤は誤り。第7段落第6文の内容と一致しない。

【6】問1　④　　問2　②　　問3　④　　問4　⑤
〈解説〉問1　第1段落第3文のthe abilityからevidenceまでの「その言語を使って他人と交流する能力が確証となる」に注目する。これと同様の意味の選択肢は④である。　問2　第2段落第2文のthe answer以下文末までの部分は主張として述べているので，「わかる」，「確認する」の

意味のseeが適切である。　問3　第3段落第2文のthe sense以下「学習者は，これらの反応を，自分の発言が理解されたという確証として受け取るかもしれない」。このような場合，いわゆる「積極的な反応」を示すものである。したがって④が適切である。　問4　①はheavily on teachersが誤り。論旨にはない。②はduringからlessonsまでが誤り。第4段落第3文のnot during以下と一致しない。③はwillingからfeedbackが誤り。第4段落第1文の内容と逆になっている。④は誤り。第3段落第6文に「いずれの反応も，誤りを修正するための学習者に対するフィードバックである」と述べている。⑤は正しい。第4段落第4文の最初からcorrect formまでに同様の内容の記述がある。

【7】問1　④　　問2　②　　問3　③　　問4　④

〈解説〉問1　直前のto stopからandまでと，第1段落第3文のthe past以下から，変化を止めて昔に戻りたがる人がいることがわかる。

問2　空欄Bの直前の第2段落第2文と，直後の第4文に，「技術や知識の発達や進歩を止めることは難しい」という意味のことを述べている。norが文頭に置かれるときは倒置が起こるので②が適切である。

問3　第3段落第2文のthe public needs以下文末までの部分と，空欄Cの直後のthe public以下文末までの部分は，ほぼ同じ意味である。したがって，「この時点では」という意味の③が適切である。　問4　①は誤り。第2段落第1文のone couldn't以下で「時間を戻すことはできない」と述べているので，選択肢の「過去100年間に起こった変化に注意を払う」はこの内容と一致しない。②はseeing advances以下が誤り。第2段落第4文のthe force以下から同第5文の文末までは「技術も科学も発展を止めることはできない」という意味なので，これと一致しない。③はquick decisionsが誤り。第4段落第1文のto make informed decisionsと逆の記述である。④は正しい。第3段落第1文の後半we canから文末までと，同第2文のthe public needsからexpertsまでに，同様の内容の記述がある。⑤は誤り。論旨にない。

【8】④

〈解説〉外国語科の特性に応じた評価の観点及びその趣旨は以下の通りである。「ア　コミュニケーションへの関心・意欲・態度」の趣旨は「コミュニケーションに関心をもち，積極的に言語活動を行い，コミュニケーションを図ろうとしている」，「イ　外国語表現の能力」の趣旨は「外国語で話したり書いたりして，自分の考えなどを表現している」，「ウ　外国語理解の能力」の趣旨は「外国語を聞いたり読んだりして，話し手や書き手の意向などを理解している」，「エ　言語や文化についての知識・理解」の趣旨は「外国語の学習を通して，言語やその運用についての知識を身に付けているとともに，その背景にある文化などを理解している」。これらを踏まえて，選択肢A～Eがどの項目に該当するか考える。

【9】問1　⑤　　問2　②　　問3　①

〈解説〉問1　中学校学習指導要領の「(1)言語活動」からの出題である。学習指導要領は同解説と併せて細部まで熟読しておきたい。なお，「中学校学習指導要領解説　外国語編」(平成20年7月)では，「第2章第2節　英語　2　内容　(1)言語活動　エ　書くこと」の項において，(ア)～(オ)の内容について次のように解説している。(ア)「書くこと」の言語活動のうち最も基本的な技能の習熟を求めたものであり，繰り返し指導することにより，文字や符号についての知識や技能の確実な定着を図り，正確に分かりやすく書けるようにする必要がある。(イ)　文構造や語法の理解が十分でなく正しい文が書けないという課題に対応したものである。「語と語のつながり」を明示して語順の重要性を強調しているのは，英語では意味の伝達において語順が重要な役割を担っているからである。　(ウ)　この指導事項では，生徒が聞いたり読んだりした内容に主体的にかかわりをもち，それを踏まえて自分の感想，内容に対しての賛否やその理由を書くことを求めたものである。　(エ)　実際に自分が体験したことなどについて自分の考えや気持ちなどを自由に書く活動のことを述べている。「身近な場面における出来事や体験したことなど」とは，家庭や学校などの日常生活の中で起こったことや，旅行や行事の体験などである。 (オ) この指導事項の「文と文のつながりなどに注意して文章を書くこと」の部分は，内容的にまとまりのある一貫した文章を書く力が十分ではないという課題に対応したものである。なお，指導要領と解説の細部まで覚えきれなかった場合，こうした問題を解くための考え方を参考までに示してみる。最初に，問題文中に空欄BとDが2カ所にあることに注目する。そして空欄Aであるが，「識別」と「認識」については，当然ながら文字や符号を「区別」するのだから，Aは「識別」である。続いて空欄Bを見る。ここでは，「語と語」及び「文と文」について述べられているが，「連結」では意味が強すぎるので「つながり」である。この時点で正解は①か⑤となる。Cは同一である。次はDであるが「自分の考えや」に続く文言としては「計画」ではなくて「気持ち」である。この時点で正解は⑤であるとわかる。 問2 学習指導要領の改訂に伴う改善点・変更点については，都度正確に把握しておく必要がある。本問は平成20年告示の学習指導要領についての出題であるが，平成29年3告示の新学習指導要領についても改訂のポイントを理解しておくこと。なお，参考までに，記載内容について正確に覚えきれていない場合に正解を導くひとつの方法を示す。学習指導要領などの公的な文書では，「弾力的な運用」などの表現が頻出する。したがって，Aは「弾力的」であると推測できる。この時点で正解は②か⑤となる。Bは同一なので，続いてCを見る。ここは「指導する語の総数」なので1200である。この数字は重要なので必ず覚えておく。この時点で正解は②であるとわかる。なお，授業時数が従来の105から140になったことも必ずおさえておく必要がある。 問3 同解説「3 指導計画の作成と内容の取扱い (1) 指導計画の作成上の配慮事項 キ」の項目からの出題である。この問題文に続く解説として次のような記述がある。「『ネイティブ・スピーカーなどの協力を得たり』とあるが，ここでいう『ネイティブ・スピーカーなど』とは，ALTのほかに，地域に住む外国人，外国からの訪問者や留学生，外国生活の経験者，海外の事情に詳しい人々など幅広い人々が考えられ，これらの人々の協力を得ることにより活発な言語活動や国際理解教育の推進を図ることが考えられる。学習形態の工夫としては，ペアワークやグループワークが挙げられているが，生徒一人一人の活動が行いやすいという利点を生かして，これらの形態を適宜取り入れながら，効果的な授業が展開できるようにする必要がある」。本問は，解説の当該箇所の文言を暗記していなくても解けると思われるが，参考までに解き方の例を示す。まず，空欄Aは，直前に「ペアワーク，グループワーク」とあるので「学習形態」である。一斉授業や個別授業も学習形態の一種である。この時点で，②と④は不正解となる。空欄Bは後の部分に「教材が」とあるので，「視聴覚機器」であるとわかる。この時点で正解は①か③である。続く空欄Cは同一である。次の空欄Dは，前の部分に「資料や情報を入手」とある。また，コンピュータや情報通信ネットワークは双方向であることを踏まえると，「入手」に対しては「発信」であり，「共有」ではないことがわかる。したがって，Dは「発信」であり，この時点で正解は①である。

【10】問1　③　　問2　④

〈解説〉問1　「グローバル化に対応した英語教育改革実施計画」(平成25年12月)は，初等中等教育段階からのグローバル化に対応した教育環境作りを進めるため，小中高等学校を通じた英語教育改革を計画的に進めることを目的に，文部科学省によって公表されたものである。同計画書は全7ページで構成されており，設問は第1ページの「1. グローバル化に対応した新たな英語教育の在り方」における「中学校」の項と，第4ページの「2. 新たな英語教育の在り方実現のための体制整備【主な施策】」の「中・高等学校における指導体制強化」から出題されている。アは「情報交換」である。イは外国語活動から正式な教科に移行することを踏まえれば「高度化」だとわかる。ウは「目標」とセットになっているので「内容」である。エは「指導力」であり，「英語力」(英語の運用能力)とは別の能力であることを明示している。オは具体的な基準を示したものである。　問2　同第1ページの「1．グローバル化に対応した新たな英語教育の在り方」及び第4ページの「2．新たな英語教育の在り方実現のための体制整備【主な施策】」の「小学校における指導体制強化」から出題されている。現在は，小学校5・6年生で外国語活動として行われている内容を小学校3・4年生から始め，5・6年生には新たに教科として導入する概要を述べたものである。キーワードは「学級担任」「モジュール授業」「専科教員」などである。

【高等学校】

【1】問1　③　　問2　④　　問3　②　　問4　②　　問5　②

〈解説〉問1　「40を過ぎて」とあるので，「大学で勉強するのに年を取りすぎていないか」と考えればよい。　問2　「講義の間は」という意味で特定の期間を示すのでduringが適切である。なお，forは不特定の期間を表す。　問3　時制の一致で，didn't likeと同一の時を表す。
問4　目的語に動名詞を取る動詞の例。主なものは，stop, miss, mind, enjoy, give up, avoid, finish, escape, put off, postponeである。　問5　道具・手段・材料などを表す用法で「…で作られている」の意味。

【2】問1　④　　問2　①　　問3　④　　問4　①

〈解説〉問1　正しい語順はwho I believe is a musical geniusでE→D→C→A→Bとなる。I believeが挿入的に用いられている。　問2　正しい語順はnever see this picture without thinkingでE→A→D→C→Bとなる。二重否定の用法である。例として，It never rains without pouring.「土砂降りなしに雨は降らない」つまり，「降れば必ず土砂降り」という意味である。　問3　正しい語順はbirds of a feather flock togetherでB→D→E→C→Aである。不定冠詞のaはsameの意味である。　問4　正しい語順はmake hay while the sun shinesでB→A→D→C→Eである。「太陽が輝いているうちに干し草を作れ」という意味である。

【3】問1　④　　問2　⑤

〈解説〉問1　A以外の選択肢の冒頭部分は，問いかけを受けてからの表現であるので，まずAが最初である。Aのroommateを受けてEが続く。このEのI thoughtの部分がDのI didにつながる。そして，Dのso以下がBの第2文につながる。全体の順番はA→E→D→B→Cである。

問2　まずBが最初にくる。B以外の選択肢の冒頭部分は，問いかけを受けてからの表現である。Bの後半を受けてEが続く。そして，Eの後半を受けてCが続く。これを受けてDのOkay以下に続く。全体の順番はB→E→C→D→Aである。

【4】問1　④　　問2　②　　問3　③　　問4　②

〈解説〉問1　第1文のability to thinkから，①から③はすべて不適切である。また第3文のto solve，to identify，to make以下の部分に注目すると，機械では対応することのできない能力について述べていることがわかる。したがって，④が適切である。　問2　第3文の冒頭のWhile「一方で～」から空欄までの部分は，in practice以下と対照的な内容を示している。したがって文末のclassroomがキーワードとなり，これと対照的な言葉を探すと，選択肢②の homeworkが対応するとわかる。

問3　第2文のfor most以下及び第3文のof second以下に注目する。これらの部分ではlearnersについて言及している。したがって，whoseの先行詞はlearnersだとわかる。そこで，文末がlearnersとなっている選択肢③，④，⑤のそれぞれthat以下を見ると，④の内容は必ずしも正しいものではなく，⑤は全く学習目的から外れていることがわかる。よって，正解は③である。　問4　①はwith以下が誤り。論旨にはない。②は正しい。第4文以下に具体例が述べられている。③はFewからofficiantsが誤り。第2文の内容と異なる。④は誤り。第1文のand stirs以下に注目する。⑤は誤り。論旨にはない。

【5】問1　③　　問2　④　　問3　②　　問4　③

〈解説〉問1　空欄Aの直前のParadoxicallyと第6段落第4文に注目。睡眠薬によって睡眠の質が悪くなることが述べられている。　問2　選択肢から誤っている文を選ぶ問題である。第5段落第1文と第2文から①は誤りではないとわかる。②は誤りではない。第7段落第1文に同様の意味の記述がある。③は誤りではない。第2段落第2文の内容と一致する。④は誤り。第5段落第3文のbut以下と一致しない。⑤は誤りではない。第4段落第2文に同様の記述がある。　問3　①は誤り。第4段落第2文の記述と一致しない。②は正しい。第2段落第3文に同様の記述がある。③，④，⑤はいずれも誤り。論旨にはない。　問4　③が正しい。第7段落第1文のdoctors以下に注目する。①と②及び④と⑤は論旨にはない。

【6】問1　②　　問2　①　　問3　③　　問4　④

〈解説〉問1　第1段落第1文のhas traditionally以下から，②と④以外は不正解だとわかり，同第2文から選択肢②が適切とわかる。　問2　第2段落第2文のa series ofからentitiesまでと，同第3文のlearners do notから最後まで及び第4文のas learners以下に注目する。「引き続く」のではなくて「徐々に」と述べているのである。したがって空欄Aは①が適切である。　問3　第3段落第3文では，学習者が目標項目を使うことを避ける傾向があることを述べている。したがって，空欄Bではこの解決策を述べることが予想される。この観点から考えると③が適切である。　問4　この文章の主題は教授法としてのPPPである。この教授法については様々な評価があるが，筆者は第4段落第1文で主張を述べているのである。したがって，この主張と一致する④が適切である。

【7】問1　③　　問2　④　　問3　①　　問4　③

〈解説〉問1「原産地がアフリカやアジア」の意味である。　問2　空欄の直後の第2段落第1文がヒントである。ここでは，具体例を述べている。　問3　第1段落第3文のthe fullからgrowthまでに答えが示されている。　問4　第2段落第5文と同第6文を受けて，まずDがくる。このDの後半を受けてBが続く。Bのin以下を受けてEが続く。このEの内容がCの冒頭のSuchに続く。最後はAである。D→B→E→C→Aとなる。

【8】問1　①　　問2　①　　問3　②

〈解説〉学習指導要領及び同解説は相互参照しながら精読しておくこと。また，「評価規準の作成，評価方法等の工夫改善のための参考資料(高等学校　外国語)」からもたびたび出題されているので，併せて目を通しておきたい。　問1 「全ての生徒に確かな学力を」という文言は，問題文の文書以外にも学習指導要領や様々な関係文書に頻出している。この表現は基本中の基本である。続く空欄Bも重要な表現である。「全ての生徒に確かな学力を付けさせることが重要である。そのためには，生徒の学習意欲を向上させることが必要である」と覚えればよい。空欄Cは直前の「多様な」という表現に注目すれば「思考力」でなく「資質能力」が適切と判断できる。　問2　空欄Aの前の部分「受け手として～，送り手として」は，双方向性を表している。ここがわかれば①か③が正解ということになる。空欄Bと空欄Cの前後には同じ表現が使われている。空欄Bの直前の部分は「場面や状況，背景，相手の」である。この次に続くのは「表情」か「ジェスチャー」だが，空欄Cが文脈上「反応」となることを考えると空欄Bは「表情」が適切である。　問3　この問題は選択肢自体にヒントがある。表現のためには何が必要かを考えれば解答を導けるであろう。なお，この選択肢の具体的な内容は，文章の構成を考えて，それを話したり書いたりして相手に伝える能力のことである。

2017年度　実施問題

福　岡　県

【中高共通】

【1】次に読まれる英文を聞き，1～3の設問に対する答として最も適切なものを，四つの選択肢の中から一つ選びなさい。(英文及び設問は2回読まれる。)

Receptionist: Hello. This is Vancouver Health Center.

Ken : I'd like to make an appointment for tomorrow.

Receptionist: What's your name?

Ken : My name is Ken Yamada. I've been having dizzy spells which won't go away.

Receptionist: OK, Ken Yamada. Have you ever visited this hospital?

Ken : No. This is my first time.

Receptionist: All right.

Ken : I'm an overseas student at Vancouver University. What should I do to see a doctor?

Receptionist: In that case, there are a few formalities to see to before you can actually be seen by one of our doctors.

Ken : What do you mean by "formalities?"

Receptionist: Well, first-time patients have to register with us, so we can create a medical file for you, and there's a simple health-check you have to do, too.

Ken : I see.

Receptionist: OK. If you register with us, then you should be able to receive free healthcare like any other patient in this country.

Ken : That sounds good.

Receptionist: You'll need to bring your passport or Student ID, and there is an initial registration fee of fifteen dollars.

Ken　　　: OK.

1　Question 1: What's the matter with Ken Yamada?

① He has a fever.

② He has a stomachache.

③ He gets dizzy.

④ He gets better.

2　Question 2: Who is talking with Ken Yamada?

① His parent

② Bank employee

③ Client

④ Receptionist

3　Question 3: Why does Ken Yamada have to pay fifteen dollars?

① Because he is a student.

② Because he has already registered.

③ Because he has a serious problem.

④ Because he has never visited that hospital.

(☆☆☆◎◎◎)

【２】次に読まれる英文《A》及び英文《B》について，それぞれの1～3の設問に対する答として最も適切なものを，四つの選択肢の中から一つ選びなさい。(英文及び設問は2回読まれる。)

《A》

Have you ever seen a rodeo? Like many other sports it is a competition using skills that were important in daily life or work. The cowboys had to be able to tame wild horses. This is represented by the saddle bronco-riding and bareback bronco-riding events. In these events the rider must stay on the horse for a specified time, holding the reins in one hand, and points are given for technique and difficulty in riding the horse. The wilder the horse is, the more points the contestant receives.

Perhaps the most exciting event is bull-riding. Like bronco-riding, the entrant is judged on technique after staying on for the required time. The difficulty in riding a bull provides a breathtaking spectacle. A dismounted rider coupled with the danger of a bull attacking. Unlike the bucking broncos, bulls will intentionally gore or trample anything in sight. Rodeo clowns are employed to distract the bulls once a ride has ended, thus providing a margin of safety, particularly to injured riders.

1 Question 1: According to the passage, what did the cowboys have to be able to do?

① They had to be able to compete with other cowboys.
② They had to be able to tame wild horses.
③ They had to be able to ride a bull.
④ They had to be able to receive many points.

2 Question 2: According to the passage, why is bull-riding so breathtaking?

① Because the rider has to stay on the horse for a long time.
② Because there is a possibility that the bull attacks the rider.
③ Because the rider has to hold the reins in one hand.
④ Because rodeo clowns are employed.

3 Question 3: According to the passage, which statement is true?

① The rodeo is a competition that is not related to daily life or work.
② The points of the rodeo depend on the difficulty in taming a horse.
③ The horse riding is the most exciting event.
④ The rodeo clowns improve the riders' safety.

《B》

In fall, we enjoy beautiful yellow-gold and orange leaves. What causes the leaves to change colors? It has something to do with the days growing shorter and the nights becoming cooler. Leaves have green pigments, the natural substances which produce the green-color. During the growing season, green pigments use the energy of water, carbon dioxide, and sunlight to produce a kind of sugar needed for the tree's food supply. As the days become shorter and the nights longer and cooler, trees respond by slowly shutting down the production of the green pigments. Once they recede, the yellow-golds and oranges, which were already present in the leaves, start to appear. These colors can usually be seen in the fall, regardless of the weather.

How about other beautiful leaves, for example, deep red or purple ones? Those colors are the result of sugar sap trapped in the trees' leaves. The cooler temperatures at night prevent the sugar sap in the leaves' veins from flowing back into the trees. Bright sunlight turns the trapped plant sugar into brilliant reds and purples, producing a spectacular array of vivid autumn colors. If the temperature is freezing, it will not produce the spectacular autumn colors. It'll only turn the leaves brown.

1　Question 1: According to the passage, why do the leaves turn yellow-gold and orange?

① Because the leaves are in the growing season in fall.
② Because the yellow-gold substances are produced in the leaves.
③ Because there's a decline in the production of green pigments.
④ Because more sugar is necessary for leaves in fall.

2　Question 2: According to the passage, what causes the leaves to turn deep red and purple?

① Lack of sunlight and an increase in sugar sap.
② Humid weather and freezing air.
③ Back-flow of sugar sap and fine weather.
④ Bright daylight and a drop in the night temperature.

3　Question 3: According to the passage, which statement is true?

① Carbon dioxide is essential for the leaves to produce natural substances which change their colors.
② Yellow-gold and orange colors are invisible when the green pigments are actively produced in the leaves.

③ The sugar sap is trapped in the leaves when the temperature remains almost unchanged.

④ The leaves sometimes don't turn vivid colors even in fall, when the temperature never goes below zero.

(☆☆☆◎◎◎◎)

【3】次に読まれる英文を聞き，1～3の設問に対する答として最も適切なものを，その後に読まれる四つの選択肢の中から一つ選びなさい。(英文，設問及び選択肢は2回読まれる。)

In West Africa, more than 700 languages exist. Cameroon alone, with a population of 22 million, is home to about 280 languages. This puzzled many linguists, because the inhabitants are not isolated by massive mountains.

One linguistic anthropologist has a theory that may explain, this diversity. He compared ecological maps of West Africa with maps showing the ranges of various languages. He noted that a direct correlation exists between the length of the rainy season and the number of languages.

In the south, where the rainy season lasts a long time, the greatest concentration of languages was found. Farther north, in the areas with fewer than four months of rain, the number of languages fell. You might say that the linguistic diversity merely reflects the region's population density. But in fact, in northern Nigeria, one of the most populous areas, one single language dominates.

The theory explains this. If you have abundant rainfall year-round, you can produce almost all the food you need. In the south, the staple crops can be harvested throughout the year, so people can live in their small communities and speak a language no outsiders understand. Contact with the outside world is not essential.

But in areas where poor harvest can bring famine, relations with outsiders are crucial. A long dry season means that food can't be produced for that period. So people need to form a social network to get enough food. And the larger the network, the greater the likelihood of a common language.

(250 words)

Question 1: According to the passage, what did the linguistic anthropologist discover?

No.1 Cameroon and northern Nigeria have a similarity in the linguistic environment.

No.2 The linguistic diversity in the area has a lot to do with the climate condition.

No.3 The mountainous environment in West Africa has a great effect on the languages.

No.4 Population density has a relationship with the number of languages to some extent.

Question 2: According to the passage, what kind of areas have the larger number of languages?

No.1 The areas where the harvest of crops is guaranteed year-round.

No.2 The north area of West Africa where the dry season lasts a long time.

No.3 The densely populated areas in the south of West Africa.

No.4 The areas where people need social networks to prevent famine.

Question 3: According to the passage, which statement is true?

No.1 Many linguists were puzzled because the number of languages in Cameroon was smaller than expected.

No.2 People want contact with outsiders when they are in danger of starvation.

No.3　The distribution of the languages suggests that life is less comfortable in areas with a variety of languages.

No.4　The theory helps explain the relation between languages and geological formations.

(☆☆☆◎◎◎)

【4】次に読まれる英文を聞き，英文の内容に合致するものを，その後に読まれる六つの選択肢の中から二つ選びなさい。(英文及び選択肢は2回読まれる。)

Many scientists are interested in how ants behave in their societies. An American scientist has obtained an understanding of a complex social structure of ant societies. He examined ants called “leaf-cutter ants.” They are known for their agricultural way of life and divisional cooperation.

They make their nests underground, where they cultivate gardens on soil made from finely chopped leaves. This is a complex operation, and requires considerable division of labor. The workers can be divided into four groups according to size. Each of the groups performs a particular job.

The jobs of the smallest workers are the making and care of the gardens and the nursing of the young ants. Slightly larger workers chop up leaves to make them suitable for use in the gardens, and for cleaning the nest. A third group of still larger ants do the construction work and collect fresh leaves from outside. The largest are the soldier ants, responsible for defending the nest.

How efficiently do they perform different tasks? The scientist measured the amount of energy they used to do a particular task. First, he examined the gathering and carrying of leaves. He selected one of the size-groups, and then measured how efficiently these ants could do the task. Then he repeated the experiment for each of the other size-groups.

It turned out that the intermediate-sized ants, which normally perform this task, were the most efficient for their energy cost. But when the scientist examined other jobs, it appeared that some sizes of worker ants were not ideally suited to the particular jobs they performed.

(261 words)

No.1　The job assignment to each group depends on the number of workers.

No.2　The workers of the smallest size mainly do the domestic jobs.

No.3　The soldier ants are mostly young and have a sense of responsibility.

No.4　In his experiment, the scientist focused on the ants' willingness to work hard.

No.5　The jobs of the intermediate-sized ants is keeping their nests safe.

No.6　Each worker's size is not necessarily the best size for their jobs.

(☆☆☆☆◎◎◎)

【5】英文の意味が通るように，(　　)に入る最も適切なものを選びなさい。

問1　One of the beauties of computer-aided instruction is that it can be (　　) the needs of the individual.

①　taught to　　②　tailored to　　③　turned into

④　looked into　　⑤　worked up to

問2　Vegetables are (　　) and expensive this summer because we've hardly had any rain for a month.

①　lack　　②　slight　　③　steady　　④　scarce　　⑤　strict

問3　He was surprised at the (　　) of e-mails from people he hardly knew.

①　influx　　②　outbreak　　③　occurrence　　④　deletion

⑤　chaos

問4　The article appearing in the latest science magazine is (　　) of the one she wrote a couple of years ago.

①　an expansion　　②　a development　　③　a corpulence

④　a growth　　⑤　an expectation

問5　The common cold, which is the most widespread disease, continues to (　　) humanity despite the efforts of scientists to find its prevention and cure.

① plead　② pledge　③ plague　④ propagate
⑤ provoke

(☆☆☆◎◎◎)

【6】次の各問の日本文の意味を表す英文を作るために，(　　)内のA～Eの語句を正しく並べかえるとき，2番目と4番目にくる最も適切な組合せを選びなさい。

ただし，組合せの左側を2番目，右側を4番目とする。

問1　今日の自動車が昔よりすぐれているかは大いに意見の分かれるところである。

There is much disagreement as to whether the cars of today ($_A$of the past $_B$are $_C$those $_D$to $_E$superior

① C－D　② C－E　③ D－A　④ E－D　⑤ E－C

問2　先週の金曜日から降り続いていた激しい雨は，今朝になってもやみそうもなかった。

The heavy rain which has been falling since last Friday ($_A$likely $_B$stop $_C$to $_D$seem $_E$did not) this morning.

① A－C　② A－D　③ D－A　④ D－C
⑤ E－C

問3　この町を歩いていると，ちりひとつ落ちていない清潔さに驚かずにはいられません。

If you walk through this town, you ($_A$help $_B$cannot $_C$its $_D$surprised at $_E$being) perfect cleanliness without a piece of rubbish on the streets.

① A－D　② B－D　③ B－E　④ D－A
⑤ E－D

問4　怒っているときこそじっくりと心を落ち着ける時間を作るべきである。

It is when ($_A$we should $_B$most angry $_C$we are $_D$make time $_E$that) to sit down and compose ourselves.

①　A－B　　②　A－C　　③　B－A　　④　B－D
⑤　D－C

(☆☆☆◎◎◎◎)

【7】次の各問のA～Eの英文を二人の会話として意味がつながるように並べかえるとき，2番目と4番目にくる最も適切な組合せを選びなさい。ただし，組合せの左側を2番目，右側を4番目とする。

問1　A: Indeed professional baseball is exciting, but my greatest pleasure is the National Senior High School Baseball Tournament held at Koshien Stadium every summer.
B: Absolutely! I'm crazy about the Fukuoka Bears. How about you?
C: Did you watch the baseball game on TV last night? The Bears came from behind to beat the Elephants 5-4 last night.
D: I like it too. I watch the games every summer.
E: Sorry, I didn't. Are you a professional baseball fan?

①　A－E　　②　D－A　　③　D－C　　④　E－D
⑤　E－A

問2　A: In Japan carp are regarded as symbols of strength and perseverance because they swim vigorously against strong currents.
B: Look! Colorful fish-like streamers are flowing. How beautiful they are!
C: I see. Parents hope that their boys will inherit these characteristics.
D: Why are they in the shape of carp? In my country carp do not evoke very good images.
E: Yes. They are so beautiful. They are called koinobori, or carp streamers. In Japan, boys' parents hoist large carp-shaped streamers outdoors to celebrate Children's Day.

①　A－C　　②　A－E　　③　D－C　　④　E－A　　⑤　E－C

(☆☆☆◎◎)

【8】次の各問の英文を読み，文脈から考えて文中の(　　)に入る最も適切なものを選びなさい。

問1　Being able to use new grammar means that students understand the meaning and the situation they use it in. Memorizing one example or model sentence won't help them use it in a conversation. It is important that (　　). When teaching new grammar, we should try to include lots of English examples as well, and have students make their own sentences.

① we teach them the example and model sentence in the textbook over and over
② we teach them how to use that grammar pattern themselves, so they can apply it to other situations
③ we avoid teaching them the meaning of that grammar pattern, so they can think of new sentences themselves
④ students spend time memorizing the model sentence in the textbook
⑤ students read one example many times, so they can remember it

問2　Motivation is a psychological feature that evokes a desire to achieve a certain goal. Students have different goals for their studies. Teachers spend the most time with their students and should be able to motivate them towards achieving their goals. But each student has their own worries. Keeping in touch with students is a key to knowing their worries. Also, communicating with them, especially asking questions, is very important. Therefore, (　　). The questions could help unearth a problem or challenge faced by a student. Some kids have low self-esteem and one-on-one sessions with a teacher can help them open up about what is troubling them.

① teachers should not be afraid to ask their students difficult questions
② teachers should not ask their students difficult questions
③ students should be afraid to answer their teacher's questions
④ students should not ask their teacher difficult questions
⑤ teachers should not be afraid to teach their students answers

問3　Previously, in most English classes in Japan, students spent a lot of time translating English into Japanese. As a result they became very good at that, but found it very difficult to produce anything in English. (　　). This was not communicative. Students need practice at expressing themselves in English, and should be encouraged to be creative.

① The emphasis was on speaking Japanese rather than reading English

② The emphasis was on writing and speaking rather than reading and listening

③ The emphasis was on speaking and listening rather than reading and writing

④ The emphasis was on 'input' rather than 'output'

⑤ The emphasis was on conversation rather than translation

問4　Hobbies have always been important. But nowadays they are coming to have much greater value for two main reasons: there is more leisure time and the tyranny of machines. Those of us with daily occupations have, on the whole, far more free time than previous generations. What is to be done with leisure time? No real satisfaction comes from a mere pastime which can do no more than while away the hours. (　　). It constitutes relaxation and a change from an ordinary occupation.

① Our satisfaction differs with the length of our leisure time

② The value of a worthwhile hobby is that it gives benefits to the mind

③ Our mind and spirit can almost be refreshed

④ In these days, so many of us do routine work in which there is no novelty or variety and no need for initiative

⑤ The demerit of having hobbies is that our ambitions may be realized in our leisure time

問5　Most parents tend to worry about what their children are eating since nutrition is so important for good health. As adults, we can more easily make the decision to eat food that is delicious and nutritious, but children can be picky eaters, liking only foods that are easy on the palate. So parents should be a healthy eating model. (　　). Also they need to develop a feeding strategy that respects their role as parents as well as their children's choices.

① It takes patience and strategy to get their children to eat a wide range of nutritious foods

② We don't need any strategies because getting their children to eat a wide range of nutritious food is a cakewalk

③ Children are not easily influenced by their parents

④ It is challenging for parents to eat a wide range of delicious food

⑤ As children do not imitate their parents, parents should be strict

(☆☆☆◎◎◎)

【9】次の英文を読んで，あとの問に答えなさい。

This may seem like a silly statement, but there are real reasons why we become hungry. Hunger is a normal condition which occurs several hours after eating, when the stomach becomes empty. Then we have a strong desire, or craving, for food. It is not only the feeling of emptiness in our stomach that makes us hungry, but several other factors as well. While food is in the stomach, the walls of the stomach contract in a rhythmic motion so that the food can be broken up for digestion. Then, about three hours after eating, the stomach empties and the contractions of the stomach wall become stronger. When the contractions become very strong, we have something which are called "hunger pangs." These hunger pangs are most intense in healthy young people. If we do not eat, they become more painful.

Another cause of hunger is the level of sugar, or glucose, in the blood. When the blood sugar level is low, certain parts of the nervous system send a message to a part of the brain called the hypothalamus. Then the brain tells us that we are hungry. In other words, we feel hungry when certain nutritive substances in the blood are missing.

Some people have a small snack at such a time if they cannot have a meal right away. This will only temporarily remove the feeling of hunger. It is important to have a regular meal as soon as possible.

Social and personal habits also influence our hunger. Most of us eat at certain times of the day and we become accustomed to having a meal at those times. We also become used to having certain types of foods at certain times. These social habits will have an influence on when we become hungry and what we become hungry for.

問1　本文の内容に合うように，次の英語に続く最も適切なものを選びなさい。

The feeling of hunger is caused by

① nutritive substances in the blood.
② eating several hours after the last meal.
③ strongly desiring or craving food,
④ the stomach becoming empty.
⑤ a high level of glucose.

問2　本文の内容に合うように，次の英語に続く最も適切なものを選びなさい。

The contraction of the stomach wall

① depends on how strong the hunger pangs are.
② helps to break food up so that it can be digested.
③ is not very intense among young people.
④ is stronger when there is food in the stomach.
⑤ occurs only when the stomach becomes empty.

問3　本文の内容に合うように，次の英語に続く最も適切なものを選びなさい。

Low blood sugar level

① indicates that the brain is sending out a signal.
② is a message sent out from the hypothalamus.
③ occurs when the brain tells us we are hungry.
④ is caused by eating a small snack.

⑤ works as a trigger for the feeling of hunger.

(☆☆☆◎◎◎)

【10】次の英文を読んで，あとの問に答えなさい。

In contemporary American society, the mass media gives a lot of attention to how people compete for status, power, and money. Parents raise their children to "try to be Number 1" to cultivate independence from the group. In social psychology, however, we recognize that more prominent characteristics of human culture are the need for social bonding, friendship, and especially, one might say, love.

This is not just an idea. There's a lot of evidence to support this interpretation of human culture. For example, children who are not held or given love when they are young much more often grow up into disturbed, scared, and dangerous people. We know this from empirical research, especially on criminals. We can even predict with reliability what percentage of a prison population has what background. Furthermore, studies show that adults who isolate themselves from the world, refusing to even own a pet, are likelier to die at a comparatively younger age than those who cultivate companionship — animal or human. Again, this is a fact borne out of scientific analysis. What this tells us is that despite the popular image of the hero and loner in film, humans are essentially social creatures and we need to be aware of these social and biological roots.

Perhaps this shouldn't surprise us so much because our social nature is shared with many of the species closest to us biologically — especially among primates like chimpanzees, bonobos, gibbons and other apes, for instance, and a variety of monkeys. Our primate relatives, like us, have strong social bonds. They are attached to their mothers and fathers, their sisters and brothers, and they even form deep friendships. Among the similar behaviors that we see are grooming (touching, petting, and holding), courtship of a boyfriend or girlfriend (even kissing), and peace-making after a fight (shaking hands, for example). This indicates that our social nature is by and large genetic.

Even though it seems that humans are naturally embedded in communities, there's a final problem. Strangely, our social nature takes hard work and experience to develop. It can't be taken for granted. Children, for example, need to bond with their parents at key times during early childhood. Throughout their lives, people need to touch each other, to eat together, and to share activities such as games and trips if they are to continue to be healthy.

問1　What is the author's main point?

① Mass media portrays humans inaccurately.
② Humans selected more social animals to keep as pets.
③ Humans are primarily social creatures.
④ People have much in common with animals.
⑤ Criminals usually fail to bond with their parents.

問2　According to the author, what happens to adults who are socially isolated?

① They commit more crime.
② They are more aggressive.
③ They miss work more often.
④ They may risk dying early.
⑤ They gain weight more easily.

問3　Why does the author mention primates, such as chimpanzees and bonobos?

① To show that other primates are more social than humans
② To suggest that humans' social nature is biological
③ To contrast human communities and primate communities
④ To illustrate behaviors that humans should avoid
⑤ To imply that hierarchy is natural in human society

問4　What does the author mention as being part of a healthy life?

① Reading books

② Staying hydrated
③ Sleeping well
④ Exercising regularly
⑤ Having communal meals

(☆☆☆◎◎◎)

【11】次の英文を読んで，あとの問に答えなさい。

There are more than 26,000 species of crustaceans, of which the most familiar are crabs, shrimps, lobsters, and barnacles. They can be found in almost every type of habitat except the most arid of deserts, Most, however, are found in the sea, where they live from the surface layers all the way down to the greatest depth of the ocean. Crustaceans exhibit an almost infinite variety of colors and patterns. Some of the smaller varieties of plankton have transparent bodies with little or no pigment. On the other hand, deep-sea shrimps and lobsters are often a uniformly brilliant red. Some marine crustaceans are self-luminescent, emitting their own light; terrestrial and freshwater crustaceans may become luminous if infected with luminescent bacteria, but are unable to produce the light by themselves. (A)

Crustaceans typically have five pairs of appendages protruding from their heads, the function of which varies depending on the species. (B) In general, the first two are primarily sensory antennae, though they may also assist in locomotion or feeding. The third set is the ア mandibles, used to chew food. (C) The latter two pairs are mainly used to set up feeding currents designed to propel food toward the jaws. (D)

No special hearing organ, or ear, has been found among the various species of crustaceans, but numerous hollow bristles, supplied with nerves, are present on the surface of the body and the appendages. イ These move when touched, making it possible for the organism to respond to and discern vibrations, including sound. (E)

Since aquatic animals' detection of dissolved substances in the water around them cannot readily be separated into smelling and tasting, it is best to refer to it by its proper scientific term, chemoreception. Chemoreception is extremely important to crustaceans that are very sensitive to chemical stimuli. These stimuli are detected by a variety of structures, especially the thin-walled, hair-like chemoreceptors most abundantly present on the antennae.

問1　本文の内容に合うように，次の英語に続く最も適切なものを番号で答えなさい。

It can be inferred from the passage that crustaceans would NOT likely be found

①　at the lower levels of the ocean.
②　at the surface of the ocean.
③　in places with very limited rainfall.
④　in conditions of high humidity.
⑤　at high mountain elevations.

問2　次の英文の(　　)には下線部アと同じ意味の語が入る。本文から探し，適語を入れなさい。

Due to many hits to the face, one of the most common injuries for boxers is that they have broken their (　　).

問3　次の一文を本文中の(A)～(E)のいずれかに挿入する場合，最も適切な箇所を記号で答えなさい。

They do this by fanning the water in an inward motion.

問4　下線部イが指している語(句)を同じ段落から抜き出して答えなさい。

(☆☆☆◎◎◎)

【中学校】

【１】「評価規準の作成，評価方法等の工夫改善のための参考資料(中学校外国語)」(平成23年11月国立教育政策研究所)において，「第2編　評価規準に盛り込むべき事項等」「第2　内容のまとまりごとの評価規準に盛り込むべき事項及び評価規準の設定例」が示されている。

次の①～⑤の評価規準は，どの観点において設定されているものか，下のア～エからそれぞれ一つずつ選び，記号で答えなさい。

① 語句や表現，文法事項などの知識を活用して短い英語の内容を正しく聞き取ることができる。

② 相づちをうったりメモをとったりするなど，相手の話に関心をもって聞いている。

③ 積極的に音読している。

④ 文構造や語法，文法などに関する知識を身に付けている。

⑤ 適切な声量や明瞭さで話すことができる。

ア コミュニケーションへの関心・意欲・態度

イ 外国語表現の能力

ウ 外国語理解の能力

エ 言語や文化についての知識・理解

(☆☆☆◎◎)

【2】「中学校学習指導要領解説　外国語編」(平成20年文部科学省)について，次の各問に答えなさい。

問1 次の文は，「第2章　外国語科の目標及び内容」「第2節　英語」「1　目標」の一部である。次の①～③に当てはまる語句を書きなさい。ただし，同じ番号には同じ語句が入るものとする。

(1) 初歩的な英語を聞いて話し手の(　①　)などを理解できるようにする。

(2) 初歩的な英語を用いて自分の(　②　)などを話すことができるようにする。

(3) 英語を読むことに(　③　)，初歩的な英語を読んで書き手の(　①　)などを理解できるようにする。

(4) 英語で書くことに(　③　)，初歩的な英語を用いて自分の(　②　)などを書くことができるようにする。

問2　次の文は，「第1章　総説」「3　外国語科改訂の要点」「(1)　目標の改善の要点」の一部である。次の④～⑧に当てはまる語句を書きなさい。ただし，同じ番号には同じ語句が入るものとする。

> 外国語科の目標は，コミュニケーション能力の(　④　)を養うことであり，次の三つを念頭に置くこととしている。
> ・外国語を通じて，言語や文化に対する理解を深める。
> ・外国語を通じて，積極的にコミュニケーションを図ろうとする(　⑤　)の育成を図る。
> ・聞くこと，話すこと，読むこと，書くことなどのコミュニケーション能力の(　④　)を養う。
> また，今回の改訂では小学校に外国語活動が導入され，特に(　⑥　)面を中心として外国語を用いたコミュニケーション能力の(　⑦　)が育成されることになったことを踏まえ，中学校段階では，「聞くこと」，「話すこと」に加え，「読むこと」，「書くこと」を明示することで，小学校における外国語活動ではぐくまれた(　⑦　)の上に，これらの四つの技能を(　⑧　)的に育成することとしている。

(☆☆☆◎◎◎◎◎)

【3】次の文は，「中学校学習指導要領解説　外国語編」(平成20年文部科学省)「第2章　外国語科の目標及び内容」「第2節　英語」「2　内容」「(1)　言語活動」「イ　話すこと」の一部である。

> (エ)　つなぎ言葉を用いるなどのいろいろな工夫をして話を続けること。

問1　「話を続ける」ために用いられる「つなぎ言葉」とはどのような表現のことか。英語で一つ書きなさい。

問2　必要な表現や技法を用いて会話を継続・発展させるための「いろいろな工夫」として，「つなぎ言葉を用いる」，「会話を始めたり発展させたりするために，相手に質問をする」ことの他に，どのようなことが示されているか。日本語で二つ書きなさい。

(☆☆☆◎◎◎◎)

【高等学校】

【1】次の問に答えなさい。

問　次の文は「評価規準の作成，評価方法等の工夫改善のための参考資料(高等学校　外国語)」(平成24年7月国立教育政策研究所)の「第2編　外国語科における評価規準の作成，評価方法等の工夫改善」「第2章　コミュニケーション英語Ⅰ」「5　評価に関する事例」の一部である。文中の①～⑤に当てはまる語句をあとの語群から一つずつ選んで記号で答えなさい。ただし，同じ番号には同じ語句が入るものとする。

(4)　観点別評価の進め方

観点別評価においては，それぞれの評価規準ごとに，「十分満足できる」状況(A),「おおむね満足できる」状況(B),「努力を要する」状況(C)のいずれの状況にあるのかを，次のような視点から判断することになる。

ア　「コミュニケーションへの関心・意欲・態度」

この観点は，コミュニケーションに取り組む様子やコミュニケーションを(　①　)させようとする努力の様子を捉えて評価することとしている。したがって，そこで用いられている英語の正確さや適切さなど，言語運用上の能力は評価しない。また，授業中の挙手や発言の回数といった表面的な状況のみに着目するのではなく，言語活動への取組や(　①　)の仕方など，実際に指導した内容に対して生徒が努力して取り組んでいるかどうかについて，活動の様子を判断材料として評価する。また，活動の観察評価だけでは読み取りにくい生徒の取組状況や関心・意欲・態度の変化についてよりよく理解するために，ワークシートや(　②　)等による評価を併用することも考えられる。

(中略)

イ 「外国語表現の能力」

この観点は，自分が伝えたい(　③　)や考えなどを，場面や状況に応じて適切に相手に伝えることができるかどうかについて評価することとしている。「言語や文化についての知識・理解」に分類される音声，語彙，文法，語法，言語の背景にある文化などに係る知識を活用して，実際に話したり書いたりすることにより，英語で表現することのできる能力を評価する。

(中略)

ウ 「外国語理解の能力」

この観点は，話し手や書き手の伝えたいことを，場面や状況を踏まえて(　④　)把握することができるかどうかについて評価することとしている。「言語や文化についての知識・理解」に分類される音声，語彙，文法，語法，言語の背景にある文化などに係る知識を活用して，実際に聞いたり読んだりした英語を理解することのできる能力を評価する。

(中略)

エ 「言語や文化についての知識・理解」

この観点は，知識や理解がコミュニケーションを目的として言語を(　⑤　)支えとなっているかについて評価することとしている。「言語」についての知識・理解は，発音，語彙，文法，語法や文章構成など，英語の仕組みやその使い方についての知識の有無を評価する。「文化」についての知識・理解は，英語を理解したり英語で表現したりするに当たって，理解をしていないとコミュニケーションに支障を来すような文化的背景についての知識・理解を評価する。

《語群》

a	おおまかに	b	インタビュー	c	経験
d	総合的に	e	習得する	f	深化
g	継続	h	情報	i	パフォーマンス

j　思い　　　k　成立　　　l　学習する
m　運用する　n　ポートフォリオ　o　的確に

(☆☆☆◎◎◎)

【2】次の文は高等学校学習指導要領(平成21年3月告示)の「第2章　各学科に共通する各教科」「第8節　外国語」「第3款　英語に関する各科目に共通する内容等」に示されている言語材料を用いるに当たって配慮すべき事項を英訳したものである。文中のア～ウに当てはまる1語をそれぞれ書きなさい。

A.　Contemporary (　ア　) English should be used. At the same time, consideration should also be given to the reality that different varieties of English are used to communicate around the world.

B.　Grammar instruction should be given as a means to (　イ　) communication through effective linkage with language activities.

C.　Phrases, sentence (　ウ　), grammatical items, etc., required for communication should be taught in a way applicable to real-life situations, without centering instruction on the distinction of terms and usage, etc.

(☆☆☆◎◎◎◎)

【3】次の文は高等学校学習指導要領(平成21年3月告示)の「第2章　各学科に共通する各教科」「第8節　外国語」「第4款　各科目にわたる指導計画の作成と内容の取扱い」の一部である。これを読んで，あとの各問に答えなさい。

2　内容の取扱いに当たっては，次の事項に配慮するものとする。

(1)　教材については，外国語を通じてコミュニケーション能力を(　①　)的に育成するため，各科目の(　②　)に応じ，実際の言語の使用場面や言語の働きに十分配慮したものを取り上げるものとすること。その際，その外国語を日常使用している人々を中心とする世界の人々及び日本人の日常生活，風俗習慣，物語，地理，歴史，伝統文化や自然科学などに関するものの中から，生徒の発達の段階及び興味・関心に即して適切な題材を変化をもたせて取り上げるものとし，次の観点に留意する必要があること。

ア　多様なものの見方や考え方を理解し，公正な(　③　)を養い豊かな心情を育てるのに役立つこと。

イ　外国や我が国の生活や文化についての理解を深めるとともに，言語や文化に対する関心を高め，これらを(　④　)する態度を育てるのに役立つこと。

ウ　広い視野から国際理解を深め，国際社会に生きる日本人としての自覚を高めるとともに，(　⑤　)の精神を養うのに役立つこと。

エ　人間，社会，自然などについての考えを深めるのに役立つこと。

(2)　音声指導の補助として，(A)発音表記を用いて指導することができること。

(3)　辞書の活用の指導などを通じ，(B)生涯にわたって，自ら外国語を学び，使おうとする積極的な態度を育てるようにすること。

(4)　各科目の指導に当たっては，指導方法や指導体制を工夫し，ペア・ワーク，グループ・ワークなどを適宜取り入れたり，視聴覚教材やコンピュータ，情報通信ネットワークなどを適宜指導に生かしたりすること。また，(C)ネイティブ・スピーカーなどの協力を得て行うティーム・ティーチングなどの授業を積極的に取り入れ，生徒のコミュニケーション能力を育成するとともに，国際理解を深めるようにすること。

問1　文中の①～⑤に当てはまる語句を書きなさい。

問2　下線部(A)について，「高等学校学習指導要領解説外国語編・英語編(平成22年文部科学省)」において，指導に当たって配慮すべきこととして示されている内容を日本語で書きなさい。

問3　下線部(B)について，「高等学校学習指導要領解説外国語編・英語編(平成22年文部科学省)」において，このような態度を育てるために，「辞書の活用の指導」に加えてどのような指導が大切であるとされているか，日本語で書きなさい。

問4　下線部(C)について，「高等学校学習指導要領解説外国語編・英語編(平成22年文部科学省)」において，このような授業において求められることとして示されている内容を日本語で書きなさい。

問5　下線部(C)について，「高等学校学習指導要領解説外国語編・英語編(平成22年文部科学省)」に示されている以下の文中の(　　)に当てはまる語句を書きなさい。

> このような授業を行う場合は，(　　)等について，教師とネイティブ・スピーカーなどの間で事前の打ち合わせを行い，共通理解を図っておくなどの配慮も必要である。

(☆☆☆◎◎◎◎)

福　岡　市

【中学校】

※高等学校は，福岡県・北九州市と同一の問題です。

【1】Please complete the following English sentences by choosing the most appropriate word or phrase to replace the blanks.

問1　I had no time to buy a souvenir for my friend (　　) my stay in Paris.

①　when　②　until　③　unless　④　since　⑤　during

問2　My new washing machine which I bought recently works (　　) than the previous machine did.

①　most quieter　②　more quieter　③　much quieter

④　more quietly　⑤　most quietly

問3 Last Wednesday, one of my friends (　　) by my house.

①　drops　②　has dropped　③　dropped　④　was dropped

⑤　was dropping

問4　(　　) the past five years, he has been working as a volunteer for reconstruction support.

① Above　② To　③ Over　④ Along　⑤ Under

問5　You can come here at any time when (　　).

① you are convenient　② it is convenient for you

③ it could be free for you　④ you are useful

⑤ it shall be useful for you

(☆☆☆◎◎◎◎)

【2】次の各問の日本文の意味を表す英文を作るために，(　　)内のA～Eの語句を正しく並べかえるとき，2番目と4番目にくる最も適切な組合せを選びなさい。ただし，組合せの左側を2番目，右側を4番目とする。

問1　科学の進歩にしたがって，私たちの生活様式がすっかり変化していく。

With the progress of science, ($_A$way $_B$has $_C$our $_D$life $_E$of) changed completely.

① A－C　② A－D　③ C－A　④ C－E　⑤ E－B

問2「精神一到何事か成らざらん」ということわざは今日でも当てはまる。

An old saying tells that where thereis a will, there is a way, ($_A$today $_B$is $_C$which $_D$of $_E$true).

① A－C　② A－D　③ B－A　④ B－D　⑤ C－E

問3　学問で大切なことは当然だと思われていることを疑ってみることである。

The important thing in learning is to doubt ($_A$be $_B$is $_C$what $_D$belived $_E$to) a matter of course.

① A－C　② B－C　③ B－E　④ D－A　⑤ D－E

問4　日本人の自然観は欧米人のそれとは異なっているようにみえる。

The Japanese view of nature seems to ($_A$from $_B$be $_C$that $_D$of $_E$different) Westerners.

① C－B　② C－D　③ E－A　④ E－C　⑤ E－D

(☆☆☆◎◎◎◎)

【3】次の各問のA～Eの英文を二人の会話として意味がつながるように並べかえるとき，2番目と4番目にくる最も適切な組合せを選びなさい。ただし，組合せの左側を2番目，右側を4番目とする。

問1　A: No. It's not that far from here. It's just five-minute walk. Here we are.

B: That's very kind of you. Is it far from here?

C: Thank you very much. It was a great help.

D: I shall be glad to. In fact I'm on my way there, too.

E: Excuse me, but would you kindly enough to tell me the way to the museum?

①　B－A　②　B－C　③　C－D　④　D－A　⑤　D－E

問2　A: I hear that the ten-o'clock coffee break is to America what the three-o'clock tea is to England.

B: It's 10 : 00. Why don't you have a cup of coffee and talk about the procedure for the interview test coming soon?

C: Each country has its own customs, I suppose. I'm fond of both of these customs.

D: So am I. I'm sure nobody would object to a coffee break in the morning and a tea break in the afternoon.

E: Good idea! I feel refreshed after a cup of coffee.

①　B－D　②　D－A　③　D－C　④　E－B　⑤　E－C

(☆☆☆◎◎◎)

【4】次の各問の英文を読み，文脈から考えて文中の(　　)に入る最も適切なものを選びなさい。

問1　It has been said that "education is not the filling of a bucket, but the lighting of a fire." In this vein, there is an important shift occurring in *ELT. In student-centered communicative classes, responsibility for "doing-English" is placed on the learner. The role of the teacher is changing from "filler of buckets" —the traditional model—to "lighter of fires" －the communicative model. Students become the star in the classroom as the teacher facilitates and stage manages, creating opportunities (　　) to take risks and speak out loud.

－Teaching English In Japan, Dale Bay

*ELT　English Language Teaching　英語教授(法)

① for self-discovery and a safe environment for students
② for self-centered and a progressive class for students
③ for interactive communication among students
④ to find out good communicative activities
⑤ to become a lighter of fires

問2　The success of Japan's economic, political and grassroots contacts with the rest of the world rests in large part on the ability of Japanese people to use English well. This is partly because English is the *de facto world language. (　　) the Japanese themselves have decided to make a commitment to learning and using English internationally.

－Teaching English In Japan, Dale Bay

*de facto　事実上

① In spite of this
② To the contrary
③ To make the matters worse
④ More often than not
⑤ But it is also because

問3　A team of researchers led by a Kyoto University professor will begin full-fledged studies next fiscal year to develop a treatment method for leukemia using induced pluripotent stem (iPS) cells. (中略)

There is no precedent for clinical tests in which cancer could be cured using immune system cells produced from iPS cells. (　　) in experiments on animals, the team will begin clinical tests on people in 2019 by injecting them with the immune system cells produced to examine the safety and effectiveness of the new method.

—The Yomiuri Shimbun, January 11, 2016

① Unless the treatment method is accepted by the government
② When there is the difficulty in cultivating cells
③ Due to the clinical tests done by using iPS cells
④ If the planned method is proven to be effective
⑤ In spite of the detailed experiments not being confirmed

問4 When native speakers of English live abroad for some time, their manner of speaking can change. Like elementary school teachers, native-speakers who live and work in Japan (　　) in slow, carefully phrased, perfectly enunciated sentences with much repetition and redundancy. This is part of a syndrome known as "teacher talk." But when they go back, their English may sound strange to "normal" i.e. unacculturated native speakers.

—Teaching English In Japan, Dale Bay

① are always used to speaking
② have never get accustomed to speaking
③ often get into the habit of speaking
④ usually get inclined to speak
⑤ sometimes hesitate to speak

(☆☆☆◎◎◎◎)

【5】Read this passage and answer the questions below.

A well-known scientist (some say it was Bertrand Russell) once gave a public lecture on astronomy. He described how the earth orbits around the sun and how the sun, in turn, orbits around the center of a vast collection of stars called our galaxy. At the end of the lecture, a little old lady at the back of the room got up and said : "What you have told us is rubbish. (　A　)" The scientist gave a superior smile before replying, "(　B　)" "You're very clever, young man, very clever," said the old lady. "(　C　)"

Most people would find the picture of our universe as an infinite tower of tortoises rather ridiculous, but why do we think we know better? What do we know about the universe, and how do we know it? Where did the universe come from, and where is it going? Did the universe have a beginning, and if so, what happened before then? What is the nature of time? Will it ever come to an end? Recent (D)breakthroughs in physics, made possible in part by fantastic new technologies, suggest answers to some of these longstanding questions. Someday these answers may seem as obvious to us as the earth orbiting the sun---or perhaps as ridiculous as a tower of tortoises. Only time (whatever that may be) will tell.

As long as 340 B.C. the Greek philosopher Aristotle, in his book *On the Heavens*, was able to put forward two good arguments for believing that the earth was a round sphere rather than a flat plate. First, he realized that eclipses of the moon were caused by the earth coming between the sun and the moon. The earth's shadow on the moon was always round, which would be true only if the earth was spherical. If the earth had been a flat disk, the shadow would have been elongated and elliptical, unless the eclipse always occurred at a time when the sun was directly under the center of the disk. Second, the Greeks knew from their travels that the North Star appeared lower in the sky when viewed in the south than it did in more northerly regions. (Since the North Star lies over the North Pole, it appears to be directly above an observer at the North Pole, but (　E　), it appears to lie just at the horizon.) From the difference in the apparent position of the North Star in Egypt and Greece, Aristotle even quoted an estimate that the distance around the earth was 400,000 stadia. It is not known exactly what length a stadium was, but it may have been about 200 yards, which would make Aristotle's estimate about twice the currently accepted figure.

—A Brief History Of Time, Stephen W. Hawking

問1　Choose the most appropriate combination of sentences (a)(b) and (c) to fill in the blanks (A), (B) and (C).

(a) But it's turtles all the way down!

(b) What is the tortoise standing on?

(c) The world is really a flat plate supported on the back of a giant tortoise.

	A	B	C
①	(a)	(c)	(b)
②	(b)	(a)	(c)
③	(b)	(c)	(a)
④	(c)	(a)	(b)
⑤	(c)	(b)	(a)

問2 Choose the most accurate statement according to the passage.

① Long time ago, a Greek philosopher proposed two reasonable points for believing that the earth was a round sphere.

② Quite a few people found that an infinite tower of tortoises was true as the old lady had explained.

③ Aristotle found out the distance around the earth and this estimate is perfect right even now.

④ If the earth were flat, the sun could not be seen from the horizon.

⑤ Nobody knows exactly the distance around the earth and no exact data would be found out even in the future.

問3 Choose the most accurate statement for the underlined part (D).

① movement

② restriction

③ invention

④ progress

⑤ experiment

問4 Fill in blank (E) with the most appropriate phrase.

① to someone looking from the Arctic Circle

② to someone looking from the equator

③ to someone looking down the European Continent
④ to someone looking over the Atlantic Ocean
⑤ to someone looking through the Antarctic

(☆☆☆◎◎◎)

【6】Read this passage and answer the questions below.

As teachers, we are always interested in finding ways we can improve our teaching practice. Even if we are new to teaching we have spent at least sixteen years in classrooms as we completed our primary, secondary and tertiary education and we probably have firm ideas about what we expect from our teachers. We can learn to apply our experience as students to give us (A)insights into our teaching practice.

As teachers, we are usually the ones who are the primary focus of attention in the classroom. This is usually how we have experienced learning ourselves. Whether our native language is English or Japanese, as English teachers, we are the model our students will follow. But who are we modeling our teaching on?

Thus, many teachers tend to do what their teachers before them did — talk, and talk and talk. As a teacher-trainer, one of the complaints I hear most frequently from students is "We never get a chance to speak!" or "Our teacher is very nice, but talks too much!" In talking to teachers, I find that some of the more common explanations for this are "They just sit there, they never speak." or "I can't (　B　) it when they just sit there looking at me — I have to say something!" Some teachers tend to think about class control and say things like "Of course I do all the talking. I'm the teacher and it's my duty to talk! If I don't control the class..." .

Well, we won't get into a debate about who is right or wrong here. (　C　). Yet it is possible for us to see old things in new ways and learn to apply new insights and attitudes to our teaching practice.

Here's a simple suggestion which we can easily use in our classes — try to see and hear ourselves as our students see and hear us. This can be called self-observation and it is a very useful technique. This method can be used by any teacher, anywhere. For example, do we do all the talking in our classes? One of the easiest exercises we can do — and we don't need any equipment for this — is to compare "teacher talk" (TT) and "student talk" (ST). The point is to be aware of how much TT and ST there is, make a decision about how much there should be and manage the class to reach the target we have decided on.

Those of us *at the chalkface can use either audio-tape or video-tape to do many more interesting types of observation. We can make good use of video to study our mannerisms, way of speaking, presentation skills, the use we make of the board or other teaching aids, in short, all aspects of our classroom practice.

—Teaching English In Japan, Dale Bay

*at the chalkface　教室の現場で

問1　Choose the most appropriate definition for the underlined part (A).

① something that you say or write which gives an opinion
② the process of carefully considering or discussing something
③ the feeling of being sorry for somebody
④ the ability to see and understand the truth about people or situations
⑤ a feeling or an opinion especially based on emotions

問2　Fill in blank (B) with the most appropriate word.

① make　② take　③ hear　④ stand　⑤ sit

問3　Fill in blank (C) with the most appropriate phrase.

① There is truth to some of the things these students say
② There is truth to all of the things these teachers say
③ It is true that everybody says the same thing
④ It is true that every student agrees to this opinion
⑤ There is no knowing what these teachers do

問4　What is the suggestion given by the writer, which could be helpful for the teachers? Choose the most appropriate statement below.

① To see and hear us teachers as students see and hear us.

② To use self-centered observation which we can see ourselves.

③ To be able to control the class as soon as possible.

④ To make good use of video to brush up our presentation skills.

⑤ To use much more teaching aids to reflect ourselves.

(☆☆☆◎◎◎)

【７】Read this passage and answer the questions below.

Should Americans say they're sorry more often? At least one Japanese friend thinks so. Her impression is that Americans rarely (A), even when it seems like they should. I know what she means. There's definitely a gap in Japanese and American expectations when it comes to saying, "I'm sorry."

I feel the gap in both places, though it's not necessarily a bad feeling. It still makes me smile every time my Japanese university students write a note, with their name and student number, saying, "I'm so sorry I slept in class today." I would never know which students slept in those big lecture classes if they didn't tell me! (B)

There are also times when American apologies surprise me. At grocery stores or walking through crowds in the U.S., I notice a lot more people saying "I'm sorry" than I expect. Having lived in Tokyo for so long, where people (C) each other without a thought, I always forget how much space people back home need. When I get into other people's space unintentionally, they often apologize even though it's my fault.

Other times though, I feel as my Japanese friend does : I expect an apology and don't get one. Like the time I went to meet my sister at the Austin airport. Her flight was two hours late, and the airline staff had already gone home. Nobody could tell me what had happened to the flight, so I got more and more scared. Finally my sister walked into the lobby. I was relieved, but still upset, and she couldn't understand why. Instead of saying, "Oh, you must have been worried. Sorry the flight was so late," she just looked at me like I was crazy.

(D)

—A Taste of Japan, Key Hetherly

問1 Fill in blank (A) with the most appropriate word below.

① appreciate ② notice ③ apologize
④ deplore ⑤ miss

問2 Fill in blank (B) with the most appropriate phrase below.

① How can I forgive them after such an honorable confession?
② How can I not forgive them after such an honorable confession?
③ How can I now forgive them after such an honest confession?
④ How can I forgive them after such an honest confession?
⑤ How can I not forgive them after such an honest confession?

問3 Fill in blank (C) with the most appropriate words.

① come about ② fall behind ③ give in
④ bump into ⑤ come down

問4 Which of the following sequences of letters shows the best logical order for the paragraph (D) in this passage.

ア In the U.S. the rules are not so clear. Instead, people tend to react according to their own mood.
イ People expect those phrases, and saying them shows your concern and makes everything O.K.
ウ In Japan, unlike the U.S., the rules are fairly clear.
エ They're not as likely to be thinking about how the other person feels, especially if they're tired or grumpy themselves.
オ You apologize in certain situations using set phrases, like when you're

late.

① イ→ア→オ→ウ→エ　② ウ→イ→ア→オ→エ
③ ウ→オ→イ→ア→エ　④ エ→ア→イ→オ→ウ
⑤ エ→ウ→ア→オ→イ

(☆☆☆◎◎◎)

【8】次の文は,「評価規準の作成, 評価方法等の工夫改善のための参考資料(中学校外国語)(平成23年11月国立教育政策研究所)において,「第2編　評価規準に盛り込むべき事項等」「第2　内容のまとまりごとの評価規準に盛り込むべき事項及び評価規準の設定例」が示されている。

次のA～Eの評価規準は, どの観点において設定されるものか, 下のア～エからそれぞれ一つずつ選び, 正しい組合せを下の［　　］の①～⑤から一つ選びなさい。

A　語句や表現, 文法事項などの知識を活用して短い英語の内容を正しく聞き取ることができる。

B　場面や状況にふさわしい表現を用いて書くことができる。

C　間違うことを恐れず積極的に自分の考えなどを話している。

D　発音の違いや音変化に関する知識を身に付けている。

E　読んだことについて, メモをとったり簡単な言葉や動作などで反応したりしている。

> ア　コミュニケーションへの関心・意欲・態度
> イ　外国語表現の能力
> ウ　外国語理解の能力
> エ　言語や文化についての知識・理解

	A	B	C	D	E
①	ア	ア	エ	ウ	イ
②	ア	イ	ウ	ア	ウ
③	イ	ア	エ	イ	ウ
④	ウ	エ	イ	ウ	ア
⑤	ウ	イ	ア	エ	ア

(☆☆☆◎◎)

【9】次の文は,「グローバル化に対応した英語教育改革実施計画」(平成25年12月文部科学省)の「2. 新たな英語教育の在り方実現のための体制整備」の一部について示したものである。文中の(ア)~(オ)に当てはまる語句の正しい組合せを,下の[ ]の①~⑤から一つ選びなさい。

○ 小学校における指導体制強化
- 小学校英語教育推進リーダーの加配措置・養成研修
- (ア)教員の指導力向上
- 小学校学級担任の英語指導力向上
- 研修用映像教材等の開発・提供
- (イ)課程・採用の改善充実

○ 中・高等学校における指導体制強化
- 中・高等学校英語教育推進(ウ)の養成
- 中・高等学校英語科教員の指導力向上
- 外部検定試験を活用し,県等ごとの教員の英語力の達成状況を定期的に検証

○ 外部人材の活用促進
- 外国語指導助手(ALT)の配置拡大,(エ)の活用促進(ガイドラインの策定等)
- (オ)向けの研修教科・充実

○ 指導用教材の開発
- 先行実施のための教材整備
- モジュール指導用ICT教材の開発・整備

	ア	イ	ウ	エ	オ
①	主 任	大学教養	専任教員	退職教員	新任教員
②	専 科	大学教養	専任教員	地域人材等	ＡＬＴ等
③	専 科	大学教養	リーダー	退職教員	新任教員
④	専 科	教員養成	リーダー	地域人材等	ＡＬＴ等
⑤	主 任	教員養成	リーダー	退職教員	新任教員

(☆☆☆◎◎◎)

【10】次の文は，中学校学習指導要領(平成20年3月告示　平成27年3月一部改正)「第2章　第9節　外国語」「第2　各言語の目標及び内容等」の「英語　2　内容」「(1)言語活動」の一部を抜粋したものである。文中の(　ア　)～(　オ　)に当てはまる語句の正しい組合せを，下の□の①～⑤から一つ選びなさい。ただし，同じ記号には同じ語句が入る。

英語を理解し，英語で表現できる(　ア　)な(　イ　)を養うため，次の言語活動を3学年間を通して行わせる。
ア　聞くこと
主として次の事項
(ア)　強勢，イントネーション，区切りなど基本的な英語の(　ウ　)の特徴をとらえ，正しく聞き取ること。
(イ)　自然な口調で話されたり読まれたりする英語を聞いて，(　エ　)を正確に聞き取ること。
(ウ)　質問や依頼などを聞いて(　オ　)に応じること。
(エ)　話し手に聞き返すなどして内容を確認しながら理解すること。
(オ)　まとまりのある英語を聞いて，概要や要点を(　オ　)に聞き取ること。

	ア	イ	ウ	エ	オ
①	実践的	運用能力	音　声	文　脈	簡　潔
②	一般的	運用能力	発　音	文　脈	適　切
③	実践的	運用能力	音　声	情　報	適　切
④	一般的	応用能力	発　音	情　報	簡　潔
⑤	実践的	応用能力	発　音	情　報	適　切

(☆☆☆◎◎◎◎)

【11】次の文は，中学校学習指導要領(平成20年3月告示　平成27年3月一部改正)「第2章　第9節　外国語」「第2　各言語の目標及び内容等」の「英語　3　指導計画の作成と内容の取扱い」の一部を抜粋したもので

ある。文中の(　ア　)～(　オ　)に当てはまる語句の正しい組合せを，下の[　　]の①～⑤から一つ選びなさい。ただし，同じ記号には同じ語句が入る。

ア　各学校においては，生徒や地域の(　ア　)に応じて，学年ごとの目標を適切に定め，3学年間を通して英語の目標の実現を図るようにすること。

イ　2の(3)の言語材料については，(　イ　)に応じて平易なものから難しいものへと段階的に指導すること。

ウ　音声指導に当たっては，日本語との違いに留意しながら，発音練習などを通して2の(3)のアに示された言語材料を継続して指導すること。

　また，音声指導の補助として，必要に応じて発音表記を用いて指導することもできること。

エ　文字指導に当たっては，生徒の学習負担に配慮し(　ウ　)を指導することもできること。

オ　語，(　エ　)及び慣用表現については，運用度の高いものを用い，活用することを通して定着を図るようにすること。

カ　辞書の使い方に慣れ，活用できるようにすること。

キ　生徒の(　ア　)や教材の内容などに応じて，コンピュータや情報通信ネットワーク，(　オ　)などを有効活用したり，ネイティブ・スピーカーなどの協力を得たりなどすること。

	ア	イ	ウ	エ	オ
①	環　境	学習段階	筆記体	熟　語	電子黒板
②	実　態	学習段階	筆記体	連　語	教育機器
③	実　態	学習段階	活字体	熟　語	電子黒板
④	実　態	発達段階	筆記体	連　語	教育機器
⑤	環　境	発達段階	活字体	連　語	電子黒板

(☆☆☆◎◎◎◎)

【12】次の文は，中学校学習指導要領解説　外国語編(平成20年文部科学省)「第2章　外国語科の目標及び内容」「第2節　英語」の「2　内容(1)言語活動」の一部を抜粋したものである。文中の(　ア　)～(　オ　)に当てはまる語句の正しい組合せを，あとの［　　］の①～⑤から一つ選びなさい。

> 中学校では，コミュニケーション能力の基礎を養うことを目標としている。そのため，英語を聞いたり，話したり，読んだり，書いたりする基礎的な言語活動をバランスよく計画的・(　ア　)に行うことが大切である。
>
> 今回の改訂では，授業時数を各学年で105時間から(　イ　)時間に増加させているが，指導すべき語数を除き，文法事項等の指導内容をほとんど増加させていない。これは，言語活動の充実を通じて，言語材料の定着を図り，コミュニケーション能力の基礎を育成することを意図したものである。
>
> この点を踏まえながら，今回の改訂では，以下に示す事項について改善を図った。
>
> (ア)　言語活動の指導事項
>
> (　ウ　)ともそれぞれ(　エ　)の指導事項で構成していたものを，今回は五つの指導事項に変更し，充実を図っている。言語材料についての知識や理解を深める言語活動から，考えや気持ちなどを伝え合う言語活動まで，特に必要な言語活動を示し，基礎的・基本的な内容についての指導を十分に行うとともに，それらを活用して(　オ　)を行う言語活動を重視している点は，改訂前と同様である。

	ア	イ	ウ	エ	オ
①	包括的	１３０	各領域	三つ	適切な表現
②	系統的	１３０	各内容	三つ	意思の伝達
③	系統的	１３０	各内容	四つ	意思の伝達
④	系統的	１４０	各領域	四つ	意思の伝達
⑤	包括的	１４０	各領域	四つ	適切な表現

(☆☆☆◎◎◎◎)

【13】次のA～Cの文は，中学校学習指導要領(平成20年3月告示　平成27年3月一部改正)「第2章　第9節　外国語」「第2　各言語の目標及び内容等」の「英語　3　指導計画の作成と内容の取扱い」の「(2)教材」の一部を英文にしたものである。文中の(　ア　)～(　ウ　)に当てはまる語句の正しい組合せを，あとの□の①～⑤から1つ選びなさい。

> A. Materials should be useful in enhancing the understanding of various ways of viewing and thinking, fostering the ability to make impartial judgments and (　ア　).
>
> B. Materials should be useful in deepening the understanding of the ways of life and cultures of foreign countries and Japan, raising interest in language and culture and (　イ　) toward these.
>
> C. Materials should be useful in deepening the international understanding from a broad perspective, (　ウ　) of being Japanese citizens living in a global community and cultivating a spirit of international cooperation.

	ア	イ	ウ
①	Heightening students' awareness	Developing respectful attitudes	Cultivating a rich sensibility
②	Heightening students' awareness	Cultivating a rich sensibility	Developing respectful attitudes
③	Cultivating a rich sensibility	Heightening students' awareness	Developing respectful attitudes
④	Cultivating a rich sensibility	Developing respectful attitudes	Heightening students' awareness
⑤	Developing respectful attitudes	Heightening students' awareness	Cultivating a rich sensibility

(☆☆☆◎◎◎◎)

解答・解説

福　岡　県

【中高共通】

【1】Question 1　③　　Question 2　④　　Question 3　④

〈解説〉Question 1　Kenの2つ目の発言にdizzy spells「めまい。立ちくらみ」とあることから判断する。　Question 2　Kenの話し相手(Receptionist)は最初の発言で「バンクーバー医療センターです」と言い，続けてKenが「明日の予約を取りたい」といっていることから，病院の受付だと判断する。　Question 3　Receptionistの6つ目の発言に「初回の患者は登録しなければなりません」とあり，最後の発言で「15ドルの新規登録料があります」と言っていることから判断する。

【2】《A》 Question 1　②　　Question 2　②　　Question 3　④

《B》 Question 1　③　　Question 2　④　　Question 3　②

〈解説〉《A》 Question 1　第1段落3文目にThe cowboy had to be able to tame wild horsesとあることから判断する。 Question 2　第2段落3文目に「雄牛に乗ることは困難で，息をのむような光景を見せてくれる」とあり，具体的な光景として4文目に「落ちた騎手は雄牛の攻撃の危険がついて回る」ことを述べていることから判断する。 Question 3　第2段落最後の文に「騎乗が終わったら雄牛の気を逸らすために，ロデオクラウンが雇われ，特にけがを負った騎手に安全を提供している」とあることから判断する。 《B》 秋に木々の葉が色づく原理が述べられている。 Question 1　第1段落2文目に「なぜ葉は色を変えるのか」と問題提起があり，同段落6～7文目に「日が短くなり，夜が長く涼しくなると，木は反応して緑の色素の生産をゆっくり止める。ひとたび緑の色素が減少すると，すでに葉の中に存在していた明るい黄色やオレンジが現れ始める」とあることから判断する。 Question 2　第2段落3～4文目に「夜に気温が下がると，葉脈にある糖質の樹液が流れて木に戻っていくことができなくなる。明るい日光が，逆流できない植物の糖質を明るい赤や紫色に変える」とあることから判断する。 Question 3　第1段落6文目を別の言い方にすると，緑の色素が多い時には明るい黄色やオレンジ色が見えないことになる。

【3】Question 1　No.2　　Question 2　No.1　　Question 3　No.2

〈解説〉Question 1　第2段落3文目に「雨季の長さと言語の数の間に直接的な相関関係があると彼(言語人類学者)は指摘した」とあり，彼が発見して指摘したと考え，No.2「地域の言語の多様性は気候によるところが大きい」が正解。 Question 2　第4段落3文目に「南部では主要生産物が1年中収穫されるので，それぞれ小さな共同体で生活することができ，外部者が理解できない言語で話す」とあり，No.1の「1年中収穫が保証される地域」なので，あえて外部者とコミュニケーションをとる必要がなく，それぞれの共同体がそれぞれの言語を話すので言語の数は減らないと考える。 Question 3　第5段落1文目に「作物の不作が飢饉を招く可能性がある地域では，外部者との関係は極めて重要である」とあり，No.2「飢餓の危険があるときには外部者と接触を持ちたい」がほぼ同じ内容を表す。

【4】No.2，No.6

〈解説〉leaf-cutter ants(ハキリアリ)の社会は，分業制で4つのグループに分かれ，それぞれが役割を果たし生活しているという話。第3段落1文目に「一番小さい働きアリの仕事は庭を作り，手入れをし，幼いアリの養育することだ」とあり，No.2「一番小さい大きさの働きアリは巣の中の仕事をする」と一致する。第5段落2文目の後半に「いくつかの大きさの働きアリは，自分たちがする仕事に理想的に適しているわけではなかった」とあり，No.6「それぞれの大きさの働きアリは，いつも自分の仕事に向いた最良の大きさというわけではない」と一致する。

【5】問1　②　　問2　④　　問3　①　　問4　①　　問5　③

〈解説〉問1「コンピュータを使った教育の利点の1つは，それが個人のニーズに～されることができることだ」から「合わせられる」と考える。　問2　ひと月の間ほとんど雨が降らなかったので，野菜は「少ない」し，値段が高いと考える。　問3「彼はほとんど知らない人からのメールの～に驚いた」からinflux「殺到」だと判断する。
問4「最新の科学雑誌に出ている記事は，彼女が数年前に書いた記事を～だ」からexpansion「発展させたもの」だと判断する。developmentは商品や土地，出来事などに対して使う。　問5「風邪は最も広範囲な疾患だが，予防や治療を見つけようとする科学者たちの努力にもかかわらず，人類を～し続けている」からplague「悩ませる」だと判断する。

【6】問1　⑤　　問2　④　　問3　①　　問4　③

〈解説〉問1　be superior toで「～よりすぐれている」，those of the pastで「昔の車」，thoseはcarsを指す。　問2　seem likely to ～で「～しそうに思える」。　問3　cannot help ～ingで「～せざるを得ない」。helpは「避

ける」という意味。　問4「～時間を作るべきであるのは怒っているときである」と考え，it is ～ that …の「～」にwhen we are most angryを入れ，強調する。

【7】問1　⑤　　問2　④

〈解説〉問1　Cの1文目「昨晩テレビで野球の試合を見たか」に，Eの1文目「ごめん，見なかった」が答えている。続く2文目の「君はプロ野球のファンなのか」に対し，Bの1文目「もちろん」と答えている。そして，2文目で「私は福岡ベアーズに夢中だが，あなたはどうか」と質問し，Aで「(福岡ベアーズのようなプロ野球もよいが,)私の楽しみは高校野球だ」と，話が高校野球のほうに展開している。それを受けて，Dで「私もそれ(高校野球)が好きだ」と答えている。

問2　Bは吹き流しのような色とりどりの魚が風になびいているのを見て，「それらは何て美しいのだろう」と言っている。これをEの1文目が受けている。そして4文目で「日本では男の子の親は，こどもの日を祝うため大きなこいのぼりを外に掲げる」と，こいのぼりの説明があり，それを受けてDで「なぜ鯉の形なのか」と展開する。その理由がAで「日本では，鯉は力強さと根気の象徴とみなされている」と述べられている。その説明を聞いて，CでI see.と納得し，「親は男の子がこれらの性質(力強さと根気)を受け継ぐことを望む」で終わる。

【8】問1　②　　問2　①　　問3　④　　問4　②　　問5　①

〈解説〉問1　1文目に「新しい文法を使うことができるとは，生徒が意味と，それを使う状況を理解しているということだ」とあり，使えるようにするためには，②「その文法パターンを，生徒自身で使う方法を教えると，生徒はそれを他の状況にも応用できる」ことが重要だと判断する。　問2　6文目に「彼ら(生徒たち)とコミュニケーションをとること，特に質問をすることはとても大切だ」とあり，「ゆえに～」と続く。空所の直後の1文には「質問は生徒が直面する問題や難題を見つけ出すのに役立つ」とある。教師は生徒に質問して心配事を解決してあげることが大切だと考え，①「教師は生徒に難しい質問をすることを恐れるべきではない」が正解。　問3　1～2文目に日本の英語の授業では英語を日本語に翻訳するので，「英語で何かを生み出すことをとても難しくしていた」とあり，それを端的に④「アウトプットよりもインプットに重きを置いていた」と言い，空所のあとに「これはコミュニケーションに関するものではなかった」と続く。

問4　空所までの文には，仕事を持つ人たちは，現代では(家庭用の)機械が広く使われ，前の世代よりも自由な時間があるが，ぶらぶら過ごすだけの気晴らしでは本当の満足は得られないとある。そのあとに，②「価値のある趣味の効用は，その趣味が心に恩恵をもたらすことだ」と続き，具体的な恩恵の説明として，「それ(価値のある趣味)は安らぎをもたらしたり，通常の仕事からの気分転換ができる」と続く。

問5　空所の直後に「子どもの食べ物の好みだけでなく，親の役割を尊重する食事戦略も立てる必要がある」とあるので，その前にも別の戦略のことが述べられていると判断し，①「子どもたちにさまざまな栄養のある食べ物を食べてもらう忍耐と戦略が必要だ」と考える。

【9】問1　④　　問2　②　　問3　⑤

〈解説〉問1　第1段落2文目に「空腹は食事の数時間後，胃が空になった時に起こるよくみられる状態だ」とあり，何が空腹を引き起こすかが述べられている。　問2　第1段落5文目に「食べ物が胃にある間に，食べ物が分解して消化されるように胃壁がリズミカルな運動で収縮する」とあり，胃の収縮が食べ物を分解すると述べられている。

問3　第2段落2～3文目に「血糖値が下がるとき，神経系のある部分が，視床下部と呼ばれる脳の一部にメッセージを送る。それからお腹が空いていると脳が私たちに知らせてくれる」とあり，低い血糖値が空腹を知らせてくれると述べられている。

【10】問1　③　　問2　④　　問3　②　　問4　⑤

〈解説〉問1　第1段落後半に「人類文化の目立つ特徴は，社会的結合や友情，特に愛情が必要なことである」とあり，第2段落でそれを裏付ける具体例がいくつか述べられている。さらに科学的分析をして「映画のヒーローや一匹オオカミは人気のあるイメージだが，人は社会的な生き物である」とある。第3段落では人類が持つ社会性は生物学的に近い霊長類も持ち合わせている」と述べられ，第4段落では社会性を育むには努力と経験が必要だとあり，すべて「人間が社会的な生き物である」ことを述べていることから判断する。　問2　第2段落6文目の「世の中から孤立して，ペットを飼うことすら拒む大人は，人との交際を育む人よりも比較的若くして死ぬ傾向にある」とあることから判断する。　問3　第3段落1文目に「私たちの社会性は生物学的に私たち(人類)に最も近い種の多く，チンパンジーやボノボ，(中略)のような霊長類が持ち合わせている」から判断する。　問4　第4段落最後の文「もし健康であり続けるつもりなら，一生を通じて，人と触れ合ったり，一緒に食事をしたり，ゲームや旅行のような活動をともにする必要がある」から判断する。

【11】問1　③　　問2　jaws　　問3　(D)　　問4　bristles

〈解説〉問1　第1段落2文目に「それら(甲殻類)は，最も乾燥している砂漠以外，ほとんどすべての自然環境で見つけることができる」とあることから，水が少ないところには生息していないことがわかる。

問2　下線部アの直後から「食物をかむために使われる」ものだとわかる。また，与えられた文は「顔面を何度も打たれることによる，ボクサーのよくある怪我の1つは～を骨折することだ」なので，その2点から甲殻類の体のどの部位なのか判断する。なお，mandibleは「下あご」の意で，jawは上下を問わず「あご」の意で用いられる。

問3　与えられた文のby以下「内側への動きで水を送り込むことによって」を手掛かりにして探す。また，前半のThey do thisは，theyが複数名詞を指し，thisが動作を表していると見当をつけて探す。第2段落1文目に「甲殻類は一般的に頭部から突き出ている5対の突起部分を持っている」とある。そのうちの2つについて4文目に「残りの2対は，あごに食物を送り込むように，水流の供給を用意するために使われている」とあり，「内側への動きで水を送り込むことによって，それら残りの2対の突起部分はこれ(水流の供給)を用意する」と判断する。問4　theseなので，下線部イより前の複数の名詞を探す。第3段落は甲殻類には聴覚器官がないが，それに代わるものがあるという内容。1文目のbut以下に，「中が空洞で神経が通っている剛毛が体の表面や突起物にたくさんある」とあり，「これらの剛毛(bristles)は触られると動き，有機体甲殻類が音を含む振動に反応し，識別できるようにする」と，剛毛が聴覚の代わりをしていると考える。

【中学校】

【1】① ウ　② ア　③ ア　④ エ　⑤ イ

〈解説〉中学校学習指導要領(平成20年3月告示)に示される指導内容に対応させると，①と②は「聞くこと」，③は「読むこと」，④は「書くこと」，⑤は「話すこと」の評価規準の設定例である。

【2】問1　① 意向　② 考え　③ 慣れ親しみ　問2　④ 基礎　⑤ 態度　⑥ 音声　⑦ 素地　⑧ 総合

〈解説〉問1　初歩的な学習を行うにあたっては，まず英語に慣れ親しむことが大切である。ただし出題の解説によると，小学校外国語活動において外国語を「聞くこと」および「話すこと」はすでに慣れ親しんでいるので，現行の中学校学習指導要領では目標の(1)および(2)では「慣れ親しみ」という語を用いていない。一方で，「実際に英語を使用してコミュニケーションを図ることを念頭に置いている」ため，より踏み込んだ能力の習得を目標にしていることも同解説では指摘している。　問2　小学校外国語活動ではコミュニケーション能力の素地を養うために音声面を中心に学ぶが，中学ではその素地をもとに，コミュニケーション能力の基礎を築くことに重点を置き，4技能を総合的に育成すると考える。

【3】問1　Let me see　　問2　・知らない表現については，身振り手振りなどを使う。／既習の表現などを使う。　　・I see.やSure.など，相づちをうつ表現を適宜用いる。

〈解説〉問1　出題の解説では解答例のもの以外に，Wellをあげている。また，同解説の記述にこだわらず，I meanやYou knowなどを解答してもよい。　問2　表現が思いつかないときは，身振り手振りなどの非言語的コミュニケーションを併用することも考えられる。また，伝えたいことと近い内容のことを既習の表現で表すことで会話がつながり，話が進んでいく。初めからスマートな表現を目指すのではなく，表現は既習のものであっても，積極的にコミュニケーションを図っていく態度や能力を育てることが大切なのである。

【高等学校】

【1】①　g　②　n　③　h　④　o　⑤　m

〈解説〉①　コミュニケーションに取り組む態度として，身振り手振りやつなぎ言葉などを用いて何とか会話を継続させようと努力することが大切である。　②　観察評価以外に，ポートフォリオに系統的に蓄積された学習者の自己評価の記録や，教師の指導と評価の記録などを用いることで，学習者の学習活動を評価するときに役立つ。　③　話し手が伝えたいものは，ある事柄についての情報や自分の考え，気持ちなど。　④　外国語を聞いたり読んだりするときに的確に把握し理解することが求められる。　⑤　言語や文化の知識を蓄えるのは，言葉を運用する自分で言葉を使ったり，相手の使う言葉を理解したりするときに役立つと考える。

【2】ア　standard　　イ　support　　ウ　structures

〈解説〉学習指導要領の英訳版は，出題頻度がかなり高い。仮訳が示されている「第8節　外国語」と「第13節　英語」については，日本語版と対照させながら内容を理解しておくこと。　ア　日本語版の「現代の標準的な英語によること」に該当する部分である。contemporaryが

「現代の」の意なので，空欄には「標準的な」という意味の語句が入る。　イ　日本語版の「文法については，コミュニケーションを支えるものであることを踏まえ」に該当する部分である。空欄の直後にcommunicationとあるので，「支える」という意味の語句が入る。
ウ　日本語版の「コミュニケーションを行うために必要となる語句や文構造，文法事項などの取扱いについては」に該当する部分である。Phrases「語句」，grammatical items, etc.「文法事項」は示されているので，sentence structures「文構造」を入れる。

【3】問1　①　総合　　②　目標　　③　判断力　　④　尊重
⑤　国際協調　　問2　(あまり専門的に詳しく指導することは生徒に過度の負担をかけることとなるおそれがあるので,)基本的な表記について，必要に応じて指導する。　　問3　図書館やインターネットなどを利用して広く情報を収集し，活用することができるようにする指導。　　問4　彼らの特性を生かしながら，生徒のコミュニケーション能力の向上につながるような豊かな言語活動を展開すること。
問5　授業の目標
〈解説〉問1　小学校ではコミュニケーションの素地を養い，中学校では4技能の総合的な基礎を築き，高等学校では中学校までの基礎をもとにコミュニケーション能力を総合的に育成する。そして，外国語の知識だけを学ぶのではなく，コミュニケーションを通して，差別や偏見のない公正な判断力を養う。また，外国の言語や文化を理解することで，自国の言語や文化との違いを知り，これらを尊重する態度，言語を通して話し合い協調し合う精神を養うと考える。　問2　発音記号を読んで正しい口や舌の形や動きができると，自分で正しい発音を身につける助けとなるが，専門家のように細分化して，正確に発音する必要はない。　問3　学校以外の場で英語に触れる機会として，図書館や地域社会の講座などの現実の世界や，インターネットのような仮想現実の世界で情報や知識を集め，それを活用するとよい。
問4　1人1人の生徒ができるだけ多くネイティブ・スピーカーとコミ

ュニケーションをとれるような言語活動を考える。その際，当該ネイティブ・スピーカーの趣味や好み，仕切るのがうまい，ほめ上手などといった特性を生かしながら授業計画を作成するとよいだろう。

問5　ネイティブ・スピーカーと協力して授業を行うので，授業をどう進め，どんな課題を生徒に与え，それをどのように達成させるかなど，事前に打ち合わせを行って授業の目標を立て，お互いに理解しておくことが大切となる。

福　岡　市

【中学校】

【1】問1　⑤　　問2　④　　問3　③　　問4　③　　問5　②

〈解説〉問1　空所のあとでmy stay ～と名詞(目的語)が来ているので前置詞だと判断し，あとは文脈から「私のパリの滞在中」とする。

問2　空所の直後にthanがあるので比較級が入ると判断する。「静かに作動する」と，動詞のworkを修飾する副詞のquietlyの比較級を選ぶ。

問3　Last Wednesdayから過去の出来事だと判断する。drop by ～で「～に立ち寄る」という意味。　問4　「この5年の間」と考え，over「(時を表して)～の間」にする。pastは「(過ぎ去った)この～」という意味で，現在完了時制でよく使われる。　問5　convenientは人を形容する単語ではなく，「時が人にとって好都合な」と考える。when it is convenient for you「いつでもあなたにとって都合のいい時に」とする。

【2】問1　②　　問2　④　　問3　③　　問4　④

〈解説〉問1　「私たちの生活様式」はour way of lifeとなる。　問2　true ofで「～に当てはまる」という意味。　問3　believe ～ to …「～を…だと信じる(思う)」。whatは関係代名詞でthe thing(s) which / thatのこと。人によって思われていることなので受け身にする。a matter of courseは「当然のこと」という意味。　問4　thatは代名詞でthe＋名詞の繰り返しを避けて使われる。be different from ～は「～と異なる」という意味。

【3】問1　④　　問2　⑤

〈解説〉問1　Eの「～していただけませんか」というていねいな依頼に対し，Dの1文目で「喜んで」と応じ，これを受けてBで「ご親切に」と応じてくれたことに感謝している。続けて「ここから遠いか」と質問したことについて，Aで「ここからそれほど遠くない」と答え，3文目で「着きました」となる。最後にCで一緒について来てくれたことへのお礼を言う，という会話の流れになっている。　問2　Bの2文目で「コーヒーを飲んで，今度の面接試験の手順について話してはどうですか」と提案して，Eの1文目で提案を受け入れている。そのあとに「コーヒーを1杯飲むと気分がスッキリする」と考えを述べると，Aで「10時のコーヒーブレイクとアメリカの関係は，3時の紅茶とイギリスの関係と同じだ」と，10時のコーヒーブレイクからイギリスの紅茶へと話題を広げている。それを受けてCで「それぞれの国にはそれぞれの習慣がある。自分はどちらも好きだ」と感想を述べると，D「私も好きだ」と同意するという会話の流れになっている。W is to be X what Y is to be Z「WとXの関係はYとZの関係と同じだ」。

【4】問1　①　　問2　⑤　　問3　④　　問4　③

〈解説〉問1　生徒中心の英語のコミュニケーションクラスでは，責任は学習者にあり，教師は「火をつける」役割をする，という文脈を受け，空所を含む文には「教室では生徒はスターで，教師は舞台監督として，生徒の手助けをし，～する機会を作り出す」とある。生徒中心のクラスなので，バケツに水を満たすように，先生から一方的に知識を与えられるのではなく，「(教師が手助けをして)生徒が自己発見をする機会と，生徒がリスクを負って大声ではっきり言える安全な環境の2つを作り出す」と考える。self-centered「自己中心的な」。　問2　日本人が経済的，政治的，そして草の根運動レベルで世界とうまく連携し合っているのは，日本人が上手に英語を使う能力に依るところが大きく，その理由として，英語が事実上の世界共通語だということと，「日本人自身が国際舞台で英語を学んで使うことに深く関わりをもつことに決めたからだ」と，理由を2つ述べていると考える。rest on ～は「～に依る」，make a commitmentは「深く関わりをもつ」という意味。
問3　第1段落に「来年度にiPS細胞を使って，白血病の治療法を開発する本格的な研究を始める」とあり，空所では「その来年度に研究が計画されている(治療)方法が動物実験で有効だと証明されたら，そのチームは2019年に人の臨床実験を始める」という話の流れになっている。
問4　「小学校の先生と同じように，日本で仕事と生活をしているネイティブ・スピーカーは，ゆっくりと，完璧な発音で，注意深く言い表された文を冗長に繰り返し～」とあり，日本で仕事と生活をしていつも日本人と接していると，日本人にわかってもらおうと，ゆっくりと話す習慣が身につくと考える。

【5】問1　⑤　　問2　①　　問3　④　　問4　②
〈解説〉問1　空所Aの前で，老婦人が「あなた(著名な科学者)が言ったこと(地球が太陽の周りを回っていて，太陽はたくさんの星の集まりである銀河系の中心を回っているという講義)はばかげている」と言い，その理由として(c)「世界は大きな亀の背中に支えられた平らな板である」と言っていると考える。それに対し科学者が(b)「亀は何の上に立っているのか」と老婦人の説に疑問を投げかけ，それに答えて老婦人は(a)「下までずっと亀がいるのだ」という話の流れになっている。
問2　第3段落1文目に「紀元前340年もの昔，ギリシャの哲学者のアリストテレスは『天体論』という自分の著作で，地球は平板というよりもむしろ球体だと信じるに足る十分な2つの主張を提示することができた」とあり，①「ずっと昔に，ギリシャの哲学者が地球は球体であると信じるに足る合理的な主張を2つ提示した」と同じ内容を表す。
問3　breakthrough(in physics)「(物理の)飛躍的進歩」と同じ意味の単語を選ぶ。　問4　第3段落5文目に「北極星が北極の真上にあるので，北極にいる観察者の真上にあるように見えるが，～人にとっては水平線のところにある」とある。北極星の高度と北緯は同じなので，北緯90度の北極にいる人が見ると真上にあり，北緯0度の赤道にいる人が見ると高度0度の水平線のところにあると考える。

【6】問1　④　　問2　④　　問3　②　　問4　①

〈解説〉問1　下線部(A)を含む文は「私たちが教育実習を深く理解できるために，学生の頃の経験を利用することができるようになる」という意味。insightは「洞察力」という意味で，④「人や状況についての真実を見極め理解する能力」が正解。　問2　第3段落2文目に「生徒からよく聞く苦情の1つに「話す機会がない」や「教師はよいが，話し過ぎる」がある」とあり，それに対する教師の言い分としてよくある説明は，「彼ら(生徒たち)はただ座って，決して話さない」や「彼らがただ座って私を見ているとき，我慢できない」と考える。can't standで「我慢できない」という意味。　問3　第3段落で生徒たちは教師が話し過ぎると言い，教師たちは生徒が全く話さないと両者の言い分が言われている。第4段落では「誰が正しくて，誰が間違っているか議論するつもりはない」とあり，空所Cで「これらの教師が言うことすべてに真実がある」と「彼ら(生徒たち)はただ座って，決して話さない」や「彼らがただ座って私を見ているとき，我慢できない」という教師の言うことを認めつつも，「しかし古いもの(教師が言うことすべて)を新しい(全く別の)視点で見て，教育実習を新しく認識し，新しい態度で臨むことを学ぶことは可能である」と判断する。　問4　第5段落1文目に「私たちがクラスですぐに利用できるシンプルな提案がある」とあり，ダーシのあとにその提案として「生徒が私たち教師を見て聞いているときに，私たちは自分自身を見て聞くようにしなさい」とある。これが①「生徒が私たち教師を見て聞いているときに，私たち教師を見て聞くこと」と同じ内容を表す。

【7】問1　③　　問2　⑤　　問3　④　　問4　③

〈解説〉問1　第1段落1文目に「アメリカ人はもっと頻繁にすみませんと

言うべきか」という話題を提供している。2文目以降で日本人の友だちはもっと言ったほうがよいと思い，「そうすべき(すみませんと言うべき)ときにめったに～ない」とあることから判断する。　問2　How can I do …?は「私はどのように～することができますか」が反語的に「どうやって～できるのか」という意味になる。第2段落で筆者が教える日本人大学生が正直に授業中に眠ってしまってすみませんと言ってきたことに対する筆者のコメントととらえ，⑤「そのような正直な告白のあとでどうやって彼らを許さないことができるのだろうか」だと判断する。honorable「尊敬に値する」。　問3　空所Cを含む文は「東京に長いこと住んでいるが，そこでは人が無意識に～するところなので，母国では人がどのくらいの(個人の)空間が必要なのかいつも忘れてしまう」となり，東京は狭くて人通りが多く，日常的に人とぶつかるので，アメリカで無意識に他の人の(個人の)空間に入り込んでしまうという話の流れになっている。　問4　第3段落では，アメリカ人は個人の空間に配慮して，たとえ相手が自分の空間に入り込んできてもI'm sorry.と言うが，第4段落では，空港で2時間待たされても相手はSorry the flight was so late.とも言わないとある。アメリカ人がいつSorryと言って，いつ言わないかわからなくなっているので，それを踏まえ，ウ「アメリカと違って日本ではルールがかなり明確だ」が最初にくる。その次にオ「遅れた時のような特定の状況で，決まった表現を使って謝る」と詳しく述べている。その話を受けて，イ「人はそういう表現を期待し，それを言うことであなたの気遣いを表し，すべてがうまくいく」と日本でどのようなルールになっているかが述べられている。そして，ア「アメリカではルールがそれほど明確ではない」とあり，「自分の気分で反応しがちである」とアメリカの状況が述べられ，具体的に，エ「とくに疲れていたり，不機嫌なとき，他の人がどう感じているか考えない傾向にある」と続く。

【8】⑤

〈解説〉中学校学習指導要領(平成20年3月告示)に示される指導内容に対

応させると，AとDは「聞くこと」，Bは「書くこと」，Cは「話すこと」，Eは「読むこと」の評価規準の設定例である。

【9】④

〈解説〉次期学習指導要領からは，現在小学校第5学年及び第6学年で行っている「聞くこと」「話すこと」を中心とした外国語活動を第3学年から行い，第5学年からは教科型の英語学習が導入される予定である。そのため，教員養成課程・採用の改善充実をする必要がある。出題の計画は比較的よく取り上げられるものなので，必ず目を通しておきたい。

【10】③

〈解説〉中学校学習指導要領解説　外国語編(平成20年文部科学省)では，「言語活動の弾力的な展開を可能にするため，聞くこと，話すこと，読むこと，書くことの4領域の言語活動の指導事項は，学年ごとに示すのではなく3学年間を通して一括して示すことで，(中略)教師が創意工夫をしやすい構成としている」としている。たとえば，「ア　聞くこと」の各指導項目のどの項目を第何学年で指導するという指示はなく，生徒の学習の習熟程度や興味・関心などに応じた指導など，柔軟に対応することができることを示している。

【11】②

〈解説〉中学校学習指導要領解説　外国語編(平成20年文部科学省)によると，言語材料について「平易なものから難しいものへと段階的に指導する」とは，たとえば，「学習の基礎の段階では単純な構造の文を取り上げ，学習が進むにつれて複雑な構造の文を主として取り上げるようにする」ことである。なお，筆記体については中学校学習指導要領(平成元年3月告示)までは適宜指導するものであったが，平成10年の改訂より「指導することもできる」となり，必ず指導するものではなくなった。

【12】④

〈解説〉イやエは具体的な数字を覚えておくこと。オは基礎的・基本的な内容についての指導を十分に行うとともに，まず意思の伝達を行う言語活動を重視して，その中で適切な表現で意思の伝達ができるようにしたい。

【13】④

〈解説〉A，B，Cの各項目が，useful inのあとに，～，～, and ～と，等位接続詞のandで3つの動名詞句を並べる構造になっている。Aは「多様なものの見方や考え方を理解する」ことで，差別や偏見のない公平な判断力を養い，いろいろな人の気持ちもわかり豊かな心情を育てると考える。Bは「外国や我が国の生活や文化についての理解を深める」ことで，言語や文化に対する関心を高め，自分たち以外の生活や文化や言語を尊重する態度を育てると考える。Cは「広い視野から国際理解を深める」ことで，日本を外から見ることができ，国際社会に生きる日本人としての自覚を高め，国際協調の精神を養うと考える。

●書籍内容の訂正等について

弊社では教員採用試験対策シリーズ（参考書，過去問，全国まるごと過去問題集），公務員試験対策シリーズ，公立幼稚園・保育士試験対策シリーズ，会社別就職試験対策シリーズについて，正誤表をホームページ（https://www.kyodo-s.jp）に掲載いたします。内容に訂正等，疑問点がございましたら，まずホームページをご確認ください。もし，正誤表に掲載されていない訂正等，疑問点がございましたら，下記項目をご記入の上，以下の送付先までお送りいただくようお願いいたします。

① **書籍名，都道府県（学校）名，年度** （例：教員採用試験過去問シリーズ　小学校教諭 過去問　2025 年度版） ② **ページ数**（書籍に記載されているページ数をご記入ください。） ③ **訂正等，疑問点**（内容は具体的にご記入ください。） （例:問題文では“ア～オの中から選べ”とあるが,選択肢はエまでしかない）

〔ご注意〕

○ 電話での質問や相談等につきましては，受付けておりません。ご注意ください。

○ 正誤表の更新は適宜行います。

○ いただいた疑問点につきましては，当社編集制作部で検討の上，正誤表への反映を決定させていただきます（個別回答は，原則行いませんのであしからずご了承ください）。

●情報提供のお願い

協同教育研究会では，これから教員採用試験を受験される方々に，より正確な問題を，より多くご提供できるよう情報の収集を行っております。つきましては，教員採用試験に関する次の項目の情報を，以下の送付先までお送りいただけますと幸いでございます。お送りいただきました方には謝礼を差し上げます。

（情報量があまりに少ない場合は，謝礼をご用意できかねる場合があります）。

◆あなたの受験された面接試験，論作文試験の実施方法や質問内容

◆教員採用試験の受験体験記

送付先	○電子メール：edit@kyodo-s.jp ○FAX：03-3233-1233（協同出版株式会社　編集制作部 行） ○郵送：〒101-0054　東京都千代田区神田錦町2-5 協同出版株式会社　編集制作部 行 ○HP:https://kyodo-s.jp/provision（右記のQRコードからもアクセスできます）

※謝礼をお送りする関係から，いずれの方法でお送りいただく際にも，「お名前」「ご住所」は，必ず明記いただきますよう，よろしくお願い申し上げます。

教員採用試験「過去問」シリーズ

福岡県・福岡市・北九州市の
英語科 過去問

編　集　Ⓒ 協同教育研究会
発　行　令和6年2月25日
発行者　小貫　輝雄
発行所　協同出版株式会社
〒101-0054　東京都千代田区神田錦町2－5
電話　03－3295－1341
振替　東京00190－4－94061
印刷所　協同出版・POD工場

落丁・乱丁はお取り替えいたします。